CONTENTS

MODERN
CABINETRY

STERLING PUBLISHING Co., INC.
NEW YORK

For my mother

Edited by Laurel Ornitz

10   9   8   7   6   5   4   3   2   1

Published by Sterling Publishing Company, Inc.
387 Park Avenue South, New York, N.Y. 10016
Originally published in 1990 as European Cabinetry
© 1990, 1995 by Jim Christ
Distributed in Canada by Sterling Publishing
% Canadian Manda Group, One Atlantic Avenue, Suite 105
Toronto, Ontario, Canada M6K 3E7
Distributed in Great Britain and Europe by Cassell PLC
Wellington House, 125 Strand, London WC2R 0BB, England
Distributed in Australia by Capricorn Link (Australia) Pty Ltd.
P.O. Box 6651, Baulkham Hills, Business Centre, NSW 2153, Australia
Manufactured in the United States of America

Sterling   ISBN 0-8069-3189-2

ACKNOWLEDGMENTS

"Change is the nursery
Of music, joy, life, and eternity."
—J. Donne

I would like to thank Tucson Architect Albert N. Hopper for turning my rather crude sketches into the good-quality line art that appears in this book.

Thanks also to the following:

Francis E. Ball;

Joe Burke of Woodcrafters Cabinet Co., Inc.;

Damon Day and Randall Hinders of Tucson Builders Hardware;

Don Kerrihard; and

Bill Lason of Creative Cabinets.

Most special thanks to Mary, Rachel, and Joseph for their patience, consideration, and support.

FOREWORD

When I wrote this volume for its 1990 publication, I was not only trying to fill a big gap in the literature of American woodworking, but also attempting to provide the first detailed comprehensive guide to the 32-millimetre system as an aid for the American woodworker. Some volumes, like *The Complete Guide to Modern Cabinetmaking,* already included some information on the subject, and at the time, there was even one book that explained how to build kitchen cabinets according to European theory using fairly primitive tools. Other printed material available in America, most of it from European tool and hardware manufacturers, was based on the premise that American woodworkers would embrace the European design system with so much enthusiasm that they would depart from their traditional methods for cabinet design, in turn rapidly enlarging the market for equipment and hardware manufactured in Italy, Germany, Austria, and other European countries. There was no thorough examination of the subject available in America: a complete guide to the 32-millimetre design system, a fair assessment of the advantages and limitations of the system, how-to information applying to small and large shops, a guide to using conventional tooling to create European results, a guide to materials and hardware usage, and an assessment of ways that this imported system could affect us cabinetmakers and the way we do what we do in the shop. And to my knowledge this book is still the only volume that meets those needs. My hope is that it meets some of your needs as well.

Your definition of the term "European cabinetry" continues to be a very important matter. If you think of European cabinetry primarily as an appearance, then you probably know that you can get that look on traditionally constructed boxes. You would probably design around face frames, but reduce the reveal around doors and drawers. Naturally, you would choose cup hinges like those distributed by Blum or Salice, and you might use melamine sheet goods for box parts. If customers or acquaintances approach you with a request for European cabinets, chances are good that this is their definition.

Within the community of cabinetmakers, however, such products would almost be considered traditional albeit with a contemporary look. On the other hand if you conceive of European cabinetry as a method of construction, then you know that it has elements that are very useful to all woodworkers and that we are free to pick and choose from its methodologies to supplement what we currently do.

The current volume has been received quite well within the craft. In fact, one of the pleasant surprises that came to me was the amount of mail that I got from knowledgeable readers. Most of the mail that came my way as a result of the book's appearance was from other craftsmen who were interested in giving me additional information, particularly in explaining ways that they had found to incorporate information from the book and extend it, so that their own shops and their own expertise had become more efficient and more productive. Some European-design tool manufacturers, like Veritas, even recommended the book in their own printed matter as a reliable guide to beginning to use elements of the system. Another pleasant surprise was that my audience was a bit broader than I thought it was going to be. As I intended for it to be, the book was deemed useful by hobbyists, small shop owners, and school officials; in addition though, the book found a solid market among medium-to-large shop operators. Just as you find intrinsic enjoyment in creating beautiful, functional, durable objects from wood, I have been gratified in writing this volume because the evidence indicates it has been a source of useful information to a wide range of woodworkers.

It is important to note that there have been several developments within the cabinetmaking trade relating directly to the implementation of European methodology in the brief span of time since this book first appeared. Much of what we see happening in cabinet shops across America tends to validate the essential notion of this book—that the new technologies are too good to ignore and that our choice to implement any of these systems depends on our individual woodworking situations. Most shops today have incorporated subsystems from the European approach into their production process. When European design first made its appearance, its proponents claimed that it would replace the American system or that we would Americanize the European cabinet. As I suggest in this book, this is not true. Instead we have Europeanized the American cabinet. Nothing makes this clearer than hardware applications. You may still build cabinets with a face frame, but you are almost certainly using hinges and drawer slides that were imported from Germany or Austria. The vast majority of hardware suppliers whom we patronize will report that European hardware claims a much larger market share of sales intended for the custom cabinet customer. Since there is such a strong preference for this hardware, we can probably find few medium-sized shops which are not equipped with a stationary hinging machine to allow a single-operation drilling of cup and mounting holes for pressing-in rather than screwing-on of the hinges. As we see more closely in chapter five, European hardware systems are superior in nearly any way that we look at them: better for overall appearance, easier to install, easier to adjust.

One of the great advantages of European construction is that it can eliminate certain steps in the milling process—dadoing for example. And you do not have to throw away your dadoing tools and begin using dowels and a case clamp. This is so even if you elect not to buy a single piece of new or expensive equipment. There is no need whatsoever to convert to dowel assembly. Ends, partitions, shelves and bottoms may be easily joined in strong butt joints using nailing tools and screws. In fact, we now have at our disposal adhesives which are specifically designed for bonding materials to the surface of the European system's favorite sheet good—melamine.

People whose shops are growing may be interested in increasing their volume and reducing labor expenses by investing in a vertical panel saw or an automatic edgebanding machine, but those of us who still depend on our ten-inch Unisaws are more interested in achieving perfect cuts and attractive edgebands on equipment that we already own. The methods for performing those operations, a variety of them, are described in some detail within this book.

Nothing signals the Europeanization of the American box-cabinet box more than the greater attention given to our choice of materials for backs and the methods that might be used to attach these backs to cabinets. I can remember a time, as many of my readers can, when backs were a bit superfluous. If the rigidity of the box comes from a face frame, then backs are primarily for sealing the rear edge of the cabinet. Many craftsmen admitted this by using eighth-inch materials for cabinet backs. As soon as we decide to build a single project "frameless" though, the importance of the back is elevated. The material has to have at least quarter-inch thickness for the sake of cabinet strength and stiffness. As you will see throughout this volume, and as you may have already found, we do not have to convert to European methodology for attaching the back. Throughout the American trade, from the smallest garage shop to the best-equipped high-volume shops, we have found that staple or nail attachment is not only very effective, it is better suited to our tooling. The appearance of the new adhesives supports this.

Shifting to the metric system is another subject that is sometimes at issue when we decide to "build European." But as I have pointed out in the following pages, Americans have not had to start thinking metric. Not only is metric measurement unnecessary, but it is also a disadvantage to the American woodworker because we still have to convert to English measurement for the sake of our clients and architects. In fact, the makers of European equipment and hardware seem to acknowledge this, since most of their tools and literature is now defined in both English and metric measurement. The American cabinetmakers to whom I have spoken agree with this underlying premise of the book as well: it is just as easy to "build European" with inches as with millimetres.

Many large American cabinet manufacturers have invested in state-of-the-art European equipment, including computerization and numeric control. But among the custom practitioners of the craft, we all have the ability to build cabinets and furniture, almost regardless of the type of equipment we use. As you will see from this book, the choice to Europeanize any part of our practices is entirely up to us. If you enjoy woodworking, or if you earn money from woodworking, and you want to round out your understanding of the processes that have come to us from abroad, then I invite you to read on.

—JIM CHRIST
1995

PREFACE

When you hear the term "European cabinetry," what do you think of?

Does a computerized numeric-controlled panel saw, a multispindle borer, or some other expensive piece of imported equipment automatically come to mind? Do you immediately think, "Oh no, converting to metric"? Or perhaps your mind turns to the 32-millimetre line-boring system—what many people in the traditional trade call the "Uzi approach" to cabinetmaking. If so, then you probably have a fairly negative view of the European cabinet system; you may even think that the entire system is overrated. After all, many people believe that the European system requires huge sums of cash just to get started, there is too much math involved, the cabinets look as if they were shot full of holes, and cabinets put together with knock-down fasteners are just modular factory cabinets anyway.

On the other hand, you may think of the "clean lines" of European cabinets and how this style adds to the streamlined, contemporary look preferred by so many modern homeowners. You may also note with pleasure how easy it is to adjust the hardware on cabinets made with the European system. And you may happily acknowledge that with European cabinetry you can often eliminate one or more steps from the traditional, or American, cabinetmaking process: face-frame making, sanding, or finishing—or all three.

The first matter then in deciding whether or not to incorporate the European system into your own repertoire of woodworking is one of definition. What are you going to be referring to when you use the term "European cabinetry"? The term can really suggest several different levels of usage or incorporation of the European system.

Obviously, "European cabinetry" can suggest completely embracing the 32-mm line-boring system. (With this system, holes are drilled into specific locations on certain cabinet components and then used for fastening the box components together, attaching door hinges, inserting adjustable-shelf supports, and other applications.)

If you have ever attended a woodworking machinery fair, you know that this is the level of adaptation that the manufacturers of European machinery would prefer us to establish. This would mean giving up most of the tooling and methodology we are accustomed to and investing tens of thousands of dollars in a radically different system. For most hobbyists, indeed for most small shops, this would simply not be very realistic. A complete conversion would not only be costly but would also require a great deal of space, electrical energy, and maintenance and setup time. Furthermore, with a complete conversion, we would have to do without all the positive aspects of the conventional system, which has evolved over hundreds of years.

A second possibility is to ignore the European system altogether—to use none of its technology and development. This, it seems to me, is not a legitimate alternative either. The products that have come to us via the 32-mm route are simply too good to be ignored. The fully concealed hinges, the vinyl-coated drawer glides, and the wide variety of edgings for particleboard have many applications, even within the traditional American system. Further, some of the European tooling is affordable in the small shop. Why should we limit ourselves? If you saw nothing of value in the European system, you probably would not be reading this book right now anyway.

The best alternative for most cabinetmakers is to pick and choose among the various European design elements. I am certainly not giving up the belt sander, the vibrator, and the hand-held power drill that my father gave me. But, like many of you, I have a lot of respect for the European hinges, not only because they are totally concealed but also because they are strong and easy to adjust. My furniture and cabinet customers have more and more frequently asked for features that have a specific European flavor—such as edge-banded particleboard components, frameless design, flat doors, and drawer fronts with European pulls. Operators of small shops, cabinetmakers such as myself, are not going to turn down these requests. Instead, we will find ways to build the requested designs. As a matter of fact, most of our customers really do not care about construction details. They are interested in the overall appearance of a piece, and in how well the piece performs the functions that it is supposed to fulfill.

Craftsmen naturally will want to make their own decisions regarding which elements from the 32-mm cabinetmaking system are suitable and affordable for their own situation. Someone with a lot of space (and more than a few dollars) may want to invest in a sliding-table dimension saw with a scoring blade because this tool can be used with such versatility. Others may see no advantage in such a machine, or they may have no space for it or may think it is a frivolous investment when they already have a well-functioning table saw. With every operation involved in producing the European cabinet, there are several choices in terms of tools and methodology. We do not need all the European equipment to produce a "Euro-look." In fact, it is even possible to construct the actual box just as it would be produced in a fully functioning European factory without any large investment in European equipment.

Whether we build pieces that possess European design characteristics in their entirety or in just some of their components, it's important for us to have a good understanding of the overall European cabinetmaking process. We need to understand all the operations, from the design stage through installation. We should know how strength is built into each unit, despite the absence of a face frame. We should also be aware of aspects of the design that create the image of "clean lines." With each stage of the 32-mm cabinetmaking system, we must consider how that particular phase affects the overall cabinet-building process. Therefore, we will be looking at each phase (cutting, edge banding, and line boring, for example) and determining whether or not it belongs in our shops. We will be looking at the purpose of each operation as well as determining which traditional operations should be changed or eliminated. We will take a look at a variety of tools and techniques that can be used to accomplish each operation, from the most to the least expensive. We will also look at alternatives to the European system itself, since we are free to choose only those aspects that we like the best.

It is certainly appropriate for us to compare the traditional American cabinetmaking process with the European system if for no other reason than that the old method will give us a good reference point for understanding the new. However, it should not be our purpose to stand in judgment as to which is the "better" system. The very idea of "better," in the woodworking context at least, is rather subjective. As I noted earlier, each of us has his or her own woodworking situation. What is important about our comparison has much more to do with determining which of the European principles are the most useful to us. Although many cabinetmakers have biases regarding the two systems, my hope is that this book will do justice to all woodworkers.

1
MATERIALS
AND CUTTING

KINDS OF MATERIALS

One way to get at the image of European cabinetry is to note the differences between the materials that are used to build European cabinets and those used for the traditional American style. Whereas nearly every part of a European cabinet is made of particleboard, conventional cabinets are generally made from solid lumber, although other materials are sometimes used. The 32-mm cabinetmaking system actually seems to have grown around particleboard rather than the other way around. In other words, the material was conceived and partially developed, and then the tools and hardware were developed to deal with it. In fact, one reason that we are beginning this book with a chapter on materials and cutting instead of planning and design is that the nature of particleboard dictates many design and assembly features in the totally European cabinet.

When people talk about the advantages of the European system, they are almost sure to bring up the dimensional stability created by using this composite material. Furthermore, when customers are interested in creating "European design" in their bathroom or kitchen, they are probably not thinking of construction techniques at all, but rather of smooth outer and inner surfaces yielded by using particleboard with an exterior of plastic laminate, melamine, or a similar coating. Therefore, in this chapter, we will look at the materials most commonly used in building the European cabinet as well as the methods employed for dimension-cutting these materials.

Substrates—Particleboards and Hardboards

Although it is certainly not necessary to know everything about particleboard when building European cabinets, some general knowledge of its characteristics can be very useful, especially in the small shop, where we will adapt parts of the system to meet our own individual needs and tastes.

The idea for gluing together tiny bits of wood to make a building material probably originated with the notion of saving scraps of wood that were otherwise useful only for burning. Our trade has always produced a substantial amount of waste, after all. Early attempts at creating such panels of wood failed, however, perhaps because suitable adhesives did not exist then.

As with so many important technological developments, effective particleboard production arose from a need. After World War II, Europe had a shortage of housing and furniture, as well as a lack of timber suitable for building. Add to these circumstances the appearance of synthetic resins suitable for binding together the fibres in wood flakes, chips, and other fragments, and you soon have a thriving particleboard industry.

As noted earlier, it was originally thought that an advantage of making particleboard was that it could reclaim wood-waste materials. Nowadays, however, the industry is no longer dependent on residues from other wood-processing operations. As part of their processing, particleboard plants often begin with logs or sections of logs, grinding them into the kinds of wood particles used at their own particular mill.

Particleboard is produced either in a matting process, where adhesive-treated particles are formed into a mat and then pressed between large platens, or in an extruding process, where such glued pieces are forced continuously between two hot dies or rollers. American mills employ the mat-forming process much more than the extrusion process, and this kind of board is generally considered superior. Since there is a difference in quality between the two kinds of boards, it is best, before a purchase, to ask your supplier which forming system was used.

The size, shape, and orientation of wood chips is fairly important in determining the quality of particleboard panels. In extrusion-processed board, for example, few of the wood particles are arranged to run parallel to the length of the board. (See Illus. 1.) This means that the extruded board has less strength where we may need it most: along the length of the board.

In the early stages of the industry, panel fabricators used particles of the same size and shape throughout the board. But since surface particles are the ones that really have the most to do with the panel's ability to bear a load, resist bending, and resist screw extraction, most modern panel manufacturers engineer the boards so that they have an inside, or core, of large, coarse, and cheap particles and an outside, or surface, of finer and more densely packed particles. Larger

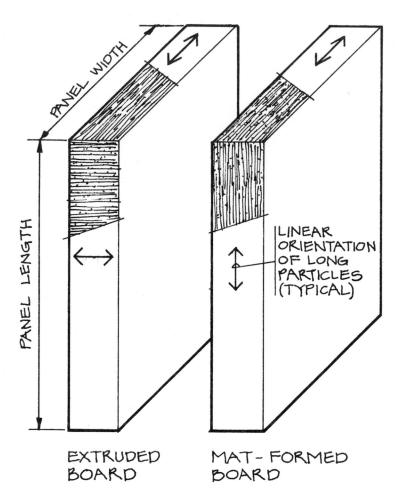

PANEL WIDTH

PANEL LENGTH

LINEAR ORIENTATION OF LONG PARTICLES (TYPICAL)

EXTRUDED BOARD

MAT-FORMED BOARD

Illus. 1. Extrusion- and mat-formed-particleboard processes result in different orientations of the particles, and consequently different qualities of board. Note the differences in linear particle alignment. The mat-formed board is stronger.

chips near the surface would contribute to board strength and resistance to screw extraction, but they would also have a tendency to "telegraph," or show through, any coverings applied to the board, especially veneer. Anyone who has done much work at all with particleboard is probably aware that it is softer in the middle, and in the core there are even tiny spaces visible to the naked eye. (See Illus. 2.)

As you might have guessed, the most prevalent wood varieties used in the production of particleboard are softwood species such as fir and pine. However, hardwoods are beginning to be used more in today's particleboard industry. Actually, hardwoods can be more economical to use in production than conifers (softwood) because hardwood fibres do not need to be compacted as tightly. It takes a greater volume of conifer to achieve the same density. Because of this compressibility, though, particleboard produced from conifer is actually stronger than the same-density board made from hardwood.[1]

Though the wood pieces that make up any composition-type board can be in a variety of shapes and sizes, the best particles seem to be flakes[2]—pieces that are as thin as veneer, less than an inch wide, and an inch or more long. These allow good overlap and provide plenty of surface area for glue to be applied. Since they lie in a sheet generally parallel to the surface, they will yield a strong, stiff board.

Cabinetmakers should also be aware of the kind of glue (resin or binder) that is used for bonding the individual bits of wood together. Urea-formaldehyde resin is most common in interior-used particleboard. It is not very water or moisture resistant, and the formaldehyde itself will seep out of any part of a particleboard cabinet member that is left exposed. Phenolic resin is more resistant to water and heat, and it should be specified in applications that will be exposed to higher levels of moisture. There is actually no particleboard really suitable for full exterior use because the wood particles are not fully coated with glue. Particleboards used in siding products must be painted or given other weathering treatments to withstand the elements.

So far, we have referred to particleboard only, making no distinction between types of particleboard and not distinguishing it from fibreboard and hardboard. Although these are all composite boards bound together with types of resin, there are some important differences among them.

Fibreboard is made somewhat like paper. Water is added to the raw material, and then the wood fibres are more or less ground into pulp. The pulp is then formed into panels via some combination of drying, heat, and pressure. The most common of the cabinetmaking materials produced in this way are medium-density fibreboard (MDF) and hardboard.

Medium-density fibreboard is denser and stronger than other particleboards such as industrial board, and it has more screw-holding power. It is available in common thicknesses (¼ in., ½ in., ⅝ in., and ¾ in.) and is frequently used for cabinet interiors built in the conventional way.

Illus. 2. A closeup view of a particleboard edge. Note that there are small gaps among the particles in the core, but few are visible near the surface of the board.

Hardboard is the thinnest (often ⅛ in. or ¼ in.), hardest, and most brittle of the fibreboards. This is because it is manufactured under higher pressure and heat (and often with the addition of oil) than other fibreboards. Hardboard is often used for cabinet backs and drawer bottoms.

Working with Substrates— Adjusting to Characteristics

So now we know something about the various particleboards, but how does this knowledge translate into technique? How do the European style builders handle particleboard, and which of our traditional systems will work with the material?

The characteristics of particleboard that have the most influence upon the way we cut, design, mill, and assemble are:

- dimensional stability;
- low cost;
- board flatness;
- board inflexibility;
- relative strength/weakness compared to other kinds of cabinet-building materials;
- stronger, rigid, more tightly compacted surfaces in contrast to weaker, looser cores in almost all particleboard;
- lack of resistance to water and humidity; and
- tendency of formaldehyde vapors to escape into the atmosphere.

Generally speaking, we can think of the first four items in the preceding list as advantages to be gained in constructing cabinetry from particleboard.

Dimensional Stability. This refers to the tendency of the board to retain its original dimensions over time and under varying conditions. As a response to heat and moisture changes, the length and width of a particleboard cabinet component will not be altered any more than those of the same component made of plywood. Plywood gets its dimensional stability from crossbanding—the alternation of grain direction in adjacent layers of panel. Common mat-formed particleboard is dimensionally stable because its tiny components almost all lie bonded parallel to the board's surfaces. There is obviously a crossband effect here, too, since the grain of some wood flakes is aligned with the length of the board while the grain of others is aligned with its width. Plywood and particleboard are both superior to most solid materials in terms of dimensional stability. Extrusion-formed board, however, does not retain its original sizing unless it is well sealed against moisture.

Low Cost. It is probably fairly obvious to everyone that the initial cost of particleboard is favorable. A sheet of A-D fir plywood (interior glue, one visual-quality face) can cost as much as 60 percent more than a sheet of industrial board and 12 percent more than a sheet of MDF in the same thickness. A precoated melamine panel of the same thickness (appearance grade on one face, with a "backer" on the other) may cost as much as 20 percent more than the A-D plywood, but it will not require surface treatment of any kind.

Perhaps less obvious are the savings derived indirectly from using particleboard. In the first place, the boards are often larger than plywood panels (49 in. x 97 in., versus 48 in. x 96 in.). This may seem insignificant, but it is not. If we are going to build cabinets without a face frame, which is another way of defining European design, then we will need the additional inch in either direction to reach our conventional standards of 24-in.-deep base cabinets and 12-in.-deep wall cabinets. You will want to stay fairly close to these standards, even if you elect to do your measuring in millimetres instead of inches, because people in all the other architectural trades think and design in terms of these same standards. Perhaps resulting in even greater indirect savings is the absence of grain on particleboard and some of its coatings. It makes absolutely no difference in our completed pieces whether we cut across the panel or along its length.

Flatness. Another great advantage in using particleboard over plywood, especially as doors and drawer components, is its superior flatness characteristic. Because of the way particleboard is engineered, the natural characteristics of the wood fibres exert less of an influence on the finished panel. Therefore, particleboard panels are especially flat. Any woodworker who has done much gluing or lamination is aware of this general rule: If a glued object cures flat, it will stay flat; if it cures crooked, it will stay crooked. Particleboard cures flat, and, as long as water absorption is controlled, it will make very flat cabinet components.

Board Inflexibility. In a kitchen that I recently built, plans called for a base-cabinet lazy-Susan-shelf unit to be installed in one of the corners. It was a small kitchen, and the users could not afford to sacrifice the space given up by a standard 28-in. prefabricated-shelf system. The cabinet interiors were made of melamine-coated particleboard. The round, pie-cut, 34-in. shelves themselves were not a difficulty, but when it came to adding a 2-in. retaining edge to the shelves, I did hit a modest snag. The ¼-in. particleboard was not flexible enough to wrap around the shelves, especially in its precoated form. So, I wound up stapling on a ⅛-in. retainer edge and then coating it with plastic laminate. (See Illus. 3.)

With the edge on my lazy-Susan shelves, inflexibility was a problem; however, in most instances, particleboard inflexibility is an advantage. For example, we want bookshelves to flex as little as possible. Even with my lazy Susan, the rigidity of the particleboard was a help in that it gave me very flat, sturdy shelves, despite their overlarge size.

Particleboard tends to be less flexible than plywood for at least a couple of reasons. First of all, recall that it is manufactured with the smallest particles at the surface. This translates into good bonding and great density at the surface of a panel, and both of these factors contribute to rigidity. Remember also that particleboard consists of flakes and other bits of wood that are overlapped, and that this over-

Illus. 3. A two-layer coating of a lazy-Susan shelf. Particleboard is not flexible enough to conform to this curve.

lapping tends to yield a crossbanding effect. Particleboard is therefore inflexible for the same reason that nine-ply panels are more inflexible than five-ply panels. As we have seen, cabinetmakers need to consider board inflexibility as they design and build.

Relative Strength/Weakness. The strength of the various boards can be measured in several ways. We can look at density, face, and edge screw-holding power as advertised by manufacturers; we can also generalize from our own experience. For the purposes of comparison, both here and in later chapters, it is probably a good idea to refer to some hard numbers. The ones that are most useful to practitioners of the trade are those regarding density and screw-holding power. These measurements are both useful and easy to understand.

Particleboard density is measured in pounds per cubic foot (pcf). Low-density boards are those less than 37 pcf, medium-density boards range from 37 to 50 pcf, and high-density boards are rated over 50 pcf. Obviously, the higher-density boards are stronger; but for cabinet work, we will most often use the medium-density board anyway. The high-density board is very heavy to handle, and in performance, it is quite similar to hardboard. Not much low-density board is manufactured, and it really does not have usefulness for the cabinetmaker. In comparing particleboard to plywood, density is not as significant as plies and crossbanding. Although usually more flexible than particleboards, plywood is probably the stronger material.

Screw-holding power is measured in pounds per square inch (psi). A rating of 200 psi should be considered rather low, whereas a measure near 300 psi can be thought of as sufficient for most cabinetmaking applications. If you have ever driven hinge screws into the surface of MDF, for example, you know that they hold quite well. On the other hand, screws driven into the edge or core of a piece of industrial particleboard are not likely to maintain a firm grasp, especially with the vibrations caused by a door. I have not seen any research on the screw-holding power of plywood, but from working the materials myself, I would contend that plywood would be superior over particleboard—although ply edges tend to delaminate when screws are driven into them. Neither plywood nor particleboard compares favorably with solid materials when it comes to resistance to screw extraction, especially with edge-driven screws.

Compacted Surfaces and Loose Cores. As to reduced sanding, the surface smoothness of particleboard isn't really an advantage because, in the European system, the particleboard will not usually be sanded or finished anyway. Instead, the surface serves as a core material for plastic, vinyl, or a similar coating. However, this surface smoothness does promote excellent bonding between the core material and its coating. As already noted, the highly compacted, well-glued surfaces also yield cabinet components that can be trusted to hold screws and other fasteners when installed through the thickness of the board.

The looser particles at the core of a piece of particleboard do present some problems for the cabinetmaker. When screws or nails are driven

into the edge of a piece of particleboard, they may not resist extraction well enough for some applications. If a given industrial board panel is rated at 285 psi for face screw-holding power, it may have an edge screw-holding power of only 225 psi. Therefore, some type of simple worked joint may be desirable in assembling the cabinet box, although the true European box is assembled with butt joints, not dadoes or rabbets. Several assembly features of the European box, based on the 32-mm system, are specially designed to overcome this weakness in the material. Whether we incorporate these assembly features or not, we need to design our own cabinetry so that this weak particleboard core will not yield inferior joints.

Resistance to Moisture. One of the characteristics of particleboard that can be a serious disadvantage is its response to water. First of all, particleboard does not resist the absorption of water as well as plywood because the tiny particles that go into each panel are not completely coated with adhesive. Naturally, anywhere that the particles are more loosely packed, as in the core, there is greater absorption than in parts of the panel that are packed more densely. The edge of a piece of particleboard can act a bit like a sponge if it comes in contact with a liquid. But this is only part of the potential problem.

Because most particleboard possesses fibres with grain direction parallel to the surface of the panel, any absorption of water will cause great swelling in panel thickness. A piece of particleboard that picks up moisture will not undergo major dimensional changes in width or length; but, if you have ever seen a piece that was left in the rain, you know that its thickness changes drastically. (See Illus. 4.) Thus, it can be said that when exposed to too much moisture, particleboard does not have dimensional stability in terms of thickness—in fact, soaked particleboard loses its flatness and strength as well. Therefore, as mentioned earlier, cabinetry with particleboard components must be effectively sealed against moisture. This is especially important with the European cabinet because it can be made entirely of particleboard members.

Formaldehyde. As already pointed out, the most common glue or adhesive found in particleboard is urea-formaldehyde resin. The trouble with this glue is that it tends to give off formaldehyde vapors, and these vapors are considered harmful. At the very least, they can cause headaches and nausea, and heavy doses of formaldehyde have been known to cause cancer in laboratory animals. The structure of most cabinet work actually compounds the problem. Since most cabinets are boxes, they collect the formaldehyde vapors in confined spaces very effectively. Then, every time the box is opened, the concentrated formaldehyde fumes come wafting out into the nostrils of the person who opened the door or drawer. The seeping of these vapors can continue for a long period of time, exposing the cabinet user to fumes again and again. Obviously not the best situation. Again, we can see the need for sealing all particleboard surfaces. In the 32-mm system, sides are generally covered with hard plastics, and edges are banded with vinyl or other material, but the line-boring operation itself opens routes of escape for formaldehyde vapor. Therefore, "extra" holes should not be drilled, or they should be filled in or coated in some way.

One way of overcoming some of the shortcomings of particleboard as a cabinetmaking material is simply to switch to a different core material, such as plywood or fibreboard. But, for the European cabinet, this is probably a poor trade-off. Plywood is stronger and lighter than particleboard, and it does not give off formaldehyde fumes; on the other hand, it is more expensive, more susceptible to warpage, more waste producing, and less reliable in terms of thickness as it comes from the mill. Fibreboards are also stronger than conventional particleboards, are at least as strong, and do not emit formaldehyde;

Illus. 4. Water can be very harmful to particleboard. Note the swelling in thickness of the darker board.

however, MDF, hardboard, and other types of fibreboard are also heavier and more expensive.

Since European cabinetry consists of plastic-coated components, we probably want to buy and work with panels that are already coated with plastic laminate, melamine-impregnated fibres, vinyl, or some other chosen finish. This may not be a major problem for high-volume users because they can specify the kind of core stock they want as well as the type of finished surface. However, the buyer of a few sheets at a time will usually not have this luxury. Most of the "European material" available to hobbyists and other small shop operators have a particleboard core.

Particleboard is certainly a suitable material from which to build cabinets, especially European style cabinets. I do not mean to suggest otherwise. But we do need to have a working knowledge of the material's shortcomings as well as its virtues in order to make use of it wisely. In later sections of the book when we look at subsystems, we will need to remember the characteristics of particleboard that have been introduced here.

Surface Materials—Plastics and Veneers

When consumers think of European design, what usually comes to mind are smooth grainless doors and finished ends, concealed hinges, and other similar attributes. On the other hand, much of the marketing for European machinery is centered around the notion that we can give either a contemporary or traditional look to the 32-mm box. Regardless of the style, what certainly seems true is that the surfaces of European cabinets are made of plastics and veneers. They have an interior that consists of particleboard coated with some variety of solid-colored plastic (in white, almond, or champagne, for example) and primary surfaces (doors, drawers, finished ends, and finished backs) of wood veneer, topcoated paper foil, wood-grain plastic, or solid-color plastic. The component edges are usually treated with materials to match adjacent surfaces.

If you have ever built a plastic laminate countertop, you already have some working knowledge of plastics. High-pressure plastic laminate, the kind you would use on a countertop, has many good qualities. It is strong and resistant to scratching and denting, while at the same time fairly easy to cut, glue, and trim.

Plastics applications in the cabinet trade are fairly recent as is the plastics industry itself, and there are still many people who would prefer to maintain cabinetmaking in as purely a woodworking mode as possible. This attitude may or may not be snobbish, but it is certainly a little unrealistic. Plastic surfaces have several functional advantages over wood surfaces, at least in secondary locations, and many of the people for whom we build will certainly benefit from them. The following are some of these advantages.

- Smoothness: Dishes and other articles slide very easily on plastic surfaces.
- Resistance to weather changes: Plastics are virtually unaffected by changes in temperature and humidity. They make a very ef-

fective seal against the penetration of moisture into and the emanation of formaldehyde from particleboard.

- Wear resistance: Since the cabinetmaking plastics are so tough, they are not worn away by everyday frictions, and the surfaces need no finishing—they protect themselves.
- Color: The tints that give plastics their coloration are an integral part of the plastic compound, not merely applied to the surface; slight scratching or abrading therefore has little effect on the color.
- Resistance to chemicals and corrosion: Plastics will stand up to any common household cleaner or solvent, and they simply do not corrode.
- Weight and strength: Plastics are very strong, particularly for their weight.

With so much going for them, plastics are hard to resist using in the cabinetmaking trade.

The plastics most commonly used in conjunction with cabinetmaking are laminated plastic, melamine-impregnated paper, and polyvinyl chloride (PVC).

Laminated Plastics. Laminated plastics are made by saturating paper or another fabric with a "thermosetting resin" such as polyester. (Thermosetting means that the plastic cannot be melted for remoulding.) Layers of the saturated fabric are then formed together by heat and pressure. The resulting sheets can then be glued onto the surface of particleboard with contact cement or similar adhesive. Laminated plastics are currently available in hundreds of colors and patterns, and marketed with names like Formica, Nevamar, and Wilsonart. We are all probably used to dealing with this material when making countertops. But when it is laminated onto sheets of particleboard, it can also be used as the raw material for European cabinet components. The advantage of using particleboard preclad with plastic laminates is that there is a great variety in color, texture, and finish. The disadvantage (and it's a major one) for anyone, except high-volume users, is expense. Even if you are willing to cement the plastic laminates onto sheets of particleboard yourself, the cost of the panels will double or triple.

Melamine. Melamine-impregnated paper is actually a type of laminated plastic. Melamine is a thermosetting plastic used for saturating the base fabric (paper). Again, sheets of the material are formed under heat and pressure. However, the material is available to us already fused onto particleboard sheets. Our choice of finishes is somewhat restricted, but what is available tends to be popular and the cost is fairly reasonable. Roseburg Forest Products Company markets such melamine panels in four wood patterns (three oak colors and a walnut) and four solid colors (white, almond, champagne, and grey). Backing sheets may be brown, black, white, or glueable. Purchasers can choose virtually any of the finishes on either the front or back of the panel. Some suppliers apply the coating only to particleboard sheets, whereas others use MDF for a core.

The National Electrical Manufacturers Association (NEMA) conducts performance tests on melamine-type panels and other laminated plastics. NEMA determines whether samples of the plastic meet or exceed standards under a variety of conditions, such as heat, light, household staining liquids, burning cigarettes, scrub cleaning, scuffing, abrasion, impact of a steel ball, and so on. Since melamine-coated panels are manufactured by a number of suppliers, and there is some variation in quality, it's best to ask for the results of the NEMA testing when you are shopping for cabinetmaking panels.

PVC. Poly-Vinyl Chloride is a "thermoplastic." This means that it can be softened by heating and then rehardened by cooling. PVC is simply a type of plastic resin formed into desired shapes. For covering particleboard or hardboard panels, the resin is formed into sheets and then applied to the substrate with an adhesive.

PVC is manufactured with varying degrees of rigidity, but most of the products that have been developed for furniture and cabinet builders are quite pliable. The more rigid products are generally used in making items for other trades, such as rain gutters and plumbing products. However, much edge-banding material is made of rigid PVC.

As with melamine-covered panels, vinyl-covered panels are available in several different solid colors and wood-grain patterns. In general, the PVC panels are less expensive than melamine panels, but they are not as tough, either. In terms of the prelaminated panels currently available, the vinyl is certainly resistant enough to solvents, water, and alcohol, but it will not stand up as well as melamine to impact and friction. In general, then, we can think of the vinyl coverings as "softer" than melamine coverings.

Veneer. When it comes to beauty, texture, and charm, no furniture material compares with real wood. Plastics may provide a harder and more destruction-resistant surface, but wood is still unmatched in providing warmth and natural beauty. When building the European style cabinet, we can still achieve those attractive features by using wood veneers laminated over a particleboard core. Naturally, it is also possible to build in the European style with veneer-core panels. (See Illus. 5.) We would certainly have lighter-weight cabinetry that way, but we would lose some virtues to be gained with the particleboard cores: reliable thickness dimensions, low warpage, and availability of plastics backings, to name a few. Actually, some veneer-core plywood on the market has a particleboard or hardboard layer for its first layer below the face. The appearance-grade veneer is thus backed up with a hard, very smooth core material, making an excellent surface for desk tops like the one in Illus. 5.

Veneers are sliced from trees either as plain slices or rotary slices. Plain-sliced veneer is generally more prized for its beauty than rotary, at least if it is matched properly on the substrate panel. Of course, it is also more expensive. This is one of the drawbacks of working with veneer anyway—it costs a good deal more than melamine coverings. Also, unlike the plastics, veneer can require sanding and finishing—two of the steps that the European system was designed to eliminate.

Veneer is readily available either as sheets to be applied over an assembled box by the cabinetmaker, or as the facing on flat panels.

Illus. 5. This European style desk was built with veneer-core oak plywood. Can you identify the elements that display a European influence?

There are a number of circumstances that call for using sheets of veneer, but none of them seem to apply here. In making the European cabinet, buying the veneer already attached to its substrate is very helpful. First of all, it eliminates an unnecessary step. Any proponent of the 32-mm system recommends beginning with preclad panels just for the sake of simplicity. Also, using preveneered panels is a way to avoid some potential problems that can occur when working with veneer: telegraphing and the tendency for splits or cracks to occur along grain lines. However, there is a fairly new veneer product that helps us with these problems; the wood veneer is actually bonded over polyester laminate so that telegraphing is virtually eliminated and the veneer is easier to work with. (See Illus. 6.)

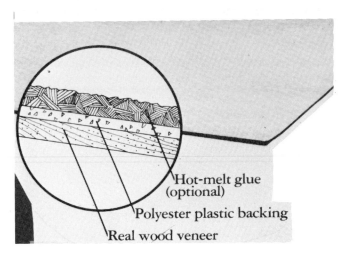

Hot-melt glue
(optional)

Polyester plastic backing

Real wood veneer

Illus. 6. Wood veneer bonded to polyester laminate. (Copyright Westvaco Corporation, 1989. All rights reserved.)

One good reason to use veneer could be the desire for a wood species outside and melamine surfaces inside the cabinet. This is an especially good idea if you want to create a traditional look while still having some of the advantages of plastic. The idea would be to make finished ends from material that has champagne or almond melamine on one side and a glueable backer on the other. Then, all you have to do is cement veneer over the backer to yield a real-wood finished end. I actually did this on kitchen cabinets—my own, although I used ⅛-in. oak plywood instead of veneer. Later, I found out that I could have purchased particleboard sheets with almond melamine on one side and oak veneer already in place on the other. I like my kitchen cabinets very much, but I don't really enjoy the smell of contact cement or wasting time and money. I could have saved 8 or 10 hours, a gallon of contact cement, and most of the cost of four sheets of ⅛-in. oak plywood if I had known about the veneer-melamine product a bit sooner. If you plan a similar project, be sure to do some investigating on the phone before diving into a materials purchase.

Probably one of the best reasons to employ veneers on a Euro-style cabinet job is if you have developed a design with curves that need veneer wrapping. I am sure there are other usages, too, but remember that veneering has its roots in traditional cabinetmaking. Veneers were originally used to extend the usage of the most attractive wood grains.

Miscellaneous Surface Coverings. There are a few other types of materials that bear mention as surface coverings. Paper foil is one, although it is generally only found on furniture and cabinetry produced in large-scale operations. Most custom cabinetmakers consider it inferior because it is simply paper with a printed design, usually simulating wood. Although it looks like wood, it is smooth like most paper that comes in rolls. Paper foil is too thin to be very protective; in fact, it must usually be protected with some sort of topcoat finish. Its generally flimsy nature makes it inappropriate in most cases as a European cabinet material.

"Painted" coatings are also available. Willamette Industries' Kortron, for example, is a plastic-type material that is applied to particleboard in liquid form and then cured, yielding a relatively hard, damage-resistant surface.

Earlier in this chapter, we looked at some of the important properties of particleboard, and we saw that it was indeed an appropriate cabinet material when properly sealed. From our brief survey of the various covering materials, it is fairly obvious that melamine-impregnated paper is one of the best substances to use over the particleboard core. It is available already clad upon panels in a variety of colors and finishes; it is cleanable, stain resistant, and very tough; and it is not expensive. However, for some cabinet components, vinyl-covered particleboard or hardboard can be the best alternative.

Edging Materials

It is imperative to cover particleboard edges with some kind of material that effectively limits penetration of moisture and release of formaldehyde fumes. Our choices are familiar materials: laminated plastic, PVC, real wood, and papers.

All of these—the plastics, the papers, and the wood veneers—are available in continuous rolls, and in various widths ranging from ⅜ in. up to 2 in. and even wider. In the smaller shop, such as the garage or basement shop, it's best to buy one width that is just slightly larger than the thickest panels you plan to use. For example, if you are going to build a bathroom vanity cabinet, you may plan to use ⅝-in. stock for the ends, bottom, and partitions; ½-in. stock for the drawer members; and ¾-in. stock for an adjustable shelf. To edge-band these components, you could buy a roll of ¹³⁄₁₆-in. panel edging. In terms of length, the rolls range from 250 ft. up to 1,000 ft., depending on the type of material, its thickness, and whether or not the material is precoated with hot-melt glue. Roller-type panel edging is available in a great variety of colors and finishes. You will generally want to choose a color or wood grain to match one of either of the adjacent surfaces on the panel. In the small shop, material that is backed with heat-activated glue is also preferred.

The characteristics of these various edge-banding materials have already been covered in some detail. In general, the laminated plastics are the hardest, and the PVC is quite pliable and therefore easy to apply. The papers are either thin and preprinted with a wood grain, or they are brownish kraft paper ready for painting. Although wood veneer must be finished, much of it is easy to apply and trim because it's backed with paper or polyester.

One material that is important not to overlook is solid wood, ⅛ in. thick or thicker. If you have built shelving, then you have probably already supplied some solid edging (perhaps ¼ in. thick) as shelf facings. This kind of panel edging has definite advantages for those of us who work in smaller shops. In the first place, we already have the right kind of tooling to cut and trim this sort of edge band: a jointer, table saw, belt sander, and router, for example. Secondly, it is easy to apply using conventional methods: glue and clamps—or glue and brads, if you are not too fussy. Furthermore, the European cabinetmakers themselves use a lot of thin, solid edge bands on their products; a trip to the furniture store confirms this. Of course, we can also build a face frame out of solid stock and then attach it to a box made from melamine-covered particleboard. The European designers have pointed out some valid drawbacks of the face-frame system, but there are still advantages as well. Many traditionalist cabinetmakers, realizing the practical virtues of plastics-covered interiors, are building this way right now. (See Illus. 7.)

Working with Panel Coverings

Anyone who has worked with A-2 plywood has already worked with preclad panels. And what you already know about working with veneer-covered materials will also apply to working with plastics-covered panels.

Basic Principles. There are three reasons for being especially concerned with the way that preclad particleboard reacts to milling. They are as follows.

- Tear away or chipping is worse with plastics (particularly the high-pressure type) than with veneer. This is because plastics have no grain direction, and bits of plastic will tear away from the underside of a board being sawn just as easily when cut along its length as when cut across its width. (See Illus. 8.)
- There may be no way to "hide" the effects of tear away because of

Illus. 7. A section of a traditional kitchen wall cabinet with a European material interior. All the secondary surfaces are made of melamine or vinyl.

Illus. 8. Tear away or chipping on the underside of a melamine panel. The effects are just as bad along the length and across the width of the panel.

the way that European style cabinets are usually put together—with butt joints.
- Plastics are "unforgiving"; that is, repairs are much more difficult with plastics than with wood, at least in smaller shops.

Nevertheless, we can work in plastics with the conventional tools that we are used to. Plastics can be cut and otherwise milled with circular and band saws, drills, routers, and other familiar tools. Still, it is fairly obvious that we need to find some solutions to the special problems presented by "European" materials.

Adaptations. As a cabinetmaker, it is up to you to choose the systems or materials that will best suit your shop and the processes you prefer. In general, then, you can adopt one or more of the following changes.

- You can buy expensive European equipment designed specifically to make smoother, more accurate cuts. This is costly, but it makes the best sense for high-volume shops and factories because reduced labor will help to pay for the investment eventually.
- You can purchase bits, blades, and other such relatively inexpensive tooling that can yield smoother and more accurate cuts and details when used in conjunction with more conventional equipment. This requires more setup time, but it is the most sensible approach for hobbyists and other low-volume operators.
- You can alter some aspects of the 32-mm construction system—using rabbets and dadoes, for example. This approach also cuts into the time-saving aspects of European design but is the route that many cabinetmakers are taking.

As we continue to explore the various elements of European cabinetmaking, keep in mind that we are examining a series of goal-directed processes. For each process, there are a number of possibilities for reaching the goal. Some choices will cost more in terms of time whereas others will cost more monetarily.

CUTTING COMPONENTS TO SIZE

Among other names for the 32-mm system is the term "flat panel processing." The more we make use of flat panels rather than solid stocks, the more we are building in the modern European style. Therefore, we will focus our attention in this section on tools and methods for cutting cabinet components from pieces of particleboard that are covered with plastic or veneer on both sides.

European Saws

The key word in European cabinetmaking is accuracy. Holes from the line-boring operation must be nearly perfectly positioned. If you were to convert utterly to the European cabinet system, you would first cut out cabinet parts, edge-band them, drill a series of holes, and then assemble and attach the accessories. Nearly every step in the 32-mm system depends upon cutting cabinet components to exactly the right sizes. The location of the line-bored holes depends upon the accuracy of the cut. These holes must be set back a certain amount from the edges of the box; they must be consistently spaced 32 mm apart, center to center; and they must have the correct diameter. All subsequent assembly and attachment depends on this. Therefore, if you were going to start buying European machinery, one piece at a time, you would first buy a saw.

Horizontal Panel Saw. The horizontal panel saw is designed for use in high-automation, high-volume cabinet factories. Many are controlled by computer or laser. They are often capable of cutting in two directions on each sheet of material set in place. In fact, a horizontal panel saw can also cut several panels at once. There is even equipment available to off-load the cut panels onto conveyor belts for the next stage of production. Obviously not a hobbyist's tool, such a saw can easily cost over $100,000 and consume hundreds of square feet of floor space. (See Illus. 9.)

Illus. 9. A computerized, numeric-controlled horizontal panel saw. (Courtesy of Holzma-U.S., Inc.)

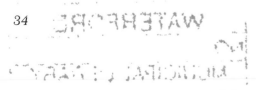

Vertical Panel Saw. The vertical panel saw not only costs far less than the horizontal panel saw, but also requires less floor space. The tool consists of a large surface support against which the operator leans each panel that is to be cut, a bottom track with rollers that makes it easy to load a panel and roll it into cutting position, and a circular saw attached to a rigid metal guide. There are also clamps to hold a piece of stock in place while it is being cut. Vertical panel saws are manually or push-button controlled. Most are capable of cutting either horizontally or vertically, depending on which way the saw head is pivoted. This tool can be loaded and operated by one person, standing upright.

In the past, panel saws were used in the European system simply to bring pieces to near-finished size for cabinet components. The pieces then had to be cut to exact size on a sliding-table dimension saw. Currently, however, very precise panel saws are being used to achieve a finished dimension with one cut.

Some cabinetmakers have been doing the cutting in their shops with conventional panel saws for years. When you build in the European mode, there is nothing wrong with this approach, especially if you intend to use your vertical panel saw as a means for getting components near size. We have already stated that this is an acceptable means of cutting out cabinet components, even in a large production-oriented business. Besides, the cutting mechanism of a vertical panel saw is more or less a portable circular saw mounted to a guiding system or frame. Saws with rigid guiding mechanisms and an effective means of keeping cutter vibrations to a minimum are the best when it comes to working with plastics-covered material. Still, reliable saws of this kind can be expensive.

Sliding-Table Dimension Saw. If I could afford the cost of a machine like this, and if I could afford the space it requires, I would own a sliding-table dimension saw. (See Illus. 10.) Though such a machine is simply a high-tech version of the table saws we are used to, it is extremely precise and possesses several fantastic features that our ordinary table saws do not.

The sliding table on this tool allows us to work with heavy panels. The mechanisms that make this possible include a swinging arm that can carry a good deal of weight, and a roller carriage that allows a portion of the table itself to slide forward and backward easily and precisely. Even full-sized panels can be cut with ease. (See Illus. 11.)

Scoring blades are a valuable feature on a saw used for cutting panels. The dimension saw can have a separate arbor and motor spinning a small blade just inches in front of the main blade and rotating in the opposite direction. The purpose of such a blade is to prevent chipping of the panel as it is fed across the table. (See Illus. 12.) Scoring blades work because they cut in the same direction as

the feed; that is, they remove each bit of material towards the inner core of the sheet's core. (See Illus. 13.)

Much of the cutting done on a sliding-table dimension saw is performed with the aid of the cross slide. This is the bar attached perpendicular to the sliding table and against which we position each piece being cut. It operates something like the mitre gauge on a conventional table saw, except that it is positioned firmly in front of the leading edge of the sheet rather than behind the stock's trailing edge. (Again, see Illus. 11.) You can make repetitious cuts in conjunction with the cross slide by using its throw-over stops.

One of the factors giving the dimension saw its stability is its weight. The base is often filled with steel-reinforced concrete. Naturally, this really limits vibration and allows the machine to bear a good deal of weight. Many have fine-adjustment capabilities for settings on blade-tilting angle, rip dimension, and scoring-blade placement. These are often set by referring to digital readouts. It is also possible to adjust RPM speeds up to 7,200 RPM and higher. The motor that drives the main saw blade can be rated at 10 horsepower.

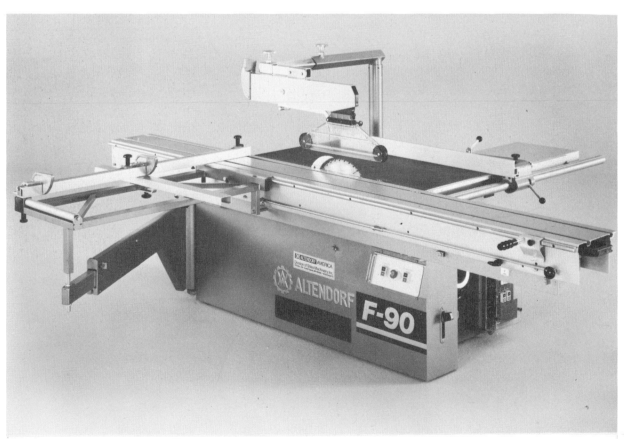

Illus. 10. A sliding-table dimension saw. (Courtesy of Altendorf America.)

In addition, a dimension saw has standard equipment, such as a rip fence and mitre fence, as well as standard optional accessories, like automatic roller feeding.

Scoring blades need to make their cuts exactly the same width as the cutting blade that follows. If the scoring kerf is too narrow, cabinet components will be splintered on the bottom side, just as if there

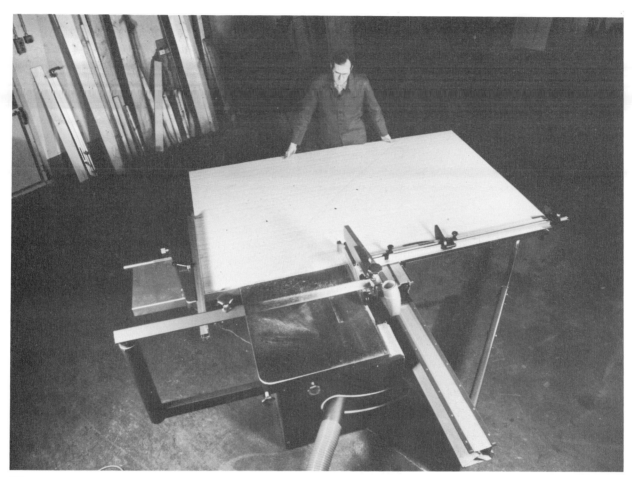

Illus. 11. The sliding table allows manageable, precise cutting with large panels. (Courtesy of Altendorf America.)

were no scoring blade at all. If the kerf is too wide, then we will wind up with four 90° corners on each cut. There are two types of scoring blades. One is a conical shaped blade, and its width of kerf is controlled by raising or lowering the blade slightly (the farther the blade projects into a panel, the wider will be its cut); the other is actually two, very thin blades separated by shims that control width.

These high-tech dimension saws are engineered to give smooth, chip-free, accurate cuts. As with the kind of table saw that you may

Illus. 12. The smaller scoring blade operates in harmony with the main blade. (Courtesy of Altendorf America.)

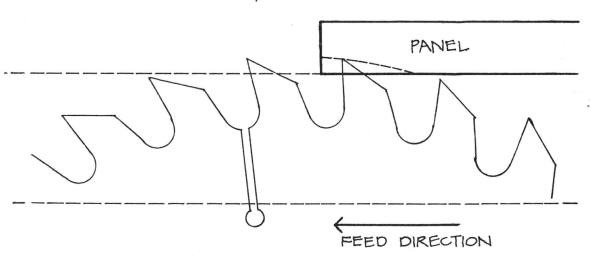

Illus. 13. Scoring-blade function is based on cutting with the direction of the feed. Tear away is reduced because each chip from the cut is driven towards the inner core of the panel.

be used to, there can be a fairly wide difference in quality (and cost) among them. I talked to one cabinetmaker who had done a good deal of cutting on such a machine. He reported that it produced excellent results and that he could cut very quickly with the machine when properly set up. On the other hand, he also said that adjustments took what seemed a substantial length of time. The best dimension

Illus. 14. In this shop, the dimension saw is used instead of a more conventional table saw. Because of space limitations, the swinging-arm mechanism is in storage. Solid stocks are ripped on this machine, but the scoring blade is used only for cutting sheet goods.

saw models are not only accurate, but they are also easy and fast to set up, quickly readjusted, and reliable. Many medium-sized traditional shops have invested in a dimension saw, either as a substitute for a conventional table saw or in addition to one as a specialized tool for cutting sheet goods. (See Illus. 14.)

Modifications to Conventional Cutting

It is fairly easy to see that most European cutting equipment was developed for medium and large cabinet shops. The purchase price alone is a big limitation. Furthermore, even if small shop operators believe that their production volume will justify the purchase of a dimension saw, its rather great space requirements are an additional problem to be overcome. Thus, unless you are willing to build a new cutting room and invest thousands of dollars instead of hundreds in your cutting operation, you need to find alternate techniques to achieve the same type of cuts. The most important characteristics to strive for in your cutting operation are straightness, nonsplintering, perpendicularity, smoothness, and accurate dimensions. There are a number of ways to achieve these characteristics, of course, but most of them call for some investment of time (rather than a great deal of money).

Saw Blades. There is no way of making a poor-quality, stationary circular saw into a decent panel-cutting tool. Even if we start with a good-quality 10-in. three-horsepower table saw, nothing is going to turn it into a sliding-table dimension saw. Still, proper blade selection can help a great deal in improving the cut quality on cabinet panels.

In general, carbide will cut plastic material much better than hardened steel. If you are not already doing most of your cutting with carbide-tipped blades, your first experience with melamine will take you irrevocably in that direction. Carbide not only yields smoother, more chip-free cuts, but it also wears far more slowly than steel when used on plastics, therefore making it more economical.

Perhaps just as important as using carbide in dealing with plastics-covered sheets is the tooth grind. For most high-pressure plastic, triple-chip-grind blades are better than either square grinds or alternating top bevels. With the triple-chip blade, every other tooth has a face with three cutting planes. (See Illus. 15.) This stabilizes the cut.

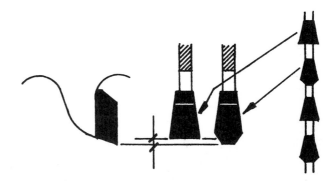

Illus. 15. Tooth configuration on a triple-chip blade.

Probably the best blade to use for the type of cuts we need in panel processing is the relatively new, hollow-ground carbide blade. (See Illus. 16.) The hollow face of each cutting tooth gives smooth, chip-free edges, even along the underside of each component. Such a blade can cost two to three times as much as one of the other grinds, but it can be a very wise investment because it really will improve the quality of your cuts.

Illus. 16. Hollow-ground, carbide-tipped blades are excellent for cutting plastics- and veneer-faced materials.

Decreasing Vibration. There are several methods for reducing extraneous vibrations that can interfere with the quality of your cuts, but again, there is no substitute for a high-quality stationary saw. We can steal an idea from the European tool designers and pour several inches of concrete into the base of our saw, for example, but this will do very little good if we do not have a saw with a smooth-operating arbor, sturdy mountings for the motor and saw, and balanced bearings.

One simple method for reducing vibration is to mount the blade on the arbor between stabilizers. These are much like oversized washers that spread out the pressure applied by the arbor-locking nut. (See Illus. 17.)

Of course, it is important to employ blades that are properly balanced. Buying blades that are guaranteed to be only a few thousandths of an inch out of perfect alignment across the plane is a sound practice. Bargain blades can be all right if you are cutting components that go behind a face frame, but they will not yield edges of good enough quality to attach laminate or PVC edge banding.

Illus. 17. Stabilizers are used somewhat like washers to reduce blade vibration.

Secondary Milling. One option that can be very effective in terms of producing high-quality panel edges is secondary milling. This basically means resigning yourself to a second or trimming cut. I know this may seem a bit ridiculous, but it is really not as bad as it seems. Oh sure, it would be idiotic if a high-volume manufacturer were trying to make a lot of money with this routine, but it is a technique that can work in smaller shops or in any shop where we want to add the capability for building in the European mode, but we don't want to replace the conventional style completely. Even the European system shows some acceptance of this approach. After all, recall that it is acceptable within the European system to bring pieces near size with a panel saw and then to cut to exact dimension with another saw.

One piece of machinery that can be used in a secondary milling operation with excellent results is the jointer. The idea is simple. First, cut cabinet components oversized by some predetermined amount—perhaps ⅛ in. The amount you cut oversize depends on the width of the largest chips torn out by cutting. Next, the jointer is set up the same way it would be for edge straightening, and the ragged edges of cut panels are removed with the jointer knives. Theoretically, cutting all pieces oversized by the same amount and then treating all edges the same will result in components of reliable dimension, but in practice, some extra care must be taken to ensure that pieces are indeed exactly the correct sizes. Also, this method is not very effective for cutting veneered pieces to length because we are planing across the veneer's grain. However, this system also has some positive features: It allows us to cut pieces to approximate size without changing saw blades, and it creates edges that are very smooth, very straight, perfectly perpendicular with the face, and usually perfectly chip free.

Kerfing. Making kerf cuts in the ply or particleboard panel is actually a type of scoring that you can perform as a double-milling operation. Kerfing may be done with either a radial arm saw or a table saw.

With the table saw, we make the scoring cut with the blade protruding only slightly above the surface of the table and by feeding backwards. In this respect, it's as if we were using a saw equipped with a scoring blade. It is very important to note, right now, that such a practice is not entirely safe with some saws. There are two key items to remember if you are contemplating using this technique: First, make sure that the rear of the saw, the end you will be feeding from, is not obstructed by the motor, the drive belts, or any other moving parts; second, make sure that you are only allowing the blade to protrude above the table enough to project through the veneer or plastics covering on the sheet's underside (similar to the arrangement in Illus. 13). It is also wise to remind yourself to proceed with an extra measure of caution since you will have to operate the saw without a splitter, and since any "kicking" or binding of the saw will have the tendency to draw your hands towards the blade rather than pushing them away. (See Illus. 18.)

Once you have completed the scoring cut, you can raise the blade up high enough to make a through cut and then feed the panel through as you would normally do (from the front).

In addition to the special safety requirements that we have already looked at, there can be some functional drawbacks to this cutting system. In order to attain straight, chip-free panel edges, both your reverse or scoring cut and your forward or through cut must be in exactly the same place—a matter made even more difficult by absence of the splitter. Besides that, large panels will be very difficult to handle in both directions. If you are like me, you use support tables to catch long or wide pieces as they come through the saw. In the two-step process just described, this is not a very good option because support tables would be in the way as soon as we switched from rear feed to front feed (or vice versa).

The radial arm saw can be a very workable station at which to cut materials to length by scoring and cutting.

I am not suggesting ripping in reverse on the radial arm saw, even for scoring cuts. Because the radial saw cuts from above, there is too much pressure on the thickness of the panel for safe feeding.

On the other hand, length-cutting of Euro-style materials is quite easy and reliable on the radial arm saw. If you are already familiar with cutting material to length on the radial saw, you know that tear away can be a real problem with this tool. However, the way to control it is to use a lockable stop for each cut. Flip-over lockable stops are commercially available, or you can make your own lockable stops with a tape measure and a block that can be clamped in place.

Raise the blade enough so that it will cut just over halfway through the thickness of your material. All you have to do then is to position the cutting panel against the rear fence and your stop (set to the desired measurement), draw the saw assembly out for the first cut (actually a deep-scoring cut), and then flip the material over and repeat the cut from the other side. (See Illus. 19.)

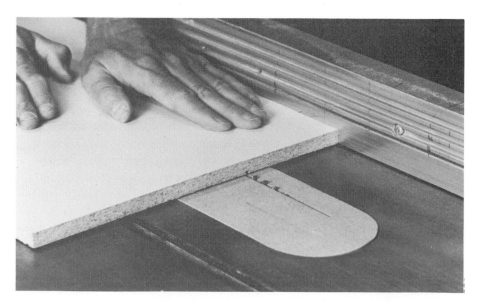

Illus. 18. Preparing to score a piece of melamine-covered material on the table saw. Notice that the feed is controlled from the back of the saw and that blade height is just high enough to score.

Illus. 19. Double milling with the radial arm saw. Here, the first cut, the deep score, is being completed.

Although this technique can yield excellent results, it doesn't work quite so well with wide pieces, panels wider than 16 in. We can still use the technique with the wider panels, but we have to position the piece four times for each cut. You would position the piece against your stop and make the first cut as usual (position #1); flip it over and cut (position #2), remove the stop, turn the piece end for end, carefully line up the saw, and make the cut (position #3); and reposition the stop, flip the piece over, and finally draw the saw forward to complete the cut (position #4).

Other Tool Modifications. There are several simple modifications that the owner of a small shop can make to improve accuracy, speed, smoothness, and straightness. One very simple modification is to make and use saw inserts that have very small clearances around the blade in your table saw. This helps a great deal in terms of reducing tear away on the undercut. (See Illus. 20.)

Another important modification is to install an accurate rip fence and gauge on your saw, if you have not already done so. Such a fence will cost in the hundreds of dollars, but it is an addition that is well worth your investment. It saves a great deal of setup time because you don't need to use a tape measure to get the right measurement, and you don't even need to turn off the saw to change cutting dimensions. (See Illus. 21.)

You can achieve remarkably good panel quality using conventional machinery, but you need to be willing to spend a little extra time in caring for your tools, setting up, and making fine adjustments. It is vital to keep blades and cutters sharp. With your table saw, make sure that the fence is always set up perfectly parallel to the blade—

and with your radial arm saw, make sure it's kept perfectly perpendicular to the blade.

Design Changes. One approach that can be taken in response to the more stringent cutting demands of European design is to alter the construction features of the system itself. We will actually look at these options in more detail in later chapters, but I will mention them generally here because all the systems of cabinetmaking are so completely interrelated. The idea here is not to improve cut quality but rather to use systems that will not require such perfection in cut quality. A purist of the European approach (or someone who is trying to sell you European machinery and hardware) might not approve of all these systems. Some of these approaches may be very familiar to you because they are traditional methods. Here are three of the most common.

- Surface selection, that is, designating a primary or "good" side and a secondary or "bad" side on all your panels as you are cutting; this way, most of the effects of chipping can be at least partly concealed next to walls and ceilings, inside drawer sections, or in other secondary locations.
- Joinery, that is, planning to use conventional cabinet joints, such as rabbets and dadoes, which will effectively hide torn edges and also conceal some ends and edges that are not perfectly straight.
- Framing, that is, planning to use a face frame, which covers the front edge of most cabinet components quite well.

It should be pointed out that the conventional approaches work quite well in terms of incorporating particleboard and plastic laminates, but every conventional technique you use in construction can

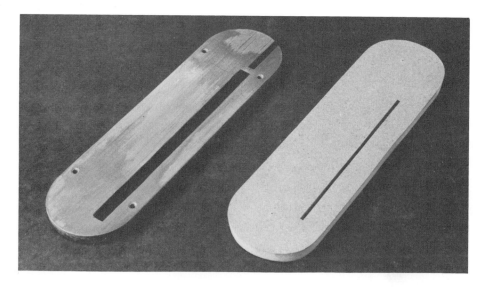

Illus. 20. Saw inserts. The homemade insert will result in much less chipping on the undercut.

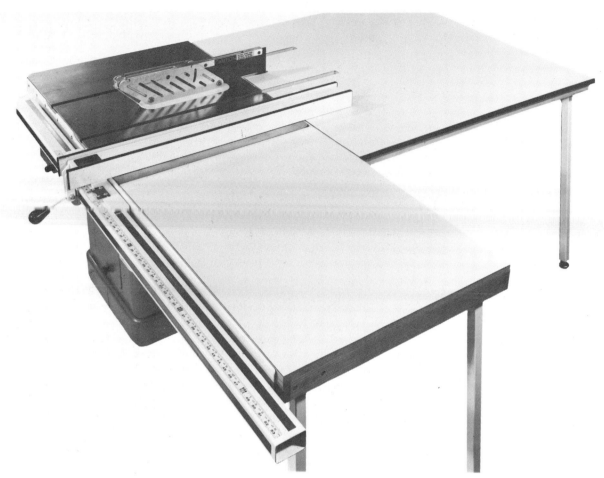

Illus. 21. Time-saving, accurate rip fences are a wise investment. (Courtesy of Biesemeyer Manufacturing Corporation.)

lessen the cabinet's "European" character. But I remind you that you are the absolute authority on determining how much of the European system is suited to you in your own particular shop.

SUMMARY

European cabinetmaking can be distinguished by the use of certain materials—specifically, particleboard that is covered with high-pressure plastic laminate, melamine-impregnated paper, vinyl, veneer, or another covering, before being cut.

Particleboards and hardboards are inexpensive, dimensionally stable, and flat with no voids—all desirable characteristics for most cabinet and furniture building. On the other hand, particleboard does not resist moisture very well. It has a weak, loose-particle inner core and it allows formaldehyde to escape as vapor through surfaces, ends, and edges that are not covered with another material.

Plastics coverings are hard, durable, and resistant to cleansers and most stains, making them very practical cabinet surfaces, but veneers are often considered more beautiful. Although precoated plastics eliminate the need for sanding and finishing, they present certain problems in the cutting operation, namely tear away and cut edges that are neither straight nor smooth—in cabinetry that seems to cry for increased quality levels. Veneer skins not only present tear-away problems but also usually require sanding and finishing.

European cabinet design also employs thin edge bands on cabinet components. There is usually not a face frame. The materials that are used for edgings are plastics, veneers, and hardwoods.

The special particleboard and plastics cutting problems can be solved by investing in some very expensive machinery, by modifying conventional tools and techniques, or by using traditional construction systems with European style materials.

RECOMMENDATIONS

Precovered particleboards definitely make sense. Even if you want to build a kitchen that looks very traditional, melamine-covered sheets are an excellent material for interiors.

Here is a list of materials that are aptly used in building conventionally joined cabinetry:

Thickness/Description		Uses
¼"	appearance-grade vinyl covering (one side—raw surface on other)	drawer bottoms and cabinet backs
½"	appearance-grade melamine covering (both sides)	drawer subfronts, drawer sides, sliding shelves, and lazy Susan shelves
⅝"	appearance-grade melamine covering (both sides)	finished ends, shelves, and partitions
⅝"	appearance-grade melamine covering (one side—backing grade on other)	wall ends, base bottoms, partitions seen on one side, wall-cabinet tops, and finished ends to be covered
¾"	appearance-grade melamine covering (both sides)	shelves, drawer backs, nailers, and finished ends

If you elect to employ Euro-assembly techniques, you would use one thickness (probably ⅝ in.) and one type of material (perhaps appearance-grade—both sides) throughout the cabinet box for the sake of simplicity.

Production levels are the key in planning for tooling and machinery. Those of us operating in basements, garages, and other small shops are not going to be very interested in large, expensive saws. But the following tools and techniques are most useful in achieving Euro-quality cuts on conventional machines:

- sharp, hollow-ground, carbide-tipped saw blades;
- stabilizers;
- edge trimming with the jointer on pieces that require perfect edges; and
- deep scoring with the radial arm saw on narrow pieces.

In addition, of course, it is possible to employ some conventional techniques to avoid the need for perfect cut quality.

[1] Moslemi, A. A. 1974. *Particleboard Volume 1: Materials,* Southern Illinois University Press, pp. 8–11.
[2] Heebink, B. G., Hann, R. A., and Haskell, K. H. 1964, Particleboard quality as affected by planer shaving geometry. For Prod J. 14(10): 486–494. [Reference from Moslemi, A. A. *Particleboard Volume 1: Materials,* pp. 50–54.]

2
DESIGNING IN THE EUROPEAN SYSTEM

GENERAL ASSUMPTIONS OF THE EUROPEAN SYSTEM

There are several assumptions that underlie the European system of cabinet designing and building. Most of these originate with the overall idea that it is desirable to reduce the amount of skilled labor necessary in cabinet production. In other words, European cabinet manufacturers show a decided preference for investment in machinery and tooling rather than in skilled labor. This is accomplished by consistently following the same procedures, and by consistently using the same measurements, again and again.

Line Boring

Every conceivable aspect of European cabinetry seems to be centered on the 32-mm line-boring system. As pointed out earlier, with this system a series of holes are drilled into specific locations of certain cabinet components, and these holes are used for fastening the box components together, for attaching door hinges, for insertion of adjustable-shelf supports, for drawer mounting, and even for fastening boxes together. There are actually two series of holes that need to be drilled for the system to work—one series 8 millimetres in diameter, drilled in a horizontal configuration on the cabinet; and another 5 millimetres in diameter, arranged vertically on the cabinet. These series of holes are called the line-boring pattern.

The 8-mm (close to ⁵/₁₆-in.) holes are used for the insertion of dowels or other types of connectors. They are drilled into the surfaces of end panels and into the ends of fixed horizontal pieces, such as bottoms, cross members, and wall-cabinet tops. (See Illus. 22.)

Some aspects of the hole positioning are critical, especially vertical placement, since this controls the exact location of all the fixed horizontal members. For example, one-half the thickness of the cabinet

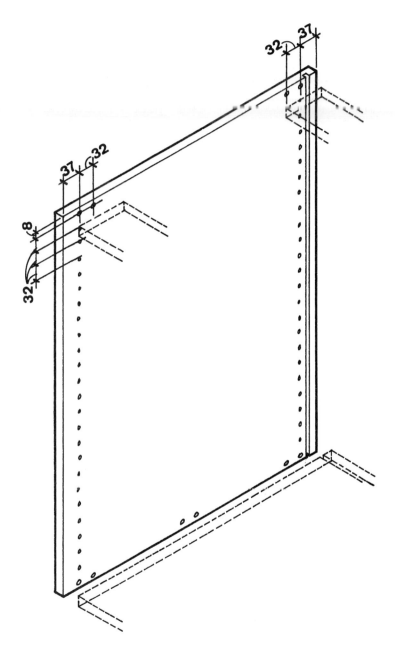

Illus. 22. Horizontal line boring for dowel assembly of a European base cabinet. Hole diameter is 8 mm, but spacings across the width of ends and other components can vary.

material is used as the distance at which to center the holes along the top edge of the ends. If we are using ⅝-in. (16-mm) stock for the cabinet, then we will center the holes for dowels exactly 5⁄16 in. (8 mm) from the top and bottom edges of the end panel. Notice that the end panel in Illus. 22 is not notched for a toe kick. Along with several other advantages, this allows us to line-bore for dowels along the top and bottom edges with exactly the same drilling setup.

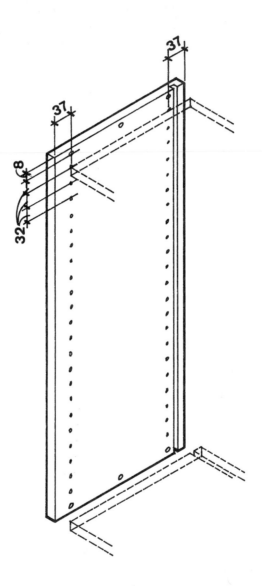

Illus. 23. The vertical line-boring pattern should be lined up exactly on center with the outer holes in the top horizontal pattern. In this example, we are using 16-mm (⅝-in.) material. Thus, the top dowel holes are centered 8 mm (5⁄16 in.) from the top edge. The center of the top hole in the vertical hole pattern is 32 mm below that. Also, note the 37-mm backset from the front edge.

The 5-mm (close to ³⁄₁₆-in.) holes are arranged vertically to allow the attachment of all the accessories that a cabinet might receive—most commonly drawers, doors, and adjustable shelves. These holes are always *exactly* 32 mm apart, center to center. Their centers are located exactly 37 mm (close to 1½ in.) from the front and rear edges. When you design a cabinet to be joined with the line-boring method, it is best to align the center of the vertical pattern's top hole with the vertical center of the dowel hole near the top edge. In our earlier example, this means that the vertical line bore pattern will begin with a hole centered ⁵⁄₁₆ in. (8 mm) from the top edge. In the end panel for a wall cabinet, the same rule applies. (See Illus. 23.) At the bottom of the cabinet, regardless of its type, we can either allow the 32-mm spacing to dictate the height of the panel, or we can simply ignore the vertical placement of the bottom hole in the vertical pattern. There is, however, some advantage in making sure that the center of the bottom 5-mm hole is exactly 32 mm from the center of the 8-mm dowel holes along the bottom edge of the panel.

European Standardization

Furniture and cabinets built in the 32-mm system are designed to conform to certain standards. Any builder of European machines or hardware will tell you that these standards are only a way of standardizing building techniques, and that you can still build custom furniture and cabinetry while obeying all the "rules" of the European system. In actual practice, though, 32-mm cabinetmakers stick to certain other standards as well, just as traditionalists do. Look at it this way: The European system is based on the 32-mm measurement because that is the minimum spacing allowed by multiple-spindle gearboxes. Hole diameters are 8 mm or 5 mm. Hole lines are centered 37 mm from the front and back and 8 mm from the top and bottom (figuring the use of 16-mm material). This is where we get the demand for precise cutting and machining. This provides the rationale for investing in the expensive, European style, 32-mm tools. However, one of the great significances of such investment levels is that cabinet factories cannot afford to do very much true custom building. Yes, such manufacturers can build cabinetry in any height, width, or depth dimension; in practice, though, most choose particular standards and stay with them.

Cabinet heights and depths are generally set at dimensions that are convenient for milling as well as convenient for the human body, but there are no hard-and-fast measurements for the European designer to adhere to in determining overall cabinet dimensions. The following are the most important matters for you to consider.

- Function as related to the user—"ergonomics" in today's parlance. This refers to how well a product meets the needs of the people for whom it is intended—for example, establishing the height of a desk near 29 in. because that is a comfortable working height for most people.

- Blending with the standards of other trades. This means staying close to our old trade standards of 24-in. base-cabinet depths and similar standards because those are what other trades are used to.

One inch equals 25.4 millimetres, and the European standard of 32 millimetres is quite close to 1¼ inches. If you were to determine cabinet standard heights with metric measures, you would wind up with the figures that follow.

- Kitchen-countertop height (we are used to 36 in.) can be set at approximately 914 mm.
- Desk height (29 in.) can be called 737 mm.
- Typing-well height (27 in.) can be easily referred to as 686 mm.
- Tall-cabinet height (such as an oven or a pantry cabinet) (84 in.) is close to 2,134 mm.
- Vanity-countertop height (32 in.) is close to 813 mm.
- Wall-cabinet height (30 in.) is 762 mm.

To come up with these figures, I simply multiplied inch measurements by 25.40. We could convert depth standards, too: Bases are 620 mm, wall cabinets are 305 mm, and so on. All the conversions are actually inaccurate by tiny amounts, but as we shall see, that doesn't matter very much.

Metric Measurements

While the scientific community has been comfortable with metric measurement for a long time, many of us in the trades have resisted any sort of conversion. I know what you may be thinking right now—something like, "Oh no, here comes another tired old argument about the great beauty of the metric system." However, if that's what you're thinking, you are mistaken. I do have a few points to make about measurement, though.

First of all, the English system is a very natural method. With measurements under an inch, it is simply a matter of splitting distances in half over and over—½ inch, then ¼ inch, then ⅛ inch, and so on. Furthermore, the normal human eye can divide short distances in half almost perfectly anyway. The concept of measuring by splitting distances in half is actually a very reliable and convenient one, indeed.

With measurements over an inch, it is simply a matter of counting or adding inches. Most cabinetmakers never convert to feet, probably because they are used to dealing with objects that are under 100 inches most of the time.

However, proponents of the metric system maintain that it is more accurate than the English system. Their argument runs something like this: The smallest unit of measure in the English system is $\frac{1}{16}$ inch. The smallest unit of measure in the European system is the millimetre. The millimetre measures a distance that is a third smaller than $\frac{1}{16}$ inch ($\frac{1}{16}$ in. = 1.59 mm). Therefore, the millimetric system is about a third more accurate.

Hogwash!

Suppose that two people measure countertop height in exactly the same spot, one using metric measurement and the other using English. The metric measurement is reported as 915 mm; the English is reported as 36 in. Now, one of the measurers may have done a better job of measuring than the other. There are several factors that can throw off a measurement—including parallax, condition and quality of the tape measure, and even temperature when the measurement is taken. The difference in the two measurements is almost exactly 1 mm (slightly more than $\frac{1}{32}$ in.). Now, even if our metric measurer is absolutely correct, is the other measurer mistaken by one third? What nonsense to quantify accuracy in this way. In most cases, there is no cumulative effect caused by using one system or the other. Besides, it may have been our English measurer who was the more careful one.

Furthermore, English measurers frequently use $\frac{1}{32}$ inch as the smallest unit of measure. I even remember a foreman once telling our detailer that the cut he was making should be $\frac{1}{64}$ in. deeper. Not only that, but the foreman left on an errand for a while. While he was gone, our detailer never touched the stock, but he convinced the foreman that the detail had been recut $\frac{1}{64}$ in. deeper. Measuring differences this tiny can indeed be difficult to distinguish. The two systems are simply different ways of measuring. As for one being more accurate than the other, as I said earlier, hogwash.

It is also important to note that it is really unnecessary to convert from one kind of measurement to the other. "No translations are necessary." If you decide to use metric measurement at one or more points in your cabinetmaking operation, you do not have to worry about 36 in. equaling 914.40 mm. Instead, you simply buy a metric tape rule.

However, you can't get away from the fact that it is easiest to use metric measurement if you decide to drill a vertical line boring pattern in your cabinets. This simply makes the most sense because all the European hardware is based on the 32-mm spacing and the 37-mm backset. Now, you could refer to 37 mm as $1\frac{7}{16}$ in. without much harm done. It can use up some of the adjustment in your

European hinges. And it is okay to refer to the 32-mm spacing between hole centers as 1¼ in., as long as you use the same reference and the same measurement system on both the cabinet box and the door. Otherwise, there will be a cumulative error of up to ¼ in. on a door opening approximately 32 in. high. Besides, with the availability of precise drilling jigs based on the 32-mm spacing, there just is no reason to go to the added trouble of conversion. Metric is just another way of counting units of length. "No translations are necessary."

European Modularization

The 32-mm cabinetmaking system is especially well suited to modularization. The expensive machinery is certainly capable of turning out highly customized products. Most traditionalists can now see this. But as already suggested, most of the expensive machinery does not turn out highly customized products. It cranks out European style modular cabinets. It does so in order to pay for itself.

One of the advantages of any modularized building mode is simplicity. If a cabinetmaker intends to employ portions of the 32-mm system in some projects, repetitive use of the same tools and techniques is vital for this very reason. You, too, should modularize to the extent that you will always build your European cabinets in the same way—with the same tools and techniques, used in the simplest ways.

Modular End Panels. In the European system, it is common to make all cabinets as much the same as possible. This means there is no difference between finished ends and wall ends on a base cabinet or any other kind of cabinet. Some modulars do have pairs of end panels: right ends and left ends. It all comes down to choosing the configuration that will be a shop standard. (See Illus. 24 for three typical end panels.) With complete modularization, it is unnecessary to distinguish between right and left ends, and it can also be unnecessary to know ahead of time what accessories are going into the cabinet or even to know the cabinet's overall length. All base end panels can be the same size, and they are all drilled in exactly the same way. This is also true for all wall-cabinet end panels, all vanity end panels, all tall-cabinet end panels, and so on.

I am not saying that a cabinetmaker or a cabinet factory cannot decide to vary end-panel height and depth, but rather that European modular cabinets are really no different from traditional modular cabinets in that they are not generally built to custom specifications.

For the small shop and the custom builder, it also makes sense to adopt some European standards when employing the line-boring patterns, in the same way that it makes sense to use ¼-in.-deep dadoes when following the traditional methodology.

Any section of European cabinetry will have two end panels. There

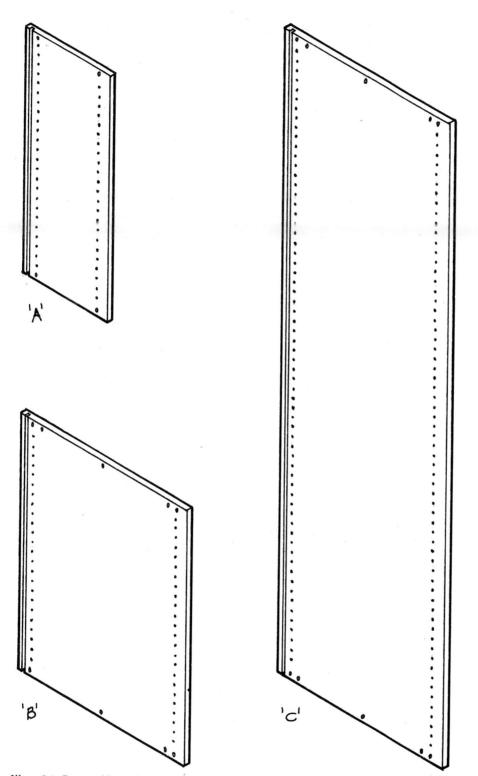

Illus. 24. Reversible end panels: (A) wall cabinet, (B) base cabinet, and (C) tall cabinet.

will usually be no partitions. If you need to build a longer piece of cabinetry, you might do either of the following:

- build the necessary length of cabinet by joining shorter modular units, which means butting end panels and connecting them; or
- join sections of cabinetry by using end panels as partitions, which means drilling all the way through the end panel so that there is an identical line-boring pattern on both sides of the same piece (see Illus. 25).

The first of these techniques, simply joining entire boxes, is the most common, just as it is in any modular system. This, again, shows a strong preference for the reduction of labor.

Notice, finally, that end panels are slotted for the installation of a thin back panel. The slot or dado can be machined at any convenient place behind the rear vertical hole line. It is usually 10 mm ($\sim 13/32$ in.) deep, 5 mm ($\sim 3/16$ in.) wide, and leaves 16 mm ($\sim 1/2$ in.) to the rear edge of the panel. Since there is no face frame, much of a European cabinet's rigidity comes from the slotted installation of this back.

It is fairly easy to see that the key to designing within the 32-mm system is understanding and taking full advantage of the modular end panel. (See Illus. 26.)

Bottoms. Cabinet bottoms made with the European system will have exactly the same depth as the end panels. They are drilled with 8-mm dowel holes on both ends in a configuration to match the boring pattern near the bottom of the end panels. The bottom is also usually slotted for the back panel. In base cabinets, the bottom can also be drilled for insertion of base-levelling hardware. When a top is needed, as in a wall cabinet or a tall unit, it can be cut the same size and milled in the same way as the bottom. Again, this saves setups and labor.

The length of a bottom allows for customizing. That is, the length of a cabinet bottom is totally independent of line-boring considerations, and even if you were to use a completely modular end panel, you could specify any cabinet length that you wanted. In fact, you can be totally committed to modularization and standardization in terms of cabinet height, but conversely committed to customization in terms of cabinet length. Therefore, if you really like the 32-mm assembly system, but you still want to customize in terms of constructing cabinets to fit into spaces of a certain length, this is a really viable alternative. Still, just as with other designing considerations in the 32-mm system, cabinet length can be customized but generally is not. Most operations that build with the European system for the American market do so employing predetermined lengths beginning with units that are 12 in. long and then going up to 48-in. lengths in

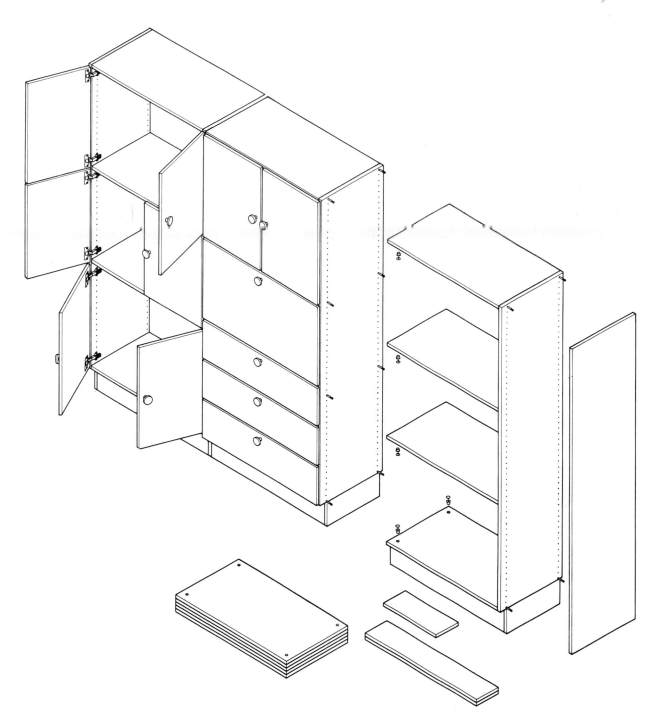

Illus. 25. One way of creating long cabinet units within the 32-mm system is to join shelves, bottoms, and cross members, or rails, to both sides of an end panel. It can be thought of as turning the end panel into a partition. We do this by extending the line-boring-pattern holes all the way through the panel and attaching horizontal pieces from both sides. (Courtesy of Häfele America Co.)

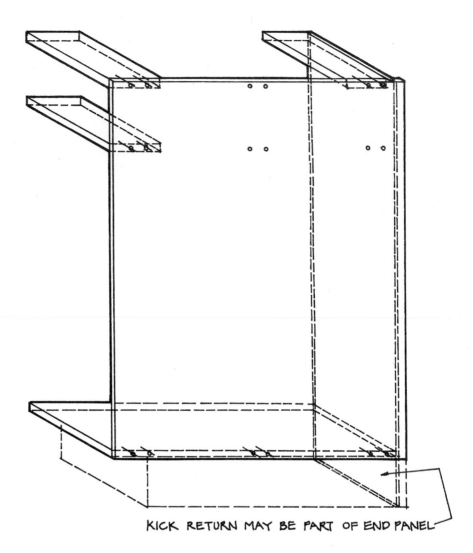

Illus. 26. Another modular end panel for a base cabinet. The top and bottom boring patterns are identical, but once horizontal boring is performed for the drawer rail, the panel is no longer reversible. Some manufacturers prefer to have the toe-kick return be an integral part of the end panel. Note the slot for installing a back.

KICK RETURN MAY BE PART OF END PANEL

increments of 3 in. This is to allow standardization of door and drawer widths along with the rest of the cabinet.

Cross Members. Base-cabinet units will have cross members, or rails. These are used as the "tops" of base cabinets, and they are also installed below each drawer. They will have the same length as the cabinet bottom and will be end-bored to match the dowel holes near the top edge of the end panels. It is naturally very desirable for this end boring to be achievable with the same setup that was used to end-bore the cabinet bottom. Sometimes the end boring for cross members will have a different configuration than the bottom. (See Illus. 27.) The rear cross member is either slotted for the back panel, or it is narrower than the front cross members, allowing the back panel to be inserted after the glued dowel joints have dried.

Shelves. In the 32-mm system, shelves are almost always adjust-

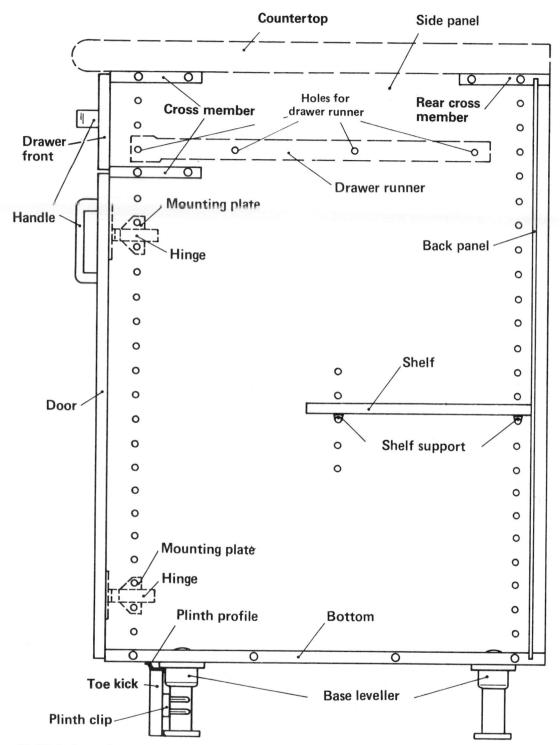

Illus. 27. With this end panel, the horizontal boring pattern is different for the bottom and the cross members. Truly reversible end panels are hard to achieve for base cabinets. (Courtesy of Häfele America Co.)

able. Fixed shelves would be stronger, but they are not in concert with the overall concept of flexibility stressed by European designers. Besides, fixed shelves would mean another horizontal line of dowel holes as well as some sort of alteration to allow installation of the back panel. Adjustable shelves need no machining after they are cut and edge-banded. Shelf length should be slightly less than the length of the cabinet bottom. Shelf width is dictated by the depth of the cabinet. Obviously, a shelf must be narrower than the distance between the back of the cabinet door and the front of the back panel. For optimum use of storage space, shelf width is only slightly less than this distance. Some cabinetmakers, however, prefer to make the adjustable shelf much narrower in base units, allowing easier access. It should be noted that this approach will create the need for another vertical line of holes to support the front edge of the shelf.

Toe Kicks. Nearly all the makers of European system machinery, hardware, and cabinets recommend the use of removable toe kicks. The toe kicks are attached with clips to the base-levelling hardware after the cabinetry is installed. This allows the base levellers to be used as furniture glides. Such a convenience is helpful to installers and to any workers in the shop who have to shift assembled units around. Furthermore, some of the levelling hardware requires access from underneath for adjustment.

Cabinet designers who adhere to the 32-mm system also contend that the removable kicks have substantial advantages for the customer. In Europe, where storage space is not ample, additional drawers are sometimes mounted to the base levellers instead of toe kicks (also with clips). Much is sometimes made of how desirable it is to be able to clean behind the removable kicks, but I have never met anyone outside the trade who considered this important.

Whether the toe kicks are removable or not, they are usually not part of a notched system the way they are in the traditional style. The kick space is often approximately 100 mm (~4 in.) high. Since there is no overhang by a bottom face-frame rail, the width of the stock is exactly the same (100 mm, or ~4 in.) in an arrangement with fixed kicks. If kicks are removable, their width is somewhat less, allowing for a rubberized sealer strip or "plinth profile." (Again, see Illus. 27.)

The length of a toe-kick board is exactly the same as the overall length of the cabinet (the length of the bottom plus the thickness of two sides). On finished ends, there needs to be a return kick, of course. It is most convenient to backset this toe-kick return from the end of the cabinet. Both this backset and the toe-kick board's backset from the front of the cabinet are rather arbitrary distances. I have nearly always used a backset of 3 in. (~76 mm). Naturally, the backset at the front of the cabinet will have a lot to do with the length of the toe-kick return on a finished end.

Doors and Drawers. Of course, whether or not you modularize the doors depends on whether the rest of the cabinet has been modularized. Even in a fairly customized, European mode shop, there is a tendency to stick with certain predetermined dimensions for the heights and widths of door and drawer components.

European style doors and drawers can be fully inset (flush inlaid), but most often they are designed to overlay the cabinet front by some predetermined amount, often 13 mm (~½ in.) when the cabinet box is made of 16-mm (⅝-in.) stock. This means that door placement leaves a reveal of 3 mm (~⅛ in.) on either side. This 3-mm spacing should be used as a guideline in determining the reveal allowed in other locations, as well: at the bottom of the door, between adjacent overlaid components, and between a door or drawer and a moulding or countertop edge to be attached later.

Actually, we may want to allow more spacing between components that are stacked vertically (for example, a base-cabinet door and the drawer above it) so that it matches the double spacing we get wherever two modular units are joined. Another important reason for allowing more spacing is to facilitate easier adjustment. The trend with most 32-mm designers, especially volume producers, is to promote larger gaps between doors and drawers. If you have ever had to mount a series of flush drawers, you know that the tiniest misalignments or errors in adjustment on the first drawer can cause bigger and bigger problems on each successive drawer that is mounted. The effect is cumulative. This cumulative effect on adjustment accounts for the current trend. Remember, though, that one of the most impressive features of European cabinet design is the modern, clean appearance that is created in part by the tiny door gaps.

The overall dimensions for doors and drawers are determined by adding the amount of overlay to the dimensions of the opening. For a closer look at the several box types and for specific information on how to design them, see the second major section of this chapter—Basic Box Types.

Sanding and Finishing

Of all the skills involved in cabinetmaking, sanding may be the most time-consuming and the least satisfying. I certainly never met any cabinetmakers who said that they actually enjoyed sanding.

The finishing process, too, is a labor-intensive job. There is staining, sealing, sanding, shading, clear coating, sanding, and more clear coating. Even if you prefer an oil or wax to lacquer or to one of the surface coatings, you have to build up the sheen and the protection in application after application. I personally love natural-wood cabinets and furniture and the way they look with a high-quality finish on them, but I have to admit that I don't really enjoy putting on a finish.

I have friends who do like the finishing process, but I would rather do design work, milling, or assembly.

One of the most important presuppositions of the 32-mm system is that sanding and finishing can be eliminated. For the committed European designer, the elimination of these steps is preferred because it means a reduction in labor. In the industry at this time, wood veneers and hardwoods used in the production of cabinet exteriors call for sanding and finishing. However, you can eliminate nearly all sanding and finishing if you build with melamine-precovered panels, and instead of using a hardwood edging for a face, you use PVC tape. Or, you can accept the extra labor of all the sanding and finishing and build your entire project with the wood surfaces showing. But you would probably like to find a piece of middle ground—a way of combining the best from both systems and their inherent selection of materials.

Facings. Of all the assumptions made regarding the 32-mm system, perhaps the most significant is that face frames should be avoided. If you embrace this idea, it will radically affect every other step in your cabinetmaking process.

If you speak to a hardware salesperson or another cabinetmaker, he or she will probably identify the presence or absence of a face frame as the greatest single distinguishing factor between the traditional system and the European system of building cabinets. And they are probably right, too, although materials-selection preferences might be nearly just as great a distinction. Precovered materials are the clear preference for European style woodworkers.

Traditionalist cabinetmakers are quick to point out the drawbacks to frameless cabinet design. There certainly are some, of course. For instance, rigidity is not as good at the front of a frameless cabinet box as it is with a box with a face frame. Whether a face frame is the product of mortise-and-tenon, dowel, or screw construction, it does yield superior strength and inflexibility at the front of the box. With the European design, the cabinet back panel can give good rigidity to the rear of the box. The particleboard or hardboard back panel does not shrink or expand much, and it can be fairly tightly inserted into dadoed slots near the back edge of end panels, the bottom, and even the rear cross member, if so desired. This back design does have the effect of projecting the cabinet's rigidity forward, but it is still not as inflexible as a well-made front frame.

I once heard basketball coach Hubie Brown speak on motivation and other topics related to basketball. One of his remarks that really stuck with me was as follows: "Shooting makes up for a multitude of sins." In other words, a player could have some deficiencies as long as he could be relied on to score. Now, before you start wondering what a reference to basketball is doing in a woodworking book, let me just say that the face frame can be considered analogous to that reliable scorer. To borrow from Hubie Brown, then, "Face frames make up for a multitude of sins." First of all, we can use the face frame to square up a cabinet box that has gone slightly out of whack. Second, a square face frame will allow us to mount doors and drawers on a cabinet in an orderly and attractive way—even if the box is not perfectly square, even if a dado or rabbet is out of its correct location by 1/8 in. or so. Since it is generally about 3/4 in. thick and its members overlap the edges of sheet goods behind, a face frame also does a good job of hiding chipped edges, saw marks, and other smaller flaws. These are all positive factors, but for traditionalists, perhaps the biggest advantage to staying with the face-frame system is that it is what they know. It is a habit, certainly not a bad habit, but a habit nonetheless. On the other hand, though, it is not so perfect a system that it can fulfill every need for every situation. There are many times when a frameless design will solve certain cabinet problems better. Let us take a look.

What are the advantages of frameless design then? To make up for the lack of rigidity, there ought to be some substantial ones, and there are.

Most important to many cabinetmakers is a freedom from overdesigning. If the box itself can be made strong enough to do what it was intended for, if the facings available for the edges of sheet goods are attractive enough, and if we do not have to hide any errors or milling imperfections, then a face frame is unnecessary. So are the machinery, blades, and cutters used to cut, lay out, mill, and assemble the face frame. Production can then be simplified. This is the standpoint of most large producers of 32-mm cabinetry.

However, the following attributes of frameless design tend to be more meaningful to hobbyists and other low-volume producers.

- Access: It is slightly easier to reach objects stored inside the frameless cabinet.
- Space savings: Drawer boxes can be wider on cabinets where there is no face frame; any face overhang around a drawer opening is wasted space (see Illus. 28).
- Cleaning ease: Face overhangs make it slightly more difficult to clean shelves and bottoms, especially in the corner directly behind a stile or mullion (see Illus. 29).
- Materials savings: All users of wood need to become more conscious of the need to extend world wood resources and forests, for the sake of everyone's quality of life; in addition, it is far less expensive to apply a thin edge band than it is to apply thick, wide face-frame stocks.
- Elimination of overdesigning: Consider the notion that building

Illus. 28. Notice that the drawer would be wider here if no face frame were used.

with a face frame actually forces you to build two things to get one, the face frame no longer being necessary with today's hinges, fasteners, and other modern considerations.

If you disagree with the last argument, I certainly understand. I, too, believe that we still have many occasions to employ face frames in building modern furniture and cabinetry. Nonetheless, it should not be dismissed without thought.

When we build entirely within the 32-mm system, we are opting for the advantages of thin facings and edge coverings in preference to the advantages of the face-frame system.

Illus. 29. The nook created here in the corner where the shelf meets the mullion is difficult to clean.

BASIC BOX TYPES

In this section, we will not only be looking at real plans and measurements for the several types of modular European cabinets, but also at how these designs might actually be used in a specific U-shaped kitchen. (See Illus. 30.)

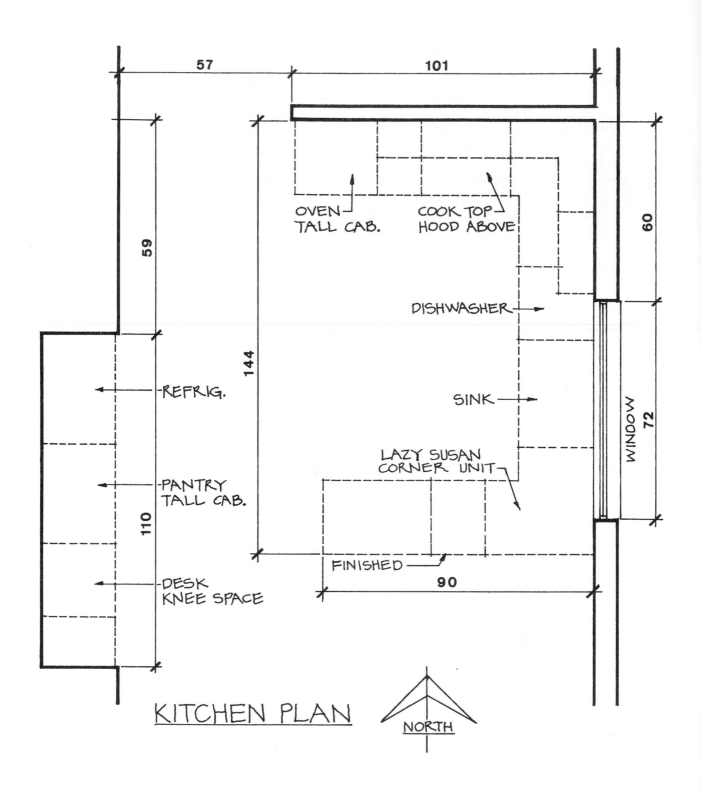

57   101

59

144

60

72   WINDOW

110

OVEN
TALL CAB.

COOK TOP
HOOD ABOVE

DISHWASHER →

SINK →

←REFRIG.

←PANTRY
TALL CAB.

LAZY SUSAN
CORNER UNIT

←DESK
KNEE SPACE

FINISHED

90

KITCHEN PLAN

NORTH

Illus. 30. The measurements and floor plan for a planned U-shaped kitchen.

The Base Cabinet

Although the exact height and width of all cabinetry is up to the individual designer, we will presume some fairly standard dimensions in our suggested design.

The key to every modular cabinet is the end panel. Adhering as closely as we can to American kitchen standards will mean specifying a width of 606 mm (~23 ⅞ in.). This will allow us to get two rips from every sheet of particleboard that we cut up, even if they are only 48-in.-wide panels. Overall height (including a separate toe kick) will be 889 mm (35 in.). There are a number of advantages to this exact dimension, as we shall see.

This height will allow us to use the standard American countertop thickness of ¾ in. (19 mm) and wind up with a countertop height very close to what we are used to—35 ¾ in. (908 mm). Most European style countertops are thicker than 19 mm (some of them are up to 38 mm thick), yielding a very sturdy top but really wasting a good deal of substrate material. The thinner tops can present another difficulty, however, that we must solve before moving on.

The traditional American top covers a portion of the cabinet face, whereas the Euro-style top does not. (See Illus. 31.) The problem is that the amount of this cover or overlap is greater than the thickness of the top cross member. If we use a top that overlaps like this, then we will probably have to do one of the following:

- Attach a second front cross member directly below the first; this will require drilling a second horizontal hole pattern 16 mm below the first and then locating the first hole in the vertical boring pattern 32 mm below that (also spoiling the concepts of simplicity and reversibility that we want to obey—see Illus. 32, A).
- Attach a second front cross member, as just stated, but without altering the vertical boring pattern; the second piece is nonstructural and can be screwed, nailed, or stapled onto the cross member above it (I like this approach, but a stapler and screws cannot be considered European fasteners—see Illus. 32, B).
- Simply accept that there is no top rail or cross member for a drawer or base-cabinet door to contact.

As shown in Illus. 31, B, we have chosen the simplest solution—no cross member visible below the countertop. This allows us to stick with our reversible design regardless of which countertop style we intend to use. An overlaid drawer front will still contact plenty of cabinet facing—along the bottom and both ends of the front.

Other advantages to the 889-mm height are that it is almost exactly 35 in. and that it allows us to maintain the 32-mm spacing from

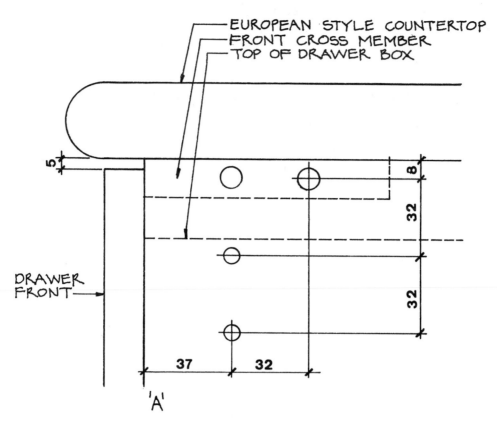

EUROPEAN STYLE COUNTERTOP
FRONT CROSS MEMBER
TOP OF DRAWER BOX

5

8

32

32

DRAWER
FRONT

37   32

'A'

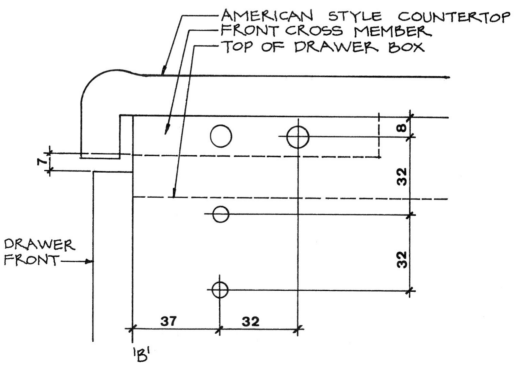

AMERICAN STYLE COUNTERTOP
FRONT CROSS MEMBER
TOP OF DRAWER BOX

7

8

32

32

DRAWER
FRONT

37   32

'B'

both the top and bottom ends (provided we use ⅝-in. stock and a 105-mm [~4⅛-in.] toe space), as follows:

Overall height . . .	889 mm
minus toe space . . .	− 105 mm
equals panel height . . .	= 784 mm

and then:

Panel height . . .	784 mm
minus ½ panel thickness times	
two (8 mm × 2) . . .	− 16 mm
equals . . .	= 768 mm

yielding a dimension that is perfectly divisible by 32 mm:

Distance between centers	
of top and bottom boring patterns . . .	768 mm
divided by 32 mm . . .	÷ 32 mm
equals a number of spaces	
(whole number) . . .	24

In our modular panel, we have identical drilling patterns at the top and bottom. The two holes closest to each end are more or less in a pair, allowing us to use the pattern for attaching either a bottom, supported by five dowels, or top cross members at the front and rear, supported by two dowels each. At this point, the end panel is totally reversible. (See Illus. 33.)

As soon as a top drawer section is planned for, it will require that we drill another horizontal line of holes, or at least the front pair of holes, so that we can attach the cross member that goes below the drawer. This will mean making the end panel nonreversible. The center of this hole line must be centered on one of the 5-mm holes in the vertical line pattern, let us say the fourth one down (not counting the 8-mm hole), yielding a new drawer-opening height of 112 mm

Illus. 31 (facing page). Two countertop end-view details. In A, the European style countertop rests on top of the base unit, allowing a drawer front to overlay the cross member, or rail. In B, the American style countertop overhangs the cabinet's front edge, and the drawer front will never contact the top rail.

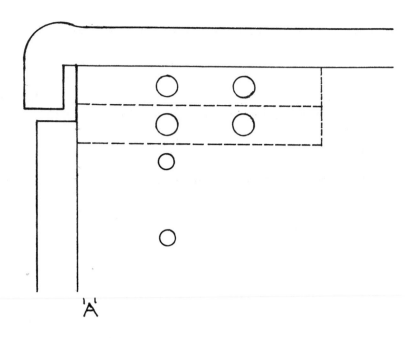

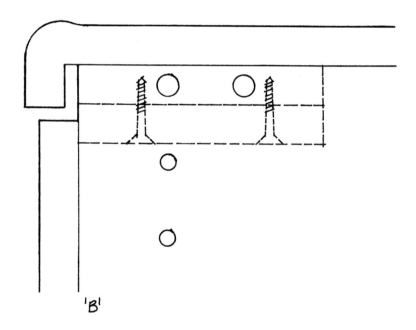

Illus. 32. Two methods for adding a second top cross member, a cross member whose only function is to allow drawer-front contact. Machining for A is not as simple as we probably desire, whereas B employs non-European fasteners.

($\sim$4 $^{13}/_{32}$ in.). We calculate the net height of the base-cabinet drawer opening as follows:

No. of holes counted times 32 mm . . .   (4 × 32 mm) or
                                                                              128 mm
minus ½ panel thickness times two (8 mm × 2) . . .
                                                                          − 16 mm
equals . . .   = 112 mm

If a stack of four drawers is called for, we will want to know ahead of time where cross members will be placed and the net vertical dimensions. Incidentally, the width of those cross members, or rails, is somewhat arbitrary. Let us specify 102 mm ($\sim$4 in.) as the width dimension for all the front rails and then subtract 18 mm (allowing

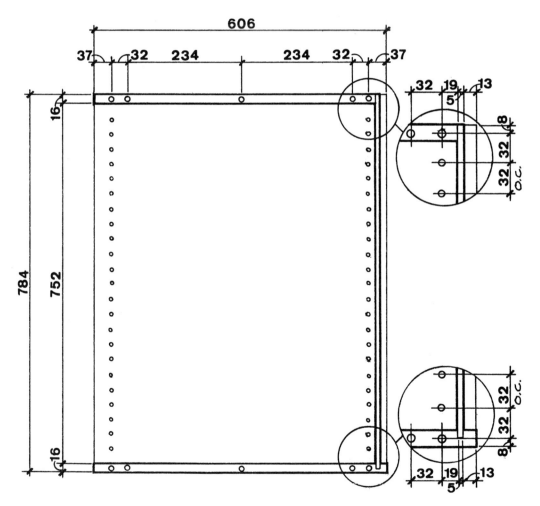

Illus. 33. Reversible end panel for a base cabinet. Look carefully at spacings.

us to slide the back panel into its slot after other assembly procedures) to determine the width of the rear rail—84 mm (~3 5/16 in.).

Instead of dividing up the remaining height for the three drawers
below as we would do in conventional American layout, we have only
to divide the remaining number of 32-mm spacings in a somewhat
equal way. Since we have 20 such spacings left, the most convenient
arrangement will be to count down six holes for locating the next
drawer rail, and seven more holes below that for the lowest drawer
rail. Below that, counting seven more holes will get us to the cabinet
bottom. (See Illus. 34.) Thus, in addition to the 112-mm opening
height for the top drawer in our base cabinet, we will have another
drawer-opening height of 176 mm (~6 15/16 in.) and two opening
heights at 208 mm (~8 3/16 in.).

Since the openings are so high, you may prefer to divide the available height into four spaces instead of three. This makes a great deal
of sense because, as any cabinet designer knows, drawer boxes
should only be slightly higher than the items they are intended to

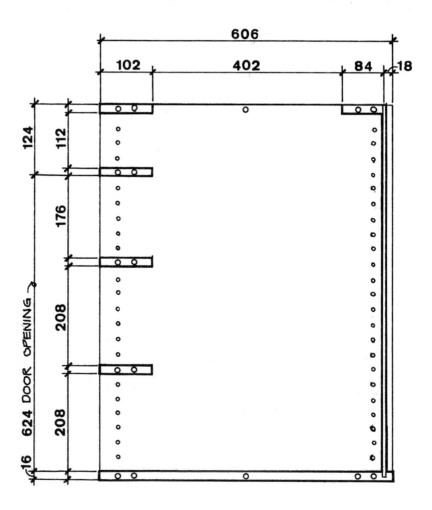

Illus. 34. Spacings on the
end panel for the
four-drawer stack of
drawers.

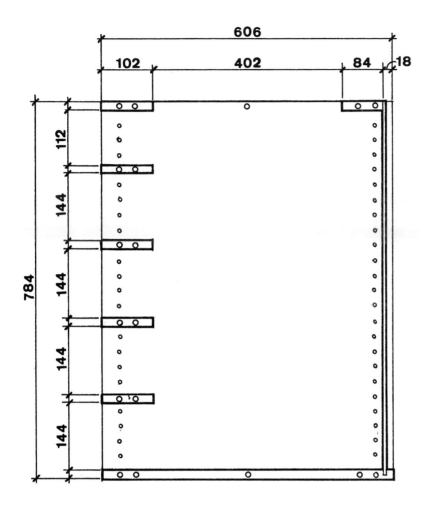

Illus. 35. Drawer spacings for a five-drawer stack.

hold. Otherwise, the result is a piled-up, junky drawer or a lot of wasted space. Here, then, is an excellent example of how the European system can make better use of space than the American face-frame system. Below the top drawer opening, which remains 112 mm high, remember that we have 20 spacings in the vertical hole pattern. This can be quite easily divided into four equivalent drawer openings of five spaces or 144 mm (~5 $^{11}/_{16}$ in.). (See Illus. 35.)

We are now finished with our designing of the end panels for base cabinets. All that remains for us to do is to count the number of such end panels needed in a given kitchen.

Consider the cabinet elevation in Illus. 36 for a moment. This is the north elevation of the kitchen shown in Illus. 30. It is easy to see that we need four base end panels here, two for each base cabinet (labelled A). From this same kitchen, the east, south, and west elevations are indicated respectively in Illus. 37, 38, and 39. We need 10 more end panels for cabinetry indicated on the east and south elevations.

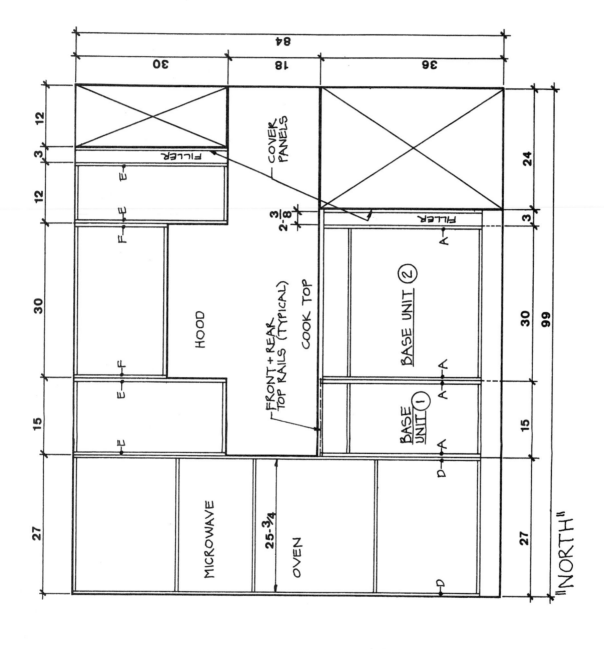

Illus. 36. Kitchen north elevation from the floor plan in Illus. 30.

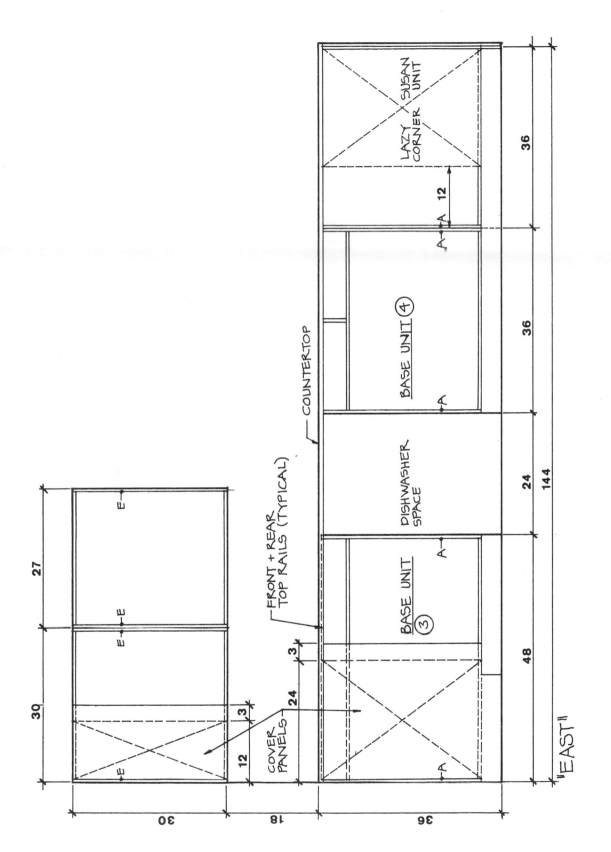

Illus. 37. East elevation.

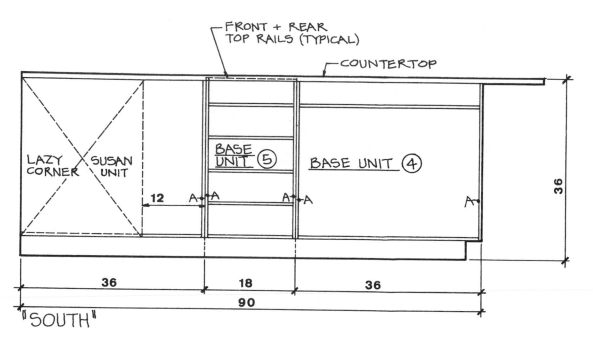

Illus. 38. South elevation.

The only base unit on the west elevation is at desk height—748 mm, or ~29 7/16 in. Subtracting 19 mm for countertop thickness and our chosen standard 105-mm toe space, we are left with end panels (labelled B) that are 624 mm high. This will yield 19 spaces of 32-mm each between the top and bottom horizontal hole lines. Right next to this short base unit, we have the need for end panels on a "knee-under" unit. Still aiming towards simplicity and standardization, let us specify the height of these very short end panels as 144 mm, or ~5 21/32 in. (labelled C). This will yield a drawer opening that is exactly the same as that for the top drawers in the rest of the kitchen—112 mm.

The bottoms for base cabinets will also be 606 mm wide, and slotted to receive a back in exactly the same way as end panels. Since these cabinets will be modular, we will only build them in predetermined lengths. What probably makes the most sense is to follow the conventional American modularizing practice. That is, the shortest overall cabinet length will be 12 in. We will make longer units, in increments of 3 in., up to 48 in. Notice that it is perfectly fine to measure and specify lengths in inches rather than millimetres because they are arbitrary, not based on hole-line spacing. You should also notice how the arbitrary 3-inch increments dictate certain other matters. On the north wall, they dictate a reveal of 2 in., since wall length is 101 in. and total cabinet length is 99 in. On the east elevation, we will actually end up with 144½ in. because we have to add a finished back. This is okay, of course, because it is not a wall-to-wall fit. Likewise, with the south elevation, an inch more or less along the length of the cabinetry will make little difference, although an 89-in. total added to a standard 12-in. eating-bar overhang would line up the end of the countertop perfectly with the end of the north wall. (Again, see Illus. 30.) The only situation that is at all troublesome is on the cabinetry indicated in the west elevation. Here, total length is only 99 in., whereas the wall-to-wall measurement is 101 in. The

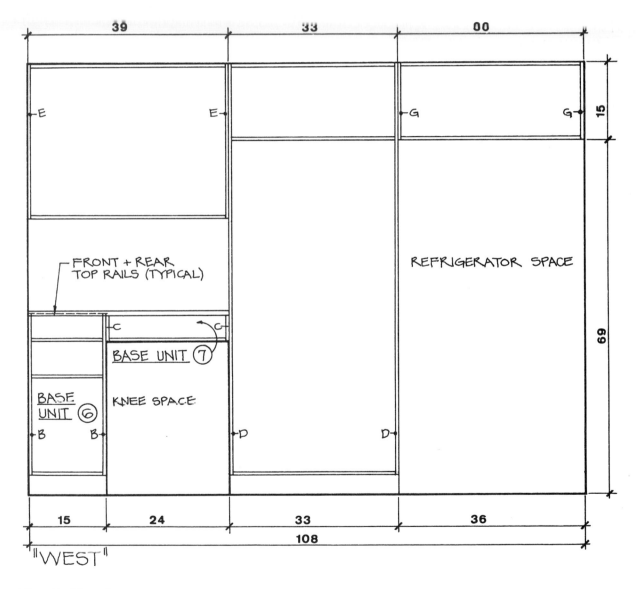

Illus. 39. West elevation.

2-inch difference is too much to ignore and also too much for standard ¾-in.-wide moulding. This is common wherever we use modular systems in a wall-to-wall situation. The possible solutions are as follows:

- build one of the cabinet units a bit longer (the logical choice is the upper unit over the refrigerator because it requires customizing only doors and the top and bottom),
- prepare strips of wider (1¼-in.) moulding, or
- prepare filler strips.

Suit yourself, of course. Preparing wide moulding or filler strips is obviously the easier adaptation, but some cabinetmakers actually customize the lengths of all their European designed cabinets and furniture. This method employs the advantages of the line-boring system, but makes no concession to modularization of length.

Regardless of whether you choose to modularize or customize the length of your projects, the actual determination of component-length dimensions is ridiculously easy. All we must do is subtract the thickness of the two end panels from the overall length of each cabinet. Lengths of cabinet bottoms and rails, then, work out as follows:

Base unit no.	Length (in.)	Length (mm)
1	13¾	349
2	28¾	730
3	46¾	~1,187
4 (2 each)	34¾	~882
5	16¾	~425
6	13¾	349
7	22¾	~578

Again, we need only count components to make a cutting list.

The overall sizes of all other components are also easy to determine. Since the back panel will be fitted into slots in the ends and bottom that have a depth of 10 mm (~13/32 in.), we can use this dimension to get overall length and height of the back panels. As we look at these figures, remember that we will employ metric units for height measurement and English units for length measurement. Of course, where appropriate I will give both. In base-cabinet 1, the back has a height equal to the end-panel height (784 mm) minus the thickness of the bottom (16 mm) plus the depth of the slot (10 mm). This equals 778 mm (~30⅝ in.). The length of the back is the same as the length of the bottom (13¾ in.) plus twice the depth of the slot (¹³⁄₁₆ in.), which equals 14⁹⁄₁₆ in. (369 mm). This kind of figuring is not really difficult, but if you are unsure of the figures in your own project, or you do not trust them on your first European projects, a very reliable method is naturally to build the box and then measure for the back panel. This will also work for components such as doors and drawers. Of course, the cabinetmaker who modularizes will only need to figure out such matters once.

The sizes of doors and drawer fronts, as pointed out in an earlier section, are determined by adding an overlay amount (13 mm, or ½ in., on each overlaid edge) to the width and height dimensions of each opening. In our model kitchen, base-unit 1 requires one door and one drawer front. The door is a single, not a pair; it and the drawer should therefore both have a width of 14¾ in. (375 mm). The door and drawer must "share" the amount of overlay on the rail, or cross member, that separates them. Door height is thus 643.5 mm (~25⅜ in.). You will recall that our kitchen has overhanging countertops, and we have to reduce the height of the drawer front enough so that it will clear this overhang. (Again, see Illus. 31, B.) If we subtract 7 mm from the drawer-opening height (112 mm) to allow this clearance, and then add the 6.5-mm overlay derived by virtue of "sharing" the rail with the door below, we arrive at a total height of 111.5 mm (~4⅜ in.).

Where paired doors are necessary, as on base-unit 2, we must first halve the opening width, then add our standard overlay, and finally subtract enough to allow clearance between the two doors. This clearance amount should be about ¹⁄₁₆ in. (1.5 mm) on each door. Each door on base-unit 2, then, should have a width of 14¹³⁄₁₆ in. (376.5 mm) or a bit less. Otherwise, the doors will rub or overlap in the middle.

The most critical dimensions on an assembled drawer box are height and width. These sizes are derived directly from the dimensions of the opening. Referring again to base-unit 1, we see that the opening is 112 mm high and 13¾ in. (349 mm) wide. With most European drawer glides, we will need no less than 22-mm (⅞-in.) total vertical clearance and exactly 1 in. (25.4 mm) for placement of the hardware. Therefore, the assembled drawer box for base-unit 1 will be no taller than 90 mm and exactly 12¾ in. wide. Depth, the overall dimension from the front of the box to its rear, is not a critical dimension. Box depth must simply be less than the net, the inside depth of the cabinet box. In our standard design here, we are using 606 mm (23⅞ in.) for the end-panel width. Net depth will be 18 mm less, or 588 mm (~23⁵⁄₃₂ in.). For the sake of simplicity, we shall specify a drawer-box depth of 22 in. (559 mm).

Once the overall dimensions of the drawer box have been established, the sizing of individual components becomes a factor of drawer-box design, and this will naturally be based on your own preferences. The spirit of European design would seem to call for butt joints, but they are a bit of a problem because of the chosen material—particleboard with a melamine covering. If you butt a raw particleboard edge against a melamine-impregnated surface (or any plastics surface), joining by glue is impossible. Furthermore, conventional fasteners, such as nails and staples, are certainly not up to the sort of heavy wear that a drawer can receive when it is put into use. Therefore, you will need to use a more effective fastening system. We can choose from the possibilities that follow.

- Use a worked joint in order to allow wood-to-wood contact; then you will be able to use conventional glue and fasteners; rabbeting the sides to receive both the subfront and back can be fairly quick.
- Use screws to fasten the components together; both drywall screws and the special European style screws are very effective because they have deep threads and straight shanks; naturally, the components need to be predrilled, or your material is likely to split.
- Use assembly fittings or some other type of knock-down fastener; here, too, there is some "extra" milling required.
- Use a manufactured-drawer assembly system that makes use of extruded or prefit parts (see Illus. 40).

Assuming that you use worked joints such as the rabbeting arrangement suggested in the first option, that you use 13-mm (½-in.) drawer-box material, and that the rabbet and dado are ¼ in. (6.35

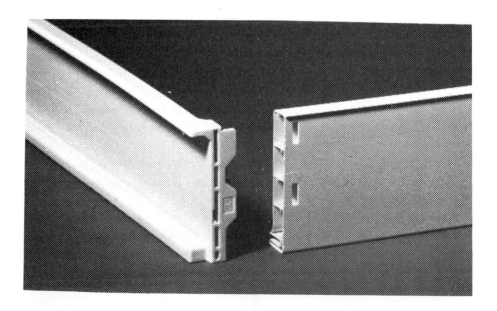

Illus. 40. Prefabricated drawer components. (Courtesy of Hettich America Corporation.)

mm) deep, you would have the following cutting list for the drawer box intended for base-unit 1:

Component	Width	Length
subfront	90 mm (~3^{17}/$_{32}$ in.)	12¼ in. (~311 mm)
back	90 mm	12¼ in.
sides (2 ea.)	90 mm	22 in. (~559 mm)

If you specify 5-mm material for the drawer bottom, and you assume that it will fit into slots that are exactly ¼ in. deep, then its dimensions for this drawer will be 12¼ in. wide and 21½ in. (~546 mm) long

Slide-out shelves or trays would be designed similarly to drawer boxes, although they would have to be shallower than the drawers in order to allow the doors to close.

Lastly, but very important to the design of any European cabinet that rests on the floor, is planning for the toe kick. In the European designing system, the toe kick itself is often cut from plywood or covered particleboard, just as are other components in the cabinet. The traditional American cabinetmaker is quite used to this. However, when we build European style, we do not attach the toe kick to the cabinet in quite the same way as we are used to. Instead of using glue and nails to fasten on sleepers and then the toe-kick board, we will attach a set of base levellers to the cabinet bottom. The toe kick is then attached to the front base levellers with clips. (See Illus. 41.)

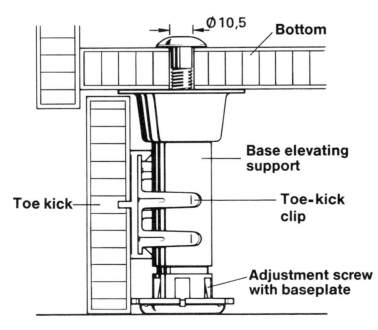

Illus. 41. Base leveller and toe-kick attachment system. Note the clip that allows the kick to be removable. (Courtesy of Häfele America Co.)

There are some advantages to the leveller-and-clip system of toe-kick attachment. Most important, this system allows the cabinet installer to level and align a set of cabinetry quite easily and reliably. The toe kick is unclipped to expose the levelling hardware. Then the adjustment screw can be turned to bring the unit into excellent alignment. It is possible to have all the levellers in contact with the floor, making for very reliable support. Actually, some levellers can be adjusted from inside the cabinet, meaning that the installer would not even have to remove the kick or reach far under the cabinet bottom to make the necessary adjustments. In many European homes and apartments, people also use this toe space for storage. Instead of toe-kick panels, drawers can be attached to the base levellers in order to make use of this otherwise wasted space.

Some cabinetmakers who use European hardware believe that the base levellers and the removable kicks have some other advantages as well. Some say that the levellers make good skids or glides, allowing us to move units around easily in the shop, on the truck, or at the job site. I never saw this as a great advantage, though, because I customize a good deal, and I stick with low-production levels. I do not need to move units around very much. Instead, I need to stack them up in order to conserve space, and the levellers just make units harder to stack. Besides, a dolly is much more convenient for moving cabinets, and I am not convinced that the attachment method for these levellers was designed for the kind of sidewards pressure created by "skidding." Removable kick panels are also supposed to be an advantage for homeowners, allowing them access underneath the cabinet for purposes of cleaning and insecticide treatment. As noted earlier, these do not really seem to be advantages, especially if removable kicks add to construction expenses by forcing us to install ceramic tile or other finished flooring beneath the cabinetry, where we otherwise would not do so.

Frankly, the good support provided by having all levellers in contact with the floor can be enough of an advantage for you to go ahead and utilize them. If you do, I suggest you use the ones that are adjustable from inside the cabinet, meaning that the toe-kick panel will never have to come off. Later on, we will look at some more traditional methods that also make sense.

The Tall Cabinet

We have already established a firm groundwork for designing the tall cabinet. The key is once again the careful designing of end panels.

In determining overall dimensions, we start with a cabinet whose total height will be approximately 84 in. (2,134 mm)—the traditional American standard. We will want to maintain the 105-mm toe space, and we will naturally want this end panel to be as similar as possible to the base end panels. This will mean a panel thickness of 16 mm. (⅝ in.) and a panel width of 606 mm (~23⅞ in.). This allows us to drill exactly the same horizontal holed patterns that we set up to bore on the base-cabinet end panels.

In terms of height, what is probably most convenient is an overall panel height of 2,032 mm. This is the product of 63 spacings of 32-mm each between top and bottom horizontal hole-line centers (63 × 32 mm = 2,106 mm), plus half the panel thickness twice (8 mm × 2 = 16 mm). Adding the 105-mm toe kick yields 2,137 mm—only a tiny bit over our desired American standard. In the kitchen design we have been referring to, there are four such end panels required (labelled D), two for the oven cabinet on the north wall and two for the pantry on the west wall. (See Illus. 36 and 39.)

Within tall cabinets, there may be no cross members unless drawers are called for. Instead, we will need a top and probably several fixed shelves to divide sections according to use. These components will be narrower than the bottom—588 mm or ~23⅛ in. This will allow insertion of the back after the other fixed components have been assembled. If such a cabinet is designed to house a conventional oven and a microwave oven, we will need three fixed shelves to separate the various sections. (See Illus. 42.) In planning any such unit, we have certain fixed measurements to work with—the appliance measurements. Suppose, then, that we have the following cutout dimensions specified:

Appliance	Height	Width
oven	590 mm (23³⁄₁₆ in.)	635 mm (25 in.)
microwave oven	338 mm (13⁷⁄₃₂ in.)	635 mm (25 in.)

The high priority here is to ensure that there is enough room for installation of these appliances, and since we are committed to the line-boring system (at least in this chapter), we need to add 16 mm to each cutout height dimension (to account for shelf thickness), and divide this total by 32. Our answer will be the number of 32-mm spaces required for the appliance. Any fraction of a 32-mm space will mean another full space.

For the oven, then, we divide 606 mm by 32 mm, yielding 18.9375 spaces. Obviously, the oven requires 19 spaces—a net dimension of 592 mm, just barely over the 590 mm required. We can hardly expect the situation to work out any better than this.

Planning for the microwave does not work out quite so nicely, however. Beginning with the cutout height (338 mm), we add the amount taken up for shelf thickness (16 mm), yielding the total space required (354 mm), which we divide by our magic measure-

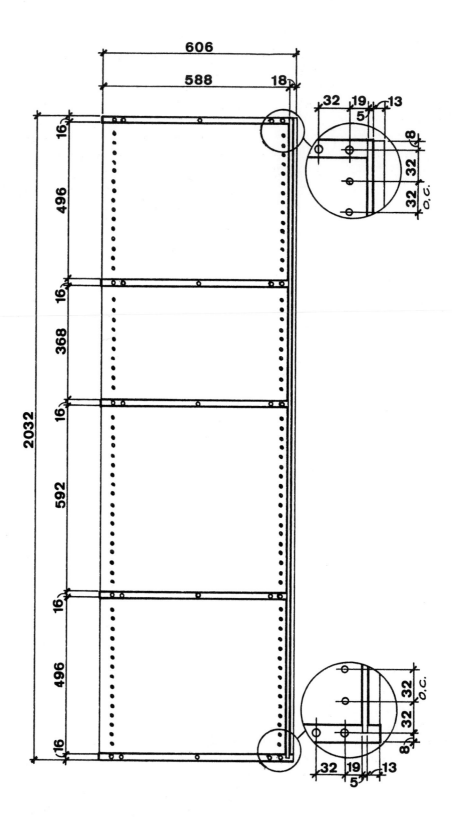

Illus. 42. Hole patterns for a tall cabinet. This end panel would be used for the oven cabinet in Illus. 36.

ment (32 mm), yielding the number of spaces required—11.0625 spaces. This is the same as 11 spaces plus $\frac{1}{16}$ of a space. The microwave oven's vertical measurement requires 12 full spaces (12 spaces × 32 mm = 384 mm) minus the 16 mm required for shelf thickness, or a total dimension of 368 mm (~14½ in.). (See Illus. 42.) This is 30 mm (1³⁄₁₆ in.) more than we need for the microwave oven. Since the 32-mm system calls for this shelf placement, we will have to use a wood or metal filler to cover the fairly large hole created.

Actually, in such a "stacked" arrangement, we can sometimes have a similar problem with the horizontal spacings, too, if different-width cutout dimensions are required for the two appliances. If we were designing within the face-frame system, this problem would be solved by additional cutting. That is, you would plan the interior width of the face frame to accommodate the smaller appliance. Then, after the frame has been assembled, you would cut away some of the material from the stiles to create an opening wide enough for the large appliance. This will not work in the European system because there is no overhanging face. Of course, a face-frame-style cabinet built to house these two appliances would have to be wider to begin with—perhaps several inches wider—than the cabinet we have called for here. The face-frame cabinet might be stronger, but it also wastes some space. In our model kitchen, this space would have to be stolen from the base cabinets next to the oven, and this is a kitchen work area (cook top and adjacent countertops) that simply must not lose any more space. Again, the solution is to plan for fillers of different widths, based on the different sizes of the two appliances. In the design called for here, we need fillers anyway, because we are planning to install 25-in.-wide ovens into openings that are 25¾ in. wide. (See Illus. 36.)

We have already looked at and answered all the horizontal design questions involved with the tall cabinet. The bottom will be sized and slotted exactly the same as for a base cabinet. The top and shelves, as already noted, will be flat panels equal in length but somewhat narrower than the bottom (18 mm, or ²³⁄₃₂ in., narrower). If you were to include drawers in such a cabinet, again you would design for these just as in a base cabinet. Door and back-panel size, too, are determined in exactly the same way as they would be for the European base cabinet.

The pantry presents some interesting possibilities that we must look at before moving along to the wall cabinets in our model kitchen. Since this storage unit is just as deep as any base cabinet in the kitchen, it is very desirable to build in some features that allow easy access. Two such options are a tall lazy Susan, or rotating-shelf unit, behind the doors and a swing-out-shelf section in front of adjustable shelves. (See Illus. 43.) In the case of the second option, it will be

Illus. 43. A tall swing-out shelf arrangement within a pantry cabinet. This particular cabinet was built face-frame style. Note the adjustable shelves visible behind.

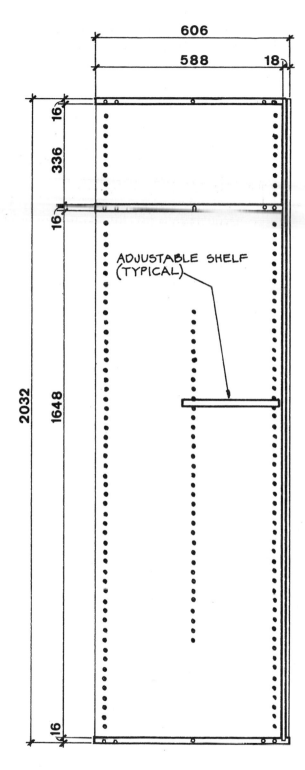

Illus. 44. The end panel with hole patterns for a tall pantry cabinet. Note the additional vertical hole line for half-depth adjustable shelves.

necessary to bore an extra vertical hole pattern somewhere near the middle of the end panel. Since the holes are used for adjustable-shelf pegs, this hole pattern will allow the kind of shelves that are only about half as deep as the cabinet, leaving room for the swing-out-shelf section in front of the adjustable shelving. (See Illus. 44.) In the model kitchen, our pantry has only one fixed shelf, located 11 spaces (336 mm, or ~13¼ in.) below the top. We need the extra vertical hole line only in the tall lower section.

The Wall Cabinet

Wall cabinetry is the simplest of the three basic box types to design and build. There are usually only four components to each box: bottom, top, and two identical end panels.

It may be redundant to say so, but again, planning the end panels is most important, and we want these end panels to be fairly close to American height standards. In spite of their complete reversibility, wall-cabinet end panels must be developed for several different heights, dependent upon application. Conventional uses, overall heights, and Europeanizations are as follows:

Use	Height (in.)	Spacings required (32-mm ea.)	Total height (mm)
standard	30	23	752
over hood	18	13	432
over sink	24	18	592
over refrig.	15	11	368

You may notice that the heights we wind up with—the total heights—are all somewhat less than the conventional English heights we began with. This is, of course, due to basing all our designing on the 32-mm hole spacings and the 16-mm stock thickness.

The 752-mm end panel can be thought of as the standard end panel. (See Illus. 45.) Notice all its similarities to the end panels called for in bases and tall cabinets, especially in spacing. There are the identical top and bottom horizontal boring patterns; there are the 37-mm backset and the exact 32-mm vertical hole spacing; and the 5-mm back panel fits into a slot in the ends and bottom but will slide past the narrower top. Width or overall cabinet depth is 301 mm (~11⅞ in.). In our model kitchen, there are 10 of these end panels (labelled E).

Most of the shorter end panels will be exactly the same, except for

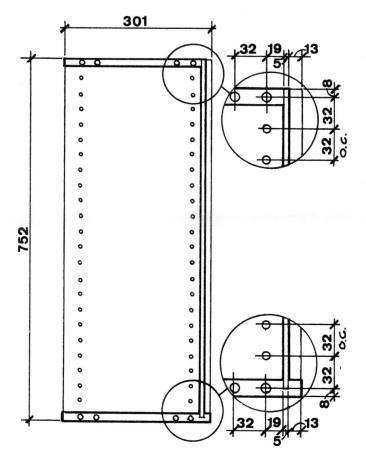

Illus. 45. The line-boring pattern for a "standard" wall-cabinet end panel.

height. (See Illus. 46.) In our model-kitchen plan, there is no cabinetry over the sink, but we are required to build one unit for the location over the hood. Thus, we will need to cut and mill two 432-mm end panels (labelled F).

In many modern kitchens, it is a fairly common practice to construct a deeper wall cabinet for the location above the refrigerator. If we suppose this to be the plan in our model, then it would probably be a good idea to think of the end panels for this wall cabinet as shortened tall-cabinet end panels. (See Illus. 47.) The top and bottom horizontal boring patterns can be drilled in the same configuration. We need a slotted bottom and a top panel that is 18 mm narrower. In the model, once more, there is a need for two such end panels (labelled G).

Naturally, there are no drawers to account for in the wall cabinets, and the dimensions for backs and doors can be determined in exactly the same way as with the other cabinets we have looked at. The only additional detailing required for wall cabinets is cutting a notch in

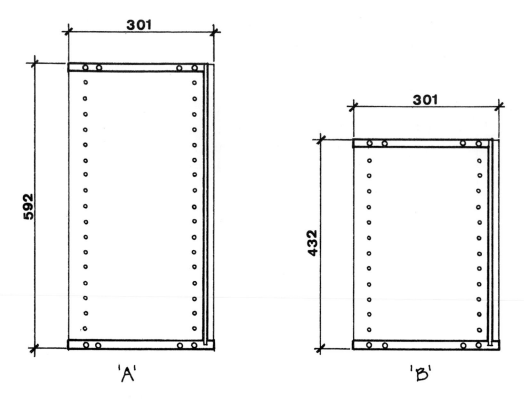

Illus. 46. Line-boring patterns for shorter wall-cabinet end panels. A is close to 24 in. and establishes a convenient height for wall cabinetry over a sink or above an eating bar. B, with a height close to 18 in., would yield the wall cabinet above a hood.

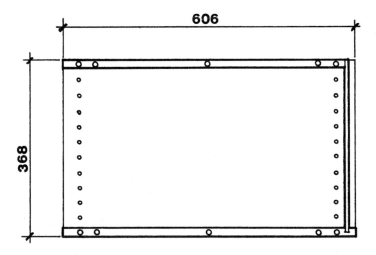

Illus. 47. A deep wall-cabinet end panel to be used above a refrigerator.

the back panel to allow for placement of special hanger hardware to be used for mounting the wall cabinet on a metal rail (see Chapter 7). The size of this notch can vary somewhat among the several European hardware companies, and some cabinetmakers still install their European designs with conventional fasteners.

With end panels and cabinet lengths planned as we have done so here, it will be a simple matter to generate a cutting list for our model kitchen, or for almost any woodworking project. Some key elements to remember in all the designing that goes on within the European system are as follows: use flat components, employ butt joints as much as possible, standardize dimensions to allow use of the same machining setups, and base vertical dimensions on the vertical hole line and its "magic" 32-mm spacings.

European Appearance

Most of the designing factors that we have looked at so far in connection with the European system have had to do with how cabinet boxes are put together. This is certainly very important because these functional matters really dictate the issues that may be most important to the woodworker—determining dimensions for a cutting list, for example, or deciding upon overall heights and depths to fulfill specific functions.

On the other hand, what may be most important to some of the people we build for is the European cabinet's appearance. There are a number of ways that people describe the European look, but some reflect individual tastes more than anything else. People who call the style "clinical" or "sterile" probably do not care for the European look at all, for example. But then, those people will not come to us or anyone else asking for European designed cabinetry. Still, the number of people who respect and even admire "Euro-style" is growing and will probably continue to grow. So, it's very important for us to know what defines the "Euro-style" as well as which design components will create this style.

Straight Lines. One of the most valued aspects of European cabinetry is its linear look. Many people simply enjoy the orderly image presented by European cabinetry, and this orderliness seems to come from the cabinetry's straight horizontal lines.

Cabinet designers know that certain elements of any cabinetry will be the most eye-catching—the most naturally interesting. And designers also know what these elements are: basically interruptions or variations in the general form of the piece. In other words, people's eyes tend to focus on an edge or a detail rather than on the middle of an unbroken mass. For example, our eyes go to the edge of a countertop or door, not the center of the component. Furthermore, designers know that straight lines will suggest movement to the human eye. Vertical lines can cause the eyes to move upwards, and horizontal lines can suggest a couple of different movements, depending on where the viewer is positioned. Viewers will likely experience a somewhat static back-and-forth movement if they are standing directly in front. But perhaps more interesting is the visual movement we can experience when we are positioned near one end of the horizontal line—a movement from close to far away that artists and architects call *perspective*. (See Illus. 48.)

All cabinetry has certain elements that tend to establish horizontal lines—the edge of the countertop, the bottom edge of base cabinetry where the toe space is located, and the top edge of wall cabinetry that is usually defined by moulding. European designers make the most of this natural eye movement by enhancing the horizontal lines in a number of ways. They can make the linear detail more attractive by changing its contour, as when they call for a profiled continuous bar pull along the top edge of base-cabinet doors. They eliminate interruptions in the horizontal lines by bringing doors and drawers closer together than they would be in most traditional cabinetry and by keeping vertical lines very simple. They keep the background fairly insignificant by selecting plain materials and simple, flat doors. If you look carefully at the base cabinetry in Illus. 48, you will see that all of these techniques were employed to achieve the European look.

Curves. With Euro-style designers showing their preference for straight horizontal lines to catch and carry the eye, and with the 32-mm assembly system dictating flat panels and butt joints, it would be very easy for European cabinet and furniture designs to become rigid and monotonous. Clearly, however, many Euro-style designers plan and execute products that are beautiful and distinctive. One way that they do this is by using rounded-edge forms and other curves, with some discrimination, to create vigorous yet subtle forms. Straight lines and flat surfaces can create the simple and functional look, but rounded forms bring a certain softness to this image. Despite an emphasis on straight horizontal lines, and even despite glossy finishes, a piece of furniture can be made to have a warm and inviting look through the use of round forms. (See Illus. 49.)

A small radius can be employed as a theme within a single piece; that is, the same clean radius can be used in several different planes and in several locations on a single article of furniture to create beauty. This is one of the methods that was used to create the desk in Illus. 49. (See Illus. 49 and 50.)

Larger, more dominant radii can also be used to superb effect. This can be especially important when you are using plastic laminates or when the confines of a small room would otherwise make a cabinet unit seem too rigid and boxlike. (See Illus. 51.) The key to using

Illus. 48. European designers can enhance unbroken horizontal lines to create a sense of perspective. Continuous bar pulls establish such lines here.

Illus. 49. Despite its glossy finish and straight-line design, this desk will create a warm environment.

Illus. 50. A close-up of rounded edges and radiused corners in a piece of European style furniture.

such forms effectively is simply not to overdo it. The curve or radius you choose should not be decoration but rather part of the overall design.

In some cases, a "radiused" furniture or cabinet component can serve not only as a visual element but also as an important functional part. One example of this is the formed post. A formed post is often simply a thick vertical slab with a fully formed (half-round) front edge, used to enhance the vertical visual effects of cabinetry produced in the European style. Its use also extends to supporting cabinet boxes or shelves that are installed between two such posts. (See Illus. 52.) Another example of this sort of double service is frequently found on desks and other furniture built Euro-style. A curved solid component can be used to join a finished end and a top by being dowelled to both pieces. The piece is not just an attractive and interesting part of the design, but it is also a kind of assembly fitting. (See Illus. 53.)

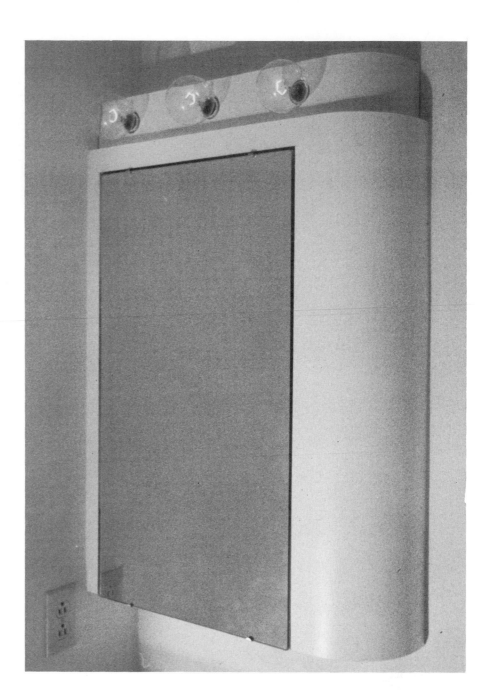

Illus. 51. This medicine cabinet, with its plastic laminate exterior, was installed in a small bathroom. Without its long-radiused vertical edge, the unit could have a very rigid and boxlike appearance.

SUMMARY

European style cabinetmaking can be thought of as a series of decisive preferences allowing for reduced dependence on skilled woodworking labor. If we are to accept this as the definition of the European system, then building in the European style means we are

Illus. 52. Formed-post construction. In this sort of application, the posts not only establish smooth, round, vertical lines, but also provide support for adjustable shelves or other cabinet components.

adopting a different method for putting cabinets together—either as a substitute for the methods that we already have or as a supplement to them.

European joining technology is based upon drilling holes in a straight line. This is referred to as the line-boring system. Horizontal

Illus. 53. The top and end of this desk were dowel-joined to the rounded solid piece shown here.

hole lines are generally used to insert fasteners, which hold together box components and reinforce the preferred joint within European design—the butt joint. Vertical hole lines are used to space cut horizontal members, to attach accessories, and to hold adjustable-shelf supports. Holes in the vertical line must be spaced exactly 32 millimetres apart, measured center to center, giving us another name for the European cabinetmaking system. To facilitate ease of design, cabinets are made to standard, modular heights and lengths. These lengths are measured in metric units—millimetres. It is most convenient to use metric measurement for vertical dimensions, but there is no need to convert from English measures to metric measures or vice versa.

The key component in designing any European cabinetry is usually the end panel, and it is desirable to make each type of end panel as totally modular as possible. The end panel receives most of the detailing that is necessary under the European system, horizontal and vertical drilling patterns, as well as a slot to accept the back. The dimension and milling of other components—such as bottoms, backs, shelves, tops, and cross members—are based on how each of these pieces will fit into the end panel. These methods for joining panels, along with the selection of precovered materials, are intended to eliminate the need for sanding and finishing, as well as certain other operations we are used to performing—operations such as face-frame making.

There are three basic box types in the European cabinet system: the base, the tall cabinet, and the wall cabinet. If you plan for each of these carefully, with a mind towards designing end panels to be as convenient to use as possible, laying out and preparing a cutting list for a European style job can be a very simple matter indeed.

European designing can also be thought of as creating a particular look—based upon sleek, long lines and some wisely used, smooth-radiused edges.

RECOMMENDATIONS

The European joining system, based on fastener-supported butt joints, can be very effective. It certainly makes design work into a simple task. It also simplifies other phases of cabinetmaking because it requires only a few different machining setups. There is no need for any rabbeting or dadoing setups, and we do not need to dowel and clamp together any face frames.

Still, many of the advantages of the modularized-component system will be the most beneficial in large shops and factories that strictly follow the 32-mm system. Total dedication to 32 mm means specialized equipment and high-volume production.

Every cabinetmaker should become familiar with the European joining system. In fact, there is no need to make a choice between it and the traditional system. Why can't we include both methodologies in our repertoire? At times, as we encounter certain types of problems in cabinetmaking, we will want to use elements of the European system. For example, when space is in short supply, we will want to build frameless—whereas when rigidity is more important, we will want to build a face frame.

Even if you conceive of the European system only as a style of appearance, it is best not to ignore the growing demand for this look—and we had better know how to include some of its elements.

In successive chapters, as we look at each operation involved in the production of European cabinets, we will consider specifics about which are most sensible to bring into the small shop. We will also consider a variety of different ways to adapt these operations to our own situations.

3
EDGE BANDING

BASIC PRINCIPLES

The term "edge banding" may be intimidating to some hobbyists and may cause others to furrow their brows in disdain. When put into its proper perspective, however, the edge-banding process should foster neither of these reactions.

Nearly all cabinetmakers perform the edge-banding operation at one time or another as part of their overall woodworking procedure. Who of us has not had the need to apply a hardwood strip to cover the raw edge of plywood shelving, for instance? Yet, as part of the European cabinetmaking system, the edge-banding operation has a more important role than it generally has within the traditional approach. Therefore, we should look at European edge-banding primarily as a shift in emphasis—not as a radical departure from what woodworkers have been doing for the past several hundred years. There are certainly some revolutionary changes in the kinds of materials being applied as edge bands and in the equipment being used to apply these materials, but these are developments that have basically arisen because of this very same shift in emphasis.

Purposes of Edge Banding

Whether you build your next cabinet project with traditional or European techniques, the primary purposes for the edge-banding process remain the same.

Probably the most obvious reason to band edges is for the sake of good appearance. This is certainly the oldest reason we have, coming along as it did with the introduction of plywood into our trade. As valuable as plywoods were as a cabinetmaking material because of their inflexibility and convenient size, their edges were anything but lovely. A strip of hardwood or pine was generally applied with glue and brads to cover any visible ply edges—usually only along the front edge of a shelf. In the traditional system, face frames covered most ply edges at the front of the cabinetry. Even when traditionalist cabinetmakers began to use particleboard for cabinet members, the primary purpose for edge banding seemed to be to hide the core edge. However, the use of particleboard in the cabinet trade created other purposes for edge banding—purposes that may be more important than simply covering an unattractive edge.

As noted in Chapter 1, most particleboards are made by mixing a binder (resin glue) with wood particles. The type of binder that is most frequently used to produce cabinetmaking panels is urea-formaldehyde resin, a substance that will leak out of the panel as formaldehyde gas if we do not seal its edges. Another major purpose for edge banding is therefore to lock this potentially dangerous substance inside the cabinet member where it will do no harm.

The third major reason to band particleboard edges is to protect the cabinet component itself. The edge band not only helps to seal formaldehyde gas *in*, but also acts to seal moisture *out*. Remember that water absorption will have very damaging effects on a piece of particleboard, both in terms of bonding between particles and dimensional stability (especially thickness). The edge band gives another kind of protection as well—by reducing the chances that a board will get its edges chipped or damaged in handling. If you cut out cabinet components using the sorts of truing and squaring technology discussed in Chapter 1, you cannot fail to see how straight and sharp the edges of these components can be. The drawback of such sharpness, along with a tendency to slice skin, is the ease with which the edges can be chipped or otherwise damaged—and damage to a plastics-covered piece is not easy to repair. (See Illus. 54.) Edge banding helps to prevent this kind of damage, too. An edge that has been banded has also usually had its sharpness "eased," meaning that it will neither cut your finger nor easily catch on protrusions that can split its core.

Sometimes an edge band, providing that it is thick and sturdy enough, can also serve as an assembly fitting in an article of furniture. (We saw an example of this in Illus. 53.)

Edge Bands: Where and When

Frameless cabinet construction suggests that we edge-band the front edge of every cabinet member, the top edge of every drawer part, and any other component with high visibility. But does this fulfill all the purposes we have just looked at? (See Illus. 55.)

If, as seems fairly clear, we want to protect people from the free formaldehyde that can escape from particleboard, then we obviously need a method or methods to afford that protection. We have already

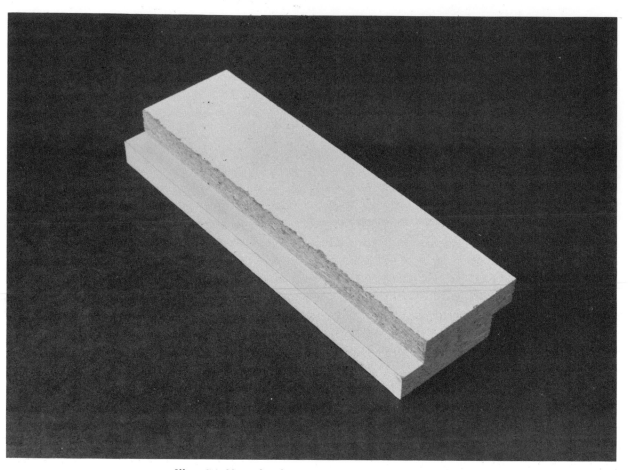

Illus. 54. Note the chipping along the edge of this unprotected piece of melamine-covered particleboard.

observed that edge banding can be used as one of these methods. But this brings up another issue—do we edge-band all four raw edges of every panel?

It is also important to lock moisture out of the cabinet parts we use to some effective degree. And protecting our skin from unnecessary cuts is a good idea, as is trying to keep square, smooth surfaces from being damaged. Again, does this mean we should band all four edges on every cabinet component? To answer this question, you really need to consider all the details involved in your overall construction plan.

If you were converting entirely to the 32-mm European cabinet-making system, I would say you should go out and find a state-of-the-art edge-banding machine and systematically band *every* raw edge that comes from your shop. There are several good reasons for the large-scale producer to do this, such as inability to control end use, preference for tool specialization and modularization, ability to perform the operation quickly, and preference for eliminating or reducing the number of finishing operations.

On the other hand, the operator of a smaller shop will find it very costly and cumbersome to perform all this edge banding. The good news is that, for us, there is really no need to do so. Remember that all the processes involved with building a cabinet are goal directed. Here, our goal is primarily to limit emissions of formaldehyde and penetrations of moisture. In many cabinet locations, we can do this simply by controlling the end use of our cabinetry; that is, by knowing where each piece will be located, we can determine which edges need banding. Although I am not aware of any research regarding the effectiveness of these blocking techniques, I have trusted them enough to use them around my own home and family. The guiding principle has been that an edge will only require banding if it is not otherwise covered or sealed. Therefore, the following edge locations

Illus. 55. An edge-banded drawer box. Note the unprotected edges, which may still "leak" free formaldehyde.

probably do not need banding due to good contact with another component or due to another kind of blocking: the tops of end panels (usually in contact with the countertop), bottoms of end panels (unless you are planning removable toe kicks), rear of most components (blocked by a wall, back panel, etc.), and ends of horizontal parts (except adjustable shelves). Some cabinetmakers also spray a clear finish over some larger areas of exposed particleboard to inhibit exchanges of gases and moisture. Three obvious locations that may call for such a finish are the underside of a countertop deck, the wall side of a back panel, and the underside of a drawer bottom. These components are often covered with a plastic on one side and are totally untreated on the other.

However, there are some locations that ought to be protected but are sometimes overlooked, including the interior edges of cross members. If you are serious about sealing the material, you will want to deal with these locations in some way. (See Illus. 56.)

In general, then, you should remember the following two guidelines in deciding where to edge-band. First, it is unnecessary to band an edge that will be otherwise sealed or blocked. Second, all raw edges should be banded if they will be exposed to the interior of the cabinet or another location where fumes can collect.

Just as important as where to edge-band is the matter of when to perform this operation. We have a much simpler answer to this question, though. The time to edge-band is as soon as possible after cutting components to size, certainly before line boring or any other milling operations are begun. Since hole locations are placed at specific distances from panel ends and edges, this practice ensures the kind of accuracy needed for modularization and standardization.

Naturally, you will have to account for the thickness of certain types of edge bands in your overall planning for end panels and other components. For example, the use of a 3-mm (⅛-in.) edge band will mean that end panels and bottoms must be listed at widths this much narrower than the intended net depth. Thus, if you decide upon base end panels with a net depth of 606 mm, you will obviously want to cut them at 603 mm and then add the edge band. Furthermore, if you do not trust the thickness of your edge-band material, you might want to band the front edge before final width-dimension cutting, although this practice is very time-consuming.

Types of Edge Banding

Edge-banding materials can be classified in several different ways. Your own circumstances, however, may be the most significant factor in determining how you would like to classify and select the type that will work best for you. We will look at three edge-band classifications, or methods of selecting an appropriate edge-band material. These three have to do with thickness, type of material, and tooling.

Selection by Thickness. Edge-banding products vary in thickness, from paper thin to as wide as a couple of inches.

The thinnest edge bands are made of PVC, wood veneer, laminated plastic, resin-saturated paper, or foil. Because these materials are generally available in rolls, they are incredibly easy to store and apply. The rolls themselves are available at reasonable prices, and

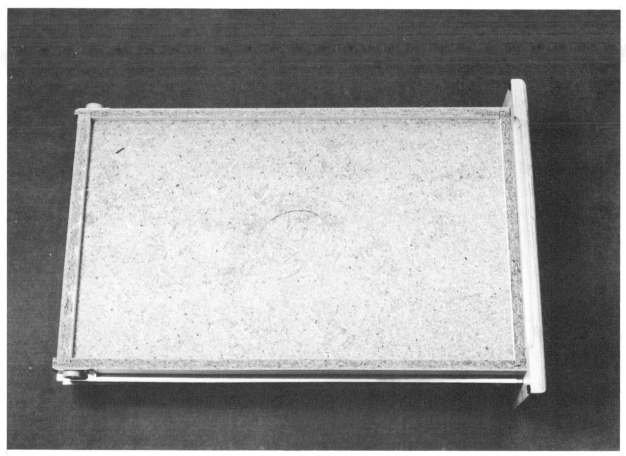

Illus. 56. The underside of this drawer is raw particleboard. This one was lacquered to seal in formaldehyde.

such materials generate further savings because they do not produce much waste. Since they are available in a great variety of colors, grains, and finishes, it is a simple matter to select an edge band that will match almost any panel covering. Matching is usually preferred with thin edge bands, especially on door edges, but using a contrasting style may work better for certain applications.

Other virtues of the rolled-up thin edging are that it gives us some choice in application methods and it's incredibly easy to cut and trim. Rolls can be purchased either with or without a precoating of hot-melt or pressure-sensitive glue. Thus, you can easily get the type of edging that works the best with your own tool system. Trimming can be performed easily with hand tools. (See Illus. 57.)

As edge-banding thickness increases, we gain certain capabilities, but we lose others. Most edge banding with a thickness of at least ⅛ in. is wood. Material in this thickness range is already less flexible than the rolled-up sort. This means that we have fewer choices when it comes to adhesives that we can use to apply the edging. It is fairly obvious, for example, that heat-sensitive glue will not be one of our options. Frequently, we have to cut this type of edging ourselves, in itself not an ideal situation for promoting tool specialization. Further-more, achieving strips of edging that are reliable in thickness, and without saw or burn marks, tends to call for additional milling. It is very likely that you will have to bring this kind of edge banding to its final thickness with a planer. In addition, thicker edge bands are more difficult to trim, generate more waste, and offer fewer choices in color, finish, and pattern.

Still, edging material in the ⅛-in. thickness range does have some virtues. First, we can mill it ourselves. This makes sense in the small shop where we do so many one-of-a-kind projects. You may get one request in a lifetime for some species of wood, for example, and few of us want the remainders of a 1,000-foot roll of expensive rosewood edge-banding material sitting around the shop after building one desk from this type of wood. It is more convenient and probably cheaper to buy a hardwood board when you need a small amount of exotic edge-band material. Second, these slightly thicker edge bands are generally tougher than veneers. Many European designers use edge bands of approximately ⅛ in. to protect products that will receive frequent bumping and other friction. Hardwood edging in this thickness also bends around a large radius without our adding moisture. (See Illus. 58.)

One of the chief reasons to use a thick edge band is so that it can be shaped or contoured. Naturally, we do this most often along door edges rather than on the front edge of box components. With edge bands of ¼ in. and thicker, we can easily round over the edge of the door. It is also sometimes efficient to apply such edging material with "white" or "yellow" resin glue and brads. Broader edging material can also improve the appearance of doors—especially where we want to create a substantial contrast on flat, melamine-covered doors and drawers. (See Illus. 59.)

Selection by Material Type. It is sometimes best to found a choice of edge-banding material on its type rather than its thickness, al-

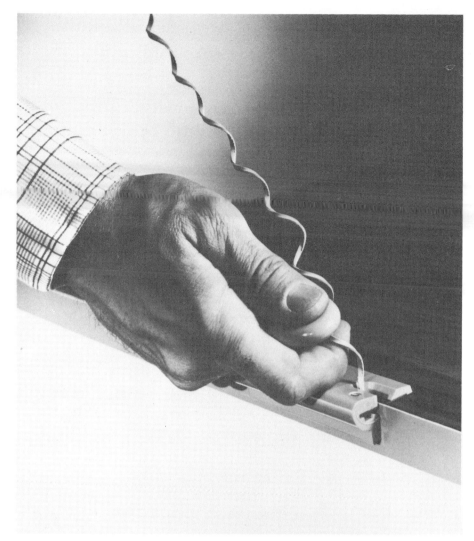

Illus. 57. This hand-held edge trimmer provides a fast, inexpensive means for edge-trimming many thin materials. (Courtesy of Adwood Corporation.)

though both are frequently interrelated. In terms of material type, in some circumstances your choice should be based on factors that have to do with durability, and in other situations it should be based on those related to appearance.

Durable banded edges are a result of at least two matters in addition to the toughness of the banding material itself. First of all, the quality of the bonding is very important. The toughest edging material in the world is useless if it separates from the panel that it is supposed to protect. This is true regardless of what type of edge-band material you elect to use, however. Secondly, the surface beneath the edge banding must provide adequate support. This kind of support

Illus. 58. This desk's top was made by banding plywood with ⅛-in. solid stock. Note the radiused corner.

depends on the density of the board used and the quality of cuts along the component's edges.

Paper edgings (printed paper, Kraft, or foil) can be surprisingly tough if they have been saturated with resin or when backed with resin-impregnated substrate. The thinness and flexibility of paper probably has a good deal to do with this strength. The paper edge bands can often be creased without tearing. In fact, the papers do not

*Illus. 59. Sleek European door styling is often largely a result of edge banding.
(Courtesy of Decore-Ative Specialties.)*

Illus. 60. A membrane moulding press. (Courtesy of Heinrich Wemhöner GmbH & Co. KG)

show significant damage from a moderate dent either because they are so supple. Paper is the most inexpensive of the roll-on-variety edgings, but it has two substantial disadvantages: It does very little to protect the material beneath it from impact, and it is easily marked.

Plastics-covered edgings can be very tough, depending on their thickness and the type of plastic resin used. Thick, rigid, laminated plastic, the kind often used for countertops, has excellent impact-resistance qualities, but it will require machine trimming. Thinner plastics—rolled, high-pressure plastic laminates and vinyl—are convenient to work with, and they are certainly tougher and more protective than the papers. Rigid PVC combines qualities that are important in the edge-banding operation. It is impact resistant and hard, yet flexible enough to be easily applied and trimmed. In fact, it has so many desirable edge-banding qualities that it could become the dominant material for this application.

When it comes to wood, resistance to impact and ability to protect the edge beneath are largely dependent on thickness. Wood veneers are not especially useful in this regard, but the thicker solid edgings are.

Appearance can be the major factor in choosing a banding material, especially if you are building a unit for someone else, and that person specifies certain appearance aspects.

As mentioned earlier, an edge band can either match the adjacent surface or contrast with it. Matching is very simple because one decision as to finish, color, and texture is usually all that is necessary. Nothing could be more obvious than to band the edge of an almond-melamine door with almond PVC or some other similar plastic. Contrasts are not always so clear cut. A huge range of colors will contrast beautifully with red oak, and there are many solid-color combinations that can be achieved to lovely effect. When creating contrast, designers look at the entire room or even the entire house in selecting hues that will accent the colors of floors, wall and window coverings, appliances, and so on.

In addition to matching or contrasting adjacent surfaces, the other significant design factor related to edge banding is contour or edge form. In European design, we generally can find only three distinct edge forms: square, rounded over, and profiled (to function as a pull). The large European cabinet manufacturers use some machinery that is capable of efficiently laminating veneer or plastic film over a preprofiled panel, but again, it is extremely expensive. (See Illus. 60.) This sort of machinery makes very good sense for the largest manufacturers of doors and other formed components; after all, it does extend the use of particleboard and edge-banding products in a way that has not been accomplished before. For most of us, though, the most efficient way of creating contours is to add a wide edge band and then round it over, or else to purchase preprofiled edgings as we do for continuous pulls. In general, then, if we want a rounded-over or broad wooden section on doors for a job, the way to accomplish it is to add thick-wood edging.

Selection by Tooling. Hobbyists will usually narrow their edging choices by first looking carefully at their own tool systems. Although low-volume cabinetmakers may admire the largest, most precise, and most versatile of the European edge banders, most may never even use one.

In fact, small and medium-sized shops have made adaptations of the European edge-banding process, largely with favorable results. Naturally, the kind of tooling that you have is also a result of the volume of work that you do in a particular style. When woodworkers are first exposed to the edge-banding process, and they see how it can benefit them and the people they craft for, they usually wind up adding a few items to their tool collection. Therefore, it probably makes the most sense for us to take a closer look at the techniques for edge banding that are available to us before trying to generalize about how tools will govern our choice of edging materials, thicknesses, and adhesives. The operation that will have the most to do with controlling our selection, though, is the actual application procedure. In general, then, we can establish a few broad guidelines.

Probably the least expensive way to incorporate rolled edging materials is to invest in a heat-type edge bander. Such a tool will rapidly melt the adhesive on preglued, rolled plastics. The tool or equipment itself may be as unsubstantial as a hand-held device and may call for only a relatively small investment. Naturally, using heat-type applicators will narrow your choice of edge bandings to the thinnest rolled styles—those with preglued backers.

A hot-melt applicator will speed up the operation a good deal, but its cost may be prohibitive. The most automatic and mechanized of these machines will also perform the other subprocesses of edge banding for you, but only the highest-volume box producers will want to pay for that kind of sophistication. Still, modern cabinetmakers can find less expensive stationary tools whose only job is to melt the adhesive, spread it evenly onto the edge of a board, and press on the edging material. Compared to the preglued edging system, this type of application system generally creates a stronger bond and allows the cabinetmaker to use much less expensive edging material.

The conventionally equipped shop allows for at least a couple of edge-banding methods, but we should note from the beginning that these methods are generally time-consuming. Woodworkers have been using contact cement to apply veneers and other thin edgings for years. Solid-wood edgings, from as thin as ⅛ in. up to about ¾ in., can be applied with aliphatic resin glue. The tools needed might include clamps and cauls, some type of nail gun, or merely a few rolls of masking tape. Wider wooden edge bands are often applied with glue and a supporting tongue-and-groove joint that requires additional milling. As already noted, the conventional application methods require less specialized tools but more time and greater woodworking skill.

THE EDGE-BANDING PROCESS

The edge-banding operation actually consists of several steps, as follows:

1. preparing and applying the adhesive,
2. affixing the edging material,
3. trimming away excess material, and
4. sanding and/or easing the edges of the component.

It should be obvious that you need to complete each of these tasks before moving to the next task in the sequence. We shall first look briefly at the European machinery that is capable of accomplishing all these steps with tremendous speed; then we will consider the alternatives available to us.

Whole-System Machinery

Modular cabinet manufacturers who plan to use the 32-mm system of production will want to take full advantage of the most advanced edge-banding technology. A whole-system edge bander will turn this entire operation into what seems like a single step. After carefully setting up this machine, we have only to feed each cabinet piece through it to get a single edge completely ready for the next step in the cabinetmaking operation. In fact, some of these tools are double-edge machines; that is, they can apply edging material to two edges of the same panel at the same time.

On one end of such a machine, we feed in the raw but perfectly smooth and flat edge of a particleboard panel. Appearing at the other end of the machine is the same panel, now with a strip of plastic or wood applied to cover the raw particle edge. The edging is firmly glued in place, with ends that have been cut off exactly at the ends of the panel, and with edges that have been bevelled and trimmed flush to the surfaces of the panel. Some of the more elaborate machines also have the capability of scraping, belt sanding, or buffing along the banded edge.

The first major subsystem of a whole-system edge bander is the melting station. The operator has only to fill a reservoir with granules of hot-melt glue and turn on the heating element. (See Illus. 61.) In

8 to 20 minutes, the glue is ready to be applied to the substrate. The application itself is performed with great speed and evenness, usually by means of a continuously turning roller that receives a steady supply of glue. As the edge of a cabinet component is fed across the roller, it receives a coating of this hot liquid glue.

All of these machines are designed to be supplied by rolls of edging material; some can also be supplied via a magazine-type mechanism that allows rapid gluing of such strip materials as rigid plastic laminates or thin lumber. (See Illus. 61 and 62.)

Illus. 61. The hot-melt station of an automatic edge bander. (Courtesy of Holz-Her U.S. Inc.)

It is very important to apply the edging material while the glue is still hot and liquid. With more rollers, the machine next presses on a section of edging. (See Illus. 63.)

Naturally, if the operator has set the machine up to feed materials out of a magazine, these pieces have already been cut to length. If the feeding is from a continuous roll, the machine also engages a set of knives to cut off the veneer or plastic just after the trail end of the component has gone past. (See Illus. 64.)

Next, the component needs trimming of the banding material at its ends and edges. One or two saw blades plunge rapidly into position for end trimming. (See Illus. 65.) Two more sets of blades rotate into position to perform flush surface trimming and bevelling at the same time. (See Illus. 66.)

Most impressive about the completion of all these subprocesses is that they are performed at separate stations, with each station en-

Illus. 62. An automatic magazine allows the feeding of strip materials. (Courtesy of Holz-Her U.S. Inc.)

gaged at precisely the right time and with the right settings as each board is fed through. A single feed on a single machine does it all. (See Illus. 67.) Larger machines also have what is called an open station—a station where the operator can install knives, belts, or buffing wheels to perform other desired operations. (See Illus. 68.)

The smallest of these multioperation machines consume about 3 feet in depth and 7 feet in length but will still require substantial

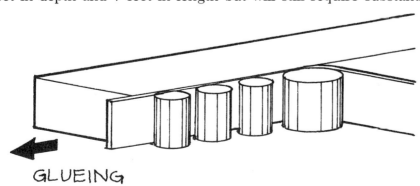

GLUEING

Illus. 63. The edge bander spreads glue with rollers.

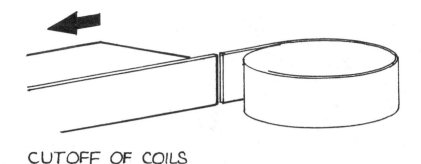

CUTOFF OF COILS

Illus. 64. The continuous feeding of the coil is automatically terminated at the tail end of a stock feed.

investments of capital because of the precise, or "low-tolerance," technology involved. Larger, single-edge, edge-banding machines weigh up to a ton and a half and consume even more space: Some are as deep as 5 feet and as long as 16 feet.

We have to admire the technology that goes into the fabulous European edge-banding machines, which allow the cabinet manufacturer to process panels very rapidly as part of a modularized system. In terms of suitability to the traditional cabinetmaker, we should perhaps consider ourselves in three general categories: manufacturers, small shops, and mid-sized shops.

Manufacturers. Owners of this sort of operation are and ought to be highly profit oriented. In reducing their dependence on skilled labor, manufacturers should incorporate the most advanced wood-

Illus. 65. The end-trimming station of an automatic edge bander. (Courtesy of Holz-Her U.S. Inc.)

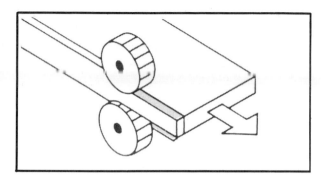

Illus. 66. The flush-trimming unit of an automatic edge bander. (Courtesy of Holz-Her U.S. Inc.)

working machinery available. Their employees do not need to be highly skilled in more than one or two phases of the cabinetmaking operation. Many traditional modular producers are converting en-

Illus. 67. Edge banders such as this will face a panel, from start to finish, in seconds. (Courtesy of Holz-Her U.S. Inc.)

Illus. 68. Scraping, belt sanding, or buffing can also be programmed into the machine.

tirely to the 32-mm system, and they are naturally investing in whole-system edge banders. Others remain successful at turning out high volumes of face-frame cabinetry.

Small Shops. This category includes all the cabinetmakers who work independently, although they may have a few employees. It includes hobbyists as well. They generally produce customized products, and they are highly skilled in many areas of woodworking. For small shop operations, efficient edge banding is obviously important, but whole-system edge banders do not make any sense.

Mid-Sized Shops. Many woodworkers are in this group. The owners of mid-sized shops usually employ more than a few employees, and try to compete both with manufacturers and with smaller shops in the kind of work they do. This calls for skilled employees. As will be obvious in the ensuing section, this is the group of cabinetmakers who will have the greatest problem incorporating European edge-banding styles and systems. The equipment itself is probably too expensive and too big for most owners of mid-sized shops, and yet these same shop owners may need a share of the modularized-cabinet market in order to survive.

Subsystem Edge Banding

The custom cabinetmaker who wants to use some European style edge banding actually has a wide variety of options. And fortunately for small shops, many of the options do not require a huge investment in dollars. Most of the systems we will look at, however, require more of the cabinetmaker's time than does a unisystem edge bander, and somewhat greater woodworking skill.

Edge Preparation. If your equipment is not capable of producing clean, chipless cuts along panel edges that are going to be banded, then you may have to take the time for some additional edge preparation. As stated in Chapter 1, the need for this additional work is partially dependent on the types of materials used in the cabinet project. Usually, if the panel itself has a covering of high-pressure laminated plastic, melamine, or some other hard-plastics material, then the edge-banding operation will not yield a very attractive edge. Pitted plastic surfaces are fairly unforgiving; that is, there is no way to repair the damage, at least nothing that will look good. The heat-sensitive glues used with rolled edge-banding materials are not intended to be gap fillers. Even if we had good fillers that could be used to repair these pits, we probably would not want to do so, for it is just as fast to cut the components oversized and then to use a jointer to trim away the pitted edges. Of course, cabinetmakers intending to use panels that are covered in unfinished veneer will have a couple of advantages: Aliphatic resin glue is a fairly good gap filler, and small voids in the veneer can be filled with paste and then sanded smooth with pretty good results.

Obviously, the best practice is to create smooth, straight, chip-free edges for edge banding. If your saw is not doing that, it is well worth the time it takes to feed each component over the jointer knives. Other options for trimming away material are to use a table-mounted router or a sander.

Setting up the router in a table to perform a trimming cut can work out fairly well. You can use the fence on the table router as an infeed/outfeed table by adding a thin strip to the outfeed side of the fence and then aligning a straight router bit's cutters with it. (See Illus. 69.) By taking some safety precautions, it is also possible to feed materials between a fence and a table-mounted router to yield perfect edges. (See Illus. 70.) The danger in this setup is that cutter rotation will tend to draw the panel away from the fence. If the feed is not smooth and steady, you can end up with panel edges that show nicely rounded dips or divots rather than pits in the plastics covering. To

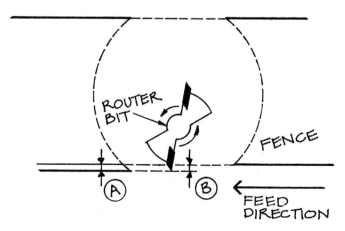

Illus. 69. The router table can be used as a jointer to prepare straight edges. A and B must be equal.

Illus. 70. Using a router and fence together to generate a straight edge. Great caution must be exercised with this setup, and featherboard should be used. This is not a recommended method.

reduce danger to the hand, and for good-quality edges, set up to take only small "bites," and feed only wide pieces in this way.

Edge sanding is not nearly as effective for this kind of edge preparation as methods that make use of cutters. The woodworker has much less control over the amount of material removed and the evenness with which it is removed. Besides that, sanding tends to pack tiny particles of wood, binder, and plastic into the edge of the panel. These tiny, loose particles will interfere with any bond attempted in the edge-banding process.

It is certainly an important enough principle to remind ourselves that good-quality edge banding begins with high-quality edges. Wise woodworkers will want to take whatever steps are necessary to generate the best possible cuts with their saws. It is far better to invest your time in setting up your saws to perform high-quality cuts than to try to correct damage later on. If secondary milling is necessary, the jointer is still far superior to a router or an edge sander.

Applying the Edge Band. Depending on the adhesive and edge-band material that you are using, the application of the edging can involve one or more steps.

Not all stationary equipment is as complex and expensive as the European unisystem machinery. For instance, some tool manufacturers have developed equipment that will simply apply edge-band materials using hot-melt glue. (See Illus. 71.) This makes a lot of sense. After all, what rule says that you have to use fantastic technology to ensure that all the steps of edge banding are coordinated? Indeed, why make the simple attachment of a piece of edging material any more sophisticated than it has to be? By handling this single step in the procedure, these tools achieve our purpose very well.

Such edge-banding machines are semiautomatic. To use one, you first turn on the glue-melting station, making sure that sufficient

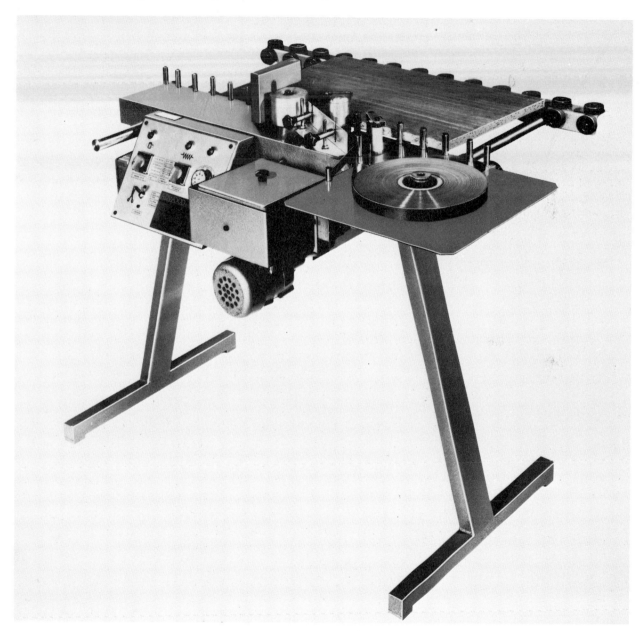

Illus. 71. This edge bander is designed for one simple function: to apply the edging material with hot-melt glue. (Courtesy of Adwood Corporation.)

glue granules have been added to the reservoir. When the glue has melted enough for application, feeding of panels can begin. A motor turns the rollers for spreading glue and pressing on the edging material. Pressure can be applied entirely by the operator or with the assistance of opposing rollers. (Again, see Illus. 71.) After the edging is in place, most of these machines have a built-in clipper station that engages to snip off the edging just after the trailing end of the panel has gone past. That's all. Trimming is left for other tools and systems.

Using this type of edge bander is not nearly as fast as using a unisystem tool, but it does allow the cabinetmaker to employ coils of plain edging material (without glue preapplied to the back). The plain material is not only less expensive than the preglued edging but also allows you to use hot-melt granulated glue. This type of glue is very reliable, at least in my experience, because it always goes on as a liquid. When the proper melting occurs, and when the rollers get a steady, even supply of the glue, it is a simple matter to achieve a strong bond all along the edge of every panel. It is even possible to apply strip materials, such as rigid plastic or lumber, with one of these machines. This type of edge bander is especially appropriate for shops where there is a good deal of edge banding to do. It may well be one of the best options for mid-sized shops, though the initial cost may be as much as a good-quality table saw.

Hot-air edge banders are another option. (See Illus. 72.) These are simpler than the hot-melt machines we have just looked at, and much less expensive. Such tools can be effective for applying preglued edging materials. There are some obvious built-in limitations here, of course: The system will not handle rigid strips of lumber or laminated plastic, and the user has to buy the more expensive preglued rolls of edging material.

The hot-air edge-banding tool uses a heating element and a blower to activate the heat-sensitive glue. Immediately thereafter, the panel is pressed into contact with the edging material and a roller. The operation is manually performed, both in terms of the rate of feed and the pressure applied. Table models and hand-held models are both available, but the hand-held models are less convenient to operate because you need an extra hand to hold the workpiece. Using hot air to activate the glue is a good idea because the heat is applied directly to the preglued side of the veneer or plastic. If the heat controls are set properly and the rate of feed is even, there should be no problem with the edging material burning or blistering. The table-top hot-air edge bander can be a good option for woodworkers in small shops if they do quite a bit of edge banding.

Irons can also be utilized with some effectiveness to apply preglued edging material. In fact, the ironing system was the first system developed to be used in conjunction with preglued, heat-sensitive edging. (See Illus. 73.) This kind of tool also uses heat to melt the glue that is already in place on the edging material. You draw the veneer or plastic across the iron, activating the glue. Then, before the glue can harden again, you press the edging into position against the panel edge, with a roller. The rolled material is generally cut with scissors or a utility knife, with the corner of the panel used as a guide. Hand-held irons are also available for smaller jobs. (See Illus. 74.) With these, it is best to clamp each piece of stock in an upright position and to snip off pieces of edging material just slightly longer than needed before attempting to do the edge banding. Then, you simply align the edging along the panel to be banded and draw the iron along to activate the glue. It's a good idea to apply pressure with a roller after ironing to ensure the best possible bonding.

Illus. 72. A table-top, hot-air edge bander. Hand-held models are also available. (Courtesy of Häfele America.)

The ironing tools can be effective, but they generally involve more time than the other edge-banding systems we have looked at. They also require some care. The major problem to be overcome with the ironing systems has to do with the heat not being applied directly to the glue as it is with the hot-air-blower technology. Instead, the heat is applied to the face of the edging, and it must penetrate the entire thickness of the edge-banding material in order to activate the glue. The potential problems include burning of veneer edgings and scorching or blistering of plastic edgings if you apply too much heat and pressure; conversely, if you don't use enough heat and pressure, bonding may not occur in some sections where it should. I am not saying these undesirable effects will occur, but they are a possibility.

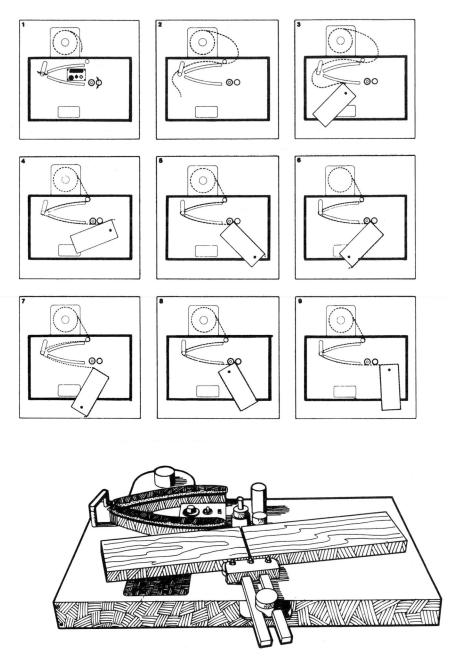

Illus. 73. An iron-style edging applicator. (Copyright Westvaco Corporation, 1989. All rights reserved.)

When applying edging material with an iron, you need to run your finger and thumb along the fresh bond to check for any sections of edging that lift away from the panel. Thus, mastery of the iron-on system can eliminate burning, blistering, and poor bonding, but application can be time-consuming.

One system that is still used fairly widely involves conventional glue. This is obviously a somewhat slow system, regardless of whether you elect to use nails or brads to secure the strips of lumber edging or allow the bonds to set up under pressure alone. In the first

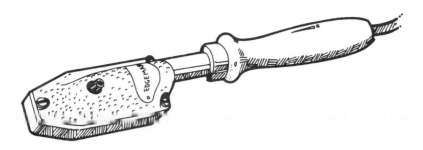

Illus. 74. A hand iron for use in small jobs. (Copyright Westvaco Corporation, 1989. All rights reserved.)

place, there is really no fast way of spreading the glue evenly. If you apply it from a glue bottle, then you will probably have to use your finger or a brush to even out the beads of glue. (See Illus. 75.) Some

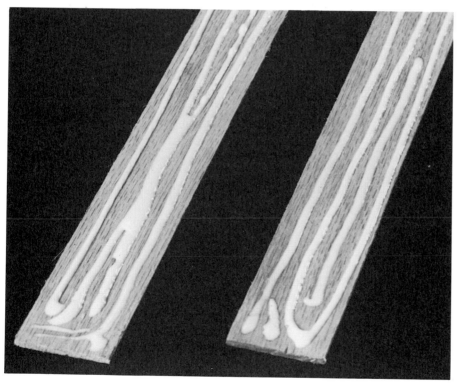

Illus. 75. This edging is lumber, ⅛ in. thick by 1½ in. wide, and designed to be attached with resin glue. Note the beads of glue.

cabinetmakers use white (polyvinyl) glue rather than the yellow (aliphatic resin) glue. The white glue cures substantially slower than yellow glue, allowing the cabinetmaker some additional working time. This is important because, if we have a good deal of edge banding to do, we can dump a quantity of white glue into an open container and then use a brush to spread it. A small amount of added water now and then keeps the adhesive workable. This approach will not work too well with yellow glue, and it may also not prove too viable in warm weather.

When using resin glues as an edge-banding adhesive, you need to plan for a method of applying pressure across seams. With thin edgings, such as the ⅛-in. edging stock shown in Illus. 75, it is almost always best to avoid the use of brads and other fasteners. Nails do not perform very well in thin stock because the edging material does a poor job of ensuring that pressure is spread over a substantial area. Edging stocks as thick as ⅝ in. do a good job of evening out the pressure applied by nails, but there are a couple of other disadvantages to using nails in thicker stocks. First is the issue of appearance, especially since it is so unusual to find face-driven nails on European cabinetry. Besides, as we have already noted, one of the main purposes of a thick-wood edge band is to allow the milling of an edge form. Steel fasteners are never too desirable close to where you intend to cut a detail.

Clamps are, of course, an effective method of applying pressure whenever you are using resin glue. After spreading glue to coat the entire edge to be banded, you align the strip, perhaps holding it in place with masking tape, and then use bar clamps for pressure. It is best to apply the edging to at least two equal-length pieces at the same time so that you can clamp them together. This procedure allows you to put clamps into double duty, and also allows you to avoid using cauls. If the banded edges face each other, then the panels themselves serve as cauls to even out the pressure across the entire glued surface. (See Illus. 76.) In building European designed cabinetry, however, we have to do a lot of edge banding—too much for all this clamping, except perhaps in the smallest shops. And even in the small shop, clamping takes too much time for many cabinetmakers. Of course, you may be building in the European mode for your own use; in this situation, some cabinetmakers think nothing of the extra time it takes to do edge banding with resin glue and clamps.

The only remaining edge-band application system involves contact cement. The advantages of contact cement are that it allows us to use virtually any edging material, we can use plain material (not preglued), and we do not need any fasteners or clamps. Contact cement creates an instant bond. On the other hand, contact cement will create some problems for woodworkers who plan to use it regularly as an edging application system. For example, contact cement can take some time to apply properly because it has to be applied on both surfaces and the only truly rapid method of applying it is by spraying. Brushes and rollers need to be dipped repeatedly into the cement can to keep them supplied with adhesive. Even spraying creates a problem because overspray can easily get onto the surfaces of the panels being edged. Therefore, you need to mask off the pre-clad surfaces or employ some other system to keep overspray from damaging panels.

Illus. 76. When clamping on a lumber edging, it makes sense to work on two pieces at the same time.

When using either contact cement or resin glue, we will generally be working with strips of edging material that are already cut to length. Each strip should be slightly longer than the panel on which it will be affixed. In fact, anyone who is using the subsystem approach to edge banding will probably have to trim away small lengths of the edging material that project beyond either end of the banded panel.

End Trimming. End trimming can be performed with a number of different tools.

Thin tapes, such as veneer and PVC, can be reliably cut with a sharp utility knife. You simply have to draw the blade of the knife along the edge of the panel. (See Illus. 77.) If a perfect trim is not required, you might want to use a pair of scissors. I confess that I have even broken or torn the edging material along a crease by first folding the overhanging edge over the end of the panel. (See Illus. 78.) This will work very well most of the time, but it is not a good idea for highly visible cabinet locations.

Illus. 77. Trimming thin edging with a utility knife.

Illus. 78. End-trimming with a finger is all right in some locations.

To trim edgings that are thicker or less pliable, most smaller shops employ saws or routers. A table-mounted router, equipped with a flush trimming bit, will do an excellent job of trimming laminated plastics. This is an extremely easy system to set up. If you decide to use this approach for end trimming, you only need to make sure that the bit projects high enough above the table for its cutters to remove the entire thickness of the edging and for the bit's roller to ride along the panel's surface. (See Illus. 79.) The router is also capable of length-trimming lumber edgings up to approximately ⅛ in. thick, providing that you feed somewhat slowly at the end of the trimming cut.

Of the several saws that can be used for end trimming, a hand saw may be the best choice. The trouble with a radial arm saw is that it can produce some tear away or chipped surfaces. Putting the front edge of the board against this saw's fence means that the blade will probably tear splinters out of the edging's face. (See Illus. 80.) With panels over 15 in. wide, we cannot trim the edging any other way. If we can flip the panel over so that the blade only tears away at the rear face of the edging, then we have to draw the blade out quite far, and there is a very good chance of damaging the surface of the panel that is resting on the table of the radial arm saw. Thus, the radial arm saw is not the best saw for end-trimming edge bands, unless you are using a sharp, fine blade.

Some cabinetmakers perform their end trimming by using their table saw in conjunction with a mitre gauge. The mitre gauge is set

Illus. 79. End-trimming
with a table-mounted
router.

up perpendicular to the blade itself. Each panel is positioned against the fence of the mitre gauge and then fed so that the blade trims only the protruding segment of edging. Again, however, this is not the most reliable of systems. If the blade comes into contact with the end

Illus. 80. End-trimming
with the radial arm saw.

of the panel, it is easy to get some chipping or splintering on its underside. The trouble is that it is almost impossible to trim the edging exactly where we want it trimmed without getting the blade in contact with the end of the panel. (See Illus. 81.) As with the

Illus. 81. End-trimming with a table saw. The system is inaccurate if the blade does contact the end of the panel, and it may yield a chipped surface if the blade makes contact.

radial arm saw, the table saw can be used for end trimming, providing that chip-free surfaces are not a critical requirement.

In a cabinetmaking system that is supposed to be based on low tolerances and great accuracy, a fine-tooth hand saw may be the best tool for end trimming. We can cut off the protruding edging exactly even with the end of the panel by simply guiding the flat part of the saw against this same end. We can turn the component over after cutting halfway through from one side. With a bit of skill, we can perform excellent trimming this way, although it means once again sacrificing a substantial amount of time to get the job done. If we make a similar sacrifice on each step of the European cabinetmaking process, we are likely to spend much longer than we should on the whole job. Therefore, cabinetmakers with a lot of edge banding to do need a fast approach.

One solution is available to cabinetmakers with a good-quality edge sander. If you have this kind of equipment, you can do "rough" end trimming with a table saw or radial arm saw and then smooth the end of the panel by pressing it against the edge sander. The idea is to perform the saw trimming so that only a tiny amount of edging material is left to remove. (See Illus. 82.)

Another possibility is naturally to invest in a table-mounted end trimmer, which is easy to operate and not terribly expensive. Anyone who needs to edge-band frequently could benefit from this kind of

Illus. 82. Fine end-trimming on the edge sander.

machine. (See Illus. 83.) However, many of these machines will only trim flexible edging materials, such as PVC, veneer, and some of the melamines. If you decide to invest in a table-mounted end trimmer, make sure that it will handle the types of edgings that you plan to use.

Surface Trimming. There are two inexpensive and efficient options for surface trimming available, one for soft materials and one for rigid plastics and wood.

For PVC, pliable melamine, and veneer, the best choice for most shops is a hand-operated edge-trimming knife. (Again, see Illus. 57.) The cabinetmaker has only to draw the knife along each edge for a rapid and lovely flush trimming job. The blade of such a knife is usually shaped so that edging material cannot escape once the cut is begun. There are edge-trimming models designed to cut curves, models for cutting in both directions, and even models that will trim two edges at once. These tools are so inexpensive, so accurate, and so easy to use that there is really no reason to resort to the chisels and utility knives that are sometimes used for this purpose.

For surface-trimming lumber and hard-plastics edgings, the router is an excellent tool. In fact, you can use a table-mounted router for both end trimming and surface trimming, employing the flush cutting bit mentioned in the previous section or a straight bit and fence.

(See Illus. 84.) To minimize tear away, it is sometimes wise to feed slowly or to use a reverse feed in this kind of setup. Carbide-tipped cutters should be used, of course. The router can naturally be used to perform flush trimming on soft materials too, but the bits have a tendency to collect a gummy mixture of adhesive and plastics, which will foul rollers and cutters alike. Again, hand-held knives work so well for soft materials that there is no need to find a substitute.

With flush trimming completed, you may need to ease the banded edges of European components before going onto the next phase of the operation. The best of the hand-operated trimming knives will have already put a tiny bevel onto the banded edge. With any of the edging materials, it is of course possible to ease the edges with a sanding block or a sharp scraper. With high-pressure laminated plastics, it is wise to use a fluted bit for easing the edges. The setup is

Illus. 83. A table-mounted end trimmer. (Courtesy of Adwood Corporation.)

very similar to the setup you would use for performing the flush trimming itself, but a fence becomes more important. You can keep each component steady for smooth, accurate milling by holding it firmly against the fence during the feed.

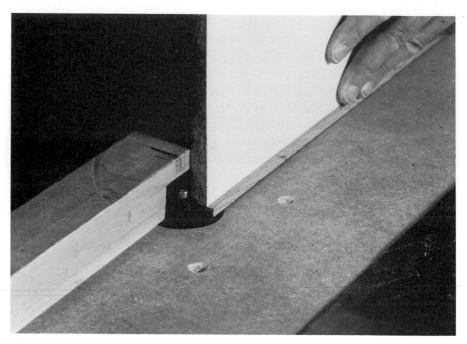

Illus. 84. Surface-trimming using a table-mounted router and fence.

As soon as the edges are banded, the components are ready for the next step of European cabinetmaking—line boring.

FACE FRAMES

Who cannot agree with Pudd'nhead Wilson's calendar that states: "Habit is habit, and not to be flung out of the window by any man, but coaxed downstairs a step at a time"[1]? Most traditional cabinetmakers are comfortable with the process of building face frames. We understand the functions and advantages of face frames, and we have at least three effective methods for building them: dowelling, toe screwing, and mortising. Very few traditional cabinetmakers are willing to "fling the face-frame notion out the window"—instead, most of us want to add the European system to our own repertoire. And why not? The face-frame system still meets some needs that flat panel processing cannot. In the context of this chapter, for example, framing would reduce the need for edge banding of materials. Furthermore, cabinetry can be given the contemporary European look, even if it is built with face frames. The cabinet shown in Illus. 48 was built face-frame style.

It is not our purpose here to give a detailed account of face-frame making. You undoubtedly have a system in place already. Instead, let us take a very brief look at ways that framed cabinetry would be different with European influence.

One of the easiest ways to begin building with European materials is to use melamine-covered sheet goods for the box and then to mount a face frame onto the assembled box. This allows you to employ the old tools and techniques you are used to. The face frame itself acts as an edge band for raw particleboard edges. That is, the face frame will seal formaldehyde in and moisture out; it will furthermore lend an attractive appearance to the face of the cabinet, protect the particleboard and covering, and also hide any minor chipping on some components. It is the way that most small and medium-sized shops begin "building European." In fact, as we shall see in the next chapter, using precovered sheets does not necessarily mean that you will have to drill a hole line for assembly either.

Effects on Cutting Procedures

Using a face frame means that you do not have to be nearly as concerned with avoiding chipping and splintering as you do in pure flat panel processing. With a face frame, you usually need only one perfectly chip-free surface on each cut. The face overhang usually does a good job of concealing the other side. If you are using a face frame then, you can cut precovered components in pretty much the same way that you have always cut plywood—being primarily concerned with achieving a chip-free cut on only one side. The use of a carbide-tipped, hollow-ground blade is sufficient guarantee that you will get the quality required, even when cutting through hard, high-pressure coverings.

The disadvantages of combining face frames and European materials are significant in terms of cutting procedures. The most obvious disadvantage is that you must cut more components than you would have to cut if you did not use face frames. Besides, the cutter has to cut up lumber to make the face frame. This involves various blades and saw setups in addition to various materials. These factors alone have led many cabinetmakers away from framing and towards edge banding.

Effects on Edge Banding

It should be obvious that the use of face frames means that we can avoid a lot of edge banding. Cabinetmakers can get by as they always have, with glue and fasteners or glue and clamps. This would seem to indicate that you do not have to buy any edge-banding tools. However, remember that you will be investing in face-frame equipment anyway. Part of the time and money that goes into maintaining a dowelling machine, for instance, might just as well go into maintaining a good hot-air edge bander. The modern cabinetmaker needs to recognize that some jobs just do not require a face frame, and that there is no need to cut, machine, build, and sand one if it is a superfluous component.

Other Effects

The decision to use a face frame or not affects every other phase of the cabinetmaking process. If you choose the face frame, you can use dadoes and rabbets as assembly details rather than line boring. Dadoing and rabbeting are less standardized than the line-boring process. Conventional construction also means that you will need additional components: nailers, hold-downs, and drawer-glide mounting rails. All of these components must be edge-banded or otherwise sealed if they are fabricated from particleboard. You also need to plan good methods for attaching these components to the other pieces of the box, a task complicated by the ineffectiveness of resin glue on plastics surfaces. A face frame involves driving nails through the frame and into the edge of precovered particleboard, so it's more important than usual to avoid missing with each nail. The damage caused by a misdirected nail is hard to correct with plastic coverings. Face frames also require finishing. Therefore, you may have to mask off plastics-covered materials when using certain stains and finishes.

A number of such problems will present themselves when you attempt to blend face frames and the European system. Of course, by blending, you will give yourself advantages as well. As you proceed through this guide to the European system, references will be made repeatedly to both the advantages and disadvantages of the European, conventional, and blended methods. In general, though, remember that one of the main purposes of European construction is to simplify—to eliminate time-consuming steps. So, we need to consider the machines and processes that can be eliminated by edge banding instead of building a face frame.

SUMMARY

Truly European cabinetmaking procedures involve edge banding or the covering of raw particleboard edges on most flat panels that go into a cabinet box. The purposes for this operation are to seal moisture out of the panel, to keep formaldehyde vapors from escaping from its particleboard core, to beautify the edges, and to protect the edges. Careful planning will often release the cabinetmaker from the obligation to edge-band every single raw edge because some panel locations will not require sealing or protection. This can be a great help in the small shop. If edge banding is planned, it should usually be performed before line boring or other milling operations.

The edging materials that you can use include PVC, pliable

melamine, high-pressure plastic laminates, paper, foil, veneer, and lumber strips. Most of these materials are available in continuous rolls, either with or without preapplied heat-sensitive glue. Lumber strips, however, must generally be cut by the cabinetmaker from solid stocks. The wider strips are intended to yield a continuous bar pull, hold an edge form, or simply modify the basically unbroken look of European cabinet components—particularly doors and drawer fronts.

Application of the plain edging material is usually performed by an automatic machine that melts glue granules, rolls the glue onto each raw panel edge, and then immediately presses a length of rolled edging into place. There are a variety of tools available for application of the preglued edging material, using either hot air or a heating iron to melt the heat-sensitive glue. Rigid edging materials, such as lumber or high-pressure laminated plastic, can be applied by an automatic machine with a special "magazine" option or by using a slower process involving resin glue or contact cement.

Unisystem edge banders are extremely expensive, but they will perform every step of the edge-banding operation in seconds. These machines are designed to be bought and used by the largest cabinetmaking firms. The smaller shop may employ a series of tools to apply the edge band, to trim it, and to ease its edges, one step at a time. Tools for applying the edge band are available in virtually any price range, depending on whether you want to use hot-melt glue, a hot-air machine, or an iron to apply the material. Routers and hand-held trimming knives are used as subsystem trimming tools. Edges are often eased with a router or a sanding block.

It is sometimes to the cabinetmaker's advantage to use a face frame instead of applying an edge band. Modern cabinetmakers must be able to do both, and they must have a criterion in order to decide when each is most appropriate.

RECOMMENDATIONS

The need for a good-quality edge-banding system seems clear. The European cabinetmaking system includes edge banding as one of its major operations, and even traditionalists have to apply edge bands fairly often. As we have already suggested, today's cabinetmakers should have a reliable system of edge banding while still maintaining their tools and methodologies for building and using face frames.

Versatility—meaning the capability to customize any cabinet or furniture product—is the most important factor in selecting an edge-banding tool system, especially in the small shop. We need to have an effective edge-banding system at our fingertips whenever we need it.

It is fairly clear that the largest cabinet manufacturers will want to modularize, and that the European 32-mm system provides the most complete and the simplest modularization. In these situations, it makes the most sense to invest in a unisystem edge bander.

Most cabinetmakers, however, do not work in the largest shops but rather in medium-sized and small shops. Many of us, in fact, work only for ourselves and a small circle of people. The key for us to remain in demand is customization. In medium-sized shops, it seems very wise to invest in a good-quality edge bander that uses hot-melt glue and can be set up to supply plain edging material from a continuous roll or rigid strips from a magazine. Edge banding is one area where the medium-sized shop can do fairly well in competing with both large manufacturers and small shops.

If you are in a small shop situation, as I am, then the best system is probably a hot-air applicator that is supplied from rolls of preglued material. This allows a wide choice in types of material, and it will not require investments that are ridiculously expensive for us. You do not have to worry too much about burned or scorched edgings, the system yields very little waste, and it is easy to switch from one kind of edging material to another. Irons can work well, too, the keys being to use the minimum heat you can get away with and to provide firm, immediate pressure to the joint. Rigid edgings require more time, so wise woodworkers will learn to favor the pliable edgings such as PVC, veneer, and flexible melamine. We will still be willing to do some work with lumber edge banding but only when there is a definite purpose for the thicker materials. With this kind of selectivity, resin glue with clamping is a viable alternative.

When it comes to trimming, nothing below a thousand dollars will beat the hand-operated knife trimmer. For rigid-edging stocks, the table-mounted router is still a very good choice.

Most traditional cabinetmakers will continue to build face frames when they are necessary or when they are the simplest method. But, as you use frameless design more and more, you will discover that it provides certain advantages that you hadn't ever planned for.

[1] Twain, Mark, *Pudd'nhead Wilson*, Bantam Books, Inc., 1971, p. 31.

4
LINE BORING

A DIFFERENCE IN KIND

The European system can be looked at as a different way of joining, a new way of putting things together. This is another way of defining the European system. As we saw in the second chapter, the European system employs the butt joint for virtually all connections in the cabinet or furniture piece. Each butt joint is strengthened and stiffened by some type of fastener. In turn, the fastener for nearly every hole is round and designed to fit into a predrilled hole that is usually 5 mm or 8 mm in diameter. In fact, the butt joints in most European cabinetry are not joints at all. There is usually no glue bond between cabinet panels, and there are no worked joints. The "joint" is either between parts of a fastener that are machined to fit snugly or between a dowel and the inner core of a cabinet component. If the panels come together as a perfectly flat end against a perfectly smooth surface, good stability results. We are used to the reverse situation, of course, where fasteners are used only to stabilize the actual joint between cabinet members.

For hundreds of years woodworkers used basically the same tools and techniques for the various phases of cabinet and furniture making. They smoothed and cut lumber; they glued together pieces to make frames and panels; they prepared pieces for assembly by cutting or shaping some type of joining detail such as a dado or dovetail; they assembled with aids such as nails and adhesives; they sanded and finished. These processes never changed very much until very recently. The machine age speeded everything up, but it did not really change the methodology involved. If you have a belt-driven jointer, you probably use it for straightening lumber, the same way that you might use a plane. An electric drill is nothing but a motor-driven hand drill. Machines sped up the woodworking processes. Machinery also undoubtedly reduced dependence on skilled labor. For most of us, a jointer makes it much easier to achieve straight edges and perfect laminations than does a jack plane. The machine age made some huge differences in the woodworking trades, but these were not differences "in kind." They had more to do with "level"—speed level and level of skill required.

The European woodworking system, on the other hand, can be viewed as a difference in kind. If you define European cabinetry in terms of line boring, then you may intend to use European joining systems. Hole lines drilled for assembly of cabinet components or for attachment of accessories indicate this difference in kind. The Europeans developed mechanized line boring primarily to accommodate their totally different construction system. Even if you use a hole line only for mounting adjustable shelves, you will immediately see the advantage in using European tools or equipment for performing this drilling.

Simplicity

In developing their entirely different cabinetmaking system, the Europeans sought to achieve the greatest degree of simplicity possible while still allowing some design flexibility. The purposes of this simplicity, remember, are to speed up cabinet and furniture production and to reduce the employer's need for costly, highly skilled workers. These purposes are extremely important to keep in mind when you are deciding whether to utilize line boring as a joining system, and what sort of line-bore tooling is necessary in your particular shop. Most hobbyists and custom builders prefer not to depend on the hole line for all their fastening. Rather, they want the flexibility to choose between line-boring construction and conventional construction on each individual job.

The European system derives its simplicity from standardization, mainly the standards of hole diameter and spacing. Of course, the conventional cabinetmaker depends on standards, too. Dadoes are usually ¼ in. deep, for example. But the level of standardization within conventional cabinetmaking is not nearly so pervasive as it is within the European system. Almost every piece of hardware, almost every component connection, almost everything that has to do with assembling or installing a European cabinet, is based on the following standards.

- Holes in the vertical line are 32 mm apart (oc).
- Holes in the vertical line are 5 mm in diameter.
- Vertical hole lines are backset 37 mm from front and back edges.
- Holes in the horizontal patterns can be 8 mm in diameter for dowels and 5 mm in diameter for other fasteners.

As we observed in Chapter 2, holes in the horizontal lines are used for fastening panels together, and holes in the vertical lines are generally used for attaching hardware and accessories. It should be obvious that the cabinetmaker does not have to do many different detail operations. The fewer the number of different details means the fewer different setups for the cabinetmaker. This is the basis of simplicity in the European system.

Advantages of Line Boring

Obviously, the line-boring operation has many advantages over the conventional detailing system. Drilling hole lines can be faster, easier, and more accurate than other methods. Let us take a look at why this is so.

Versatility. Cabinetmakers who use the vertical hole line only for mounting adjustable shelves—that is, without using it for other kinds of attachment—will gain very little. In fact, this really means drilling a hole line in addition to performing other milling operations, such as dadoing, rabbeting, and so on. If you do this by marking out hole centers on each panel and drilling with a hand drill or a drill press, then it is a very tedious and time-consuming operation. (See Illus. 85.) On the other hand, if you use some piece of European equip-

Illus. 85. A vertical line-boring pattern intended only for adjustable shelves. Note the faint pencil lines on the plywood.

ment for this drilling, the process will go much faster, but you may not be taking full advantage of your tooling.

A hole line can be used for many purposes if it has been milled according to the European standards previously listed. All European hardware is designed to fit the vertical European hole line. For example, a hinge mounting plate is designed so that it can be attached to the cabinet box by simply pressing in two specially designed screws. The countersunk mounting holes are located exactly 32 mm apart, and the 37-mm backset is the perfect placement for this part of the hinge. The mounting screws themselves are designed so that they can be snugly pressed into the 5-mm holes in the vertical hole line. (See Illus. 86.) Contrast this with the way that a hinge is usually

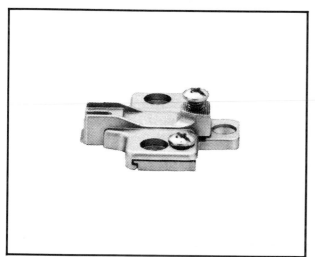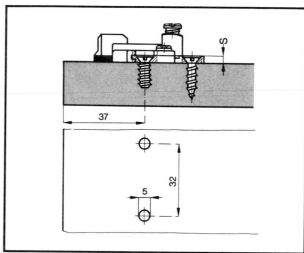

Illus. 86. A hinge-mounting plate. Note the dimensions so perfectly adapted to the 32-mm system. (Courtesy of Julius Blum, Inc.)

mounted—with an awl, a drill, and a screwdriver. Using demountable hinges is fairly fast, of course, but you will need some special equipment for them. And neither the router-type tooling required for demountable hinges nor the demountable-hinge details themselves can be used for anything else. The 5-mm holes in the European vertical boring pattern can be employed to mount virtually any European style accessory.

Drawers are a good example of the hole line's versatility, too, as the 5-mm holes can also be used to support drawer runners. (See Illus. 87.) Many cabinetmakers mount drawer glides with screws or staples, reasoning that their system is just about as fast as the hole-line system. I doubt it. For most of my jobs, I mount the drawer glides with screws. Positioning the guide member itself takes longer this way than it does with a hole line. In fact, positioning is not even a concern in the European system because the 32-mm spacings and the 37-mm backset automatically take care of positioning. Instead of simply pressing the glide into place, I need to go to my tool box and get out a few more tools—at least the drill I use as a screwdriver and some flat-head screws. The point is that the vertical hole line can be used for attaching any accessory. No additional machining is necessary.

The horizontal hole pattern also creates great versatility. The holes can be used in conjunction with a variety of fasteners that will hold the cabinet box together.

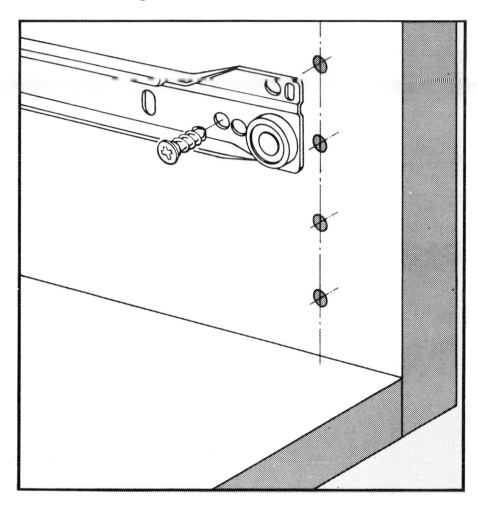

Illus. 87. European drawer runners are designed specifically to fit the vertical boring pattern. (Courtesy of Hettich America Corporation.)

Accuracy and Standardization. One of the difficulties with doing a lot of dadoing and rabbeting is that the dimensions of these details often have to be changed. It is true that the depth of most dadoes is exactly ¼ in., but the width of a dado is usually only specified by the thickness of the material that fits into the dado. The trouble here is that material thicknesses are nominal specifications. For instance, a piece of ¾-in. plywood can actually be less than ¹¹⁄₁₆ in., or it can be slightly thicker than a full ¾ in. Particleboard panels, even preclad ones, also vary somewhat. Getting a perfect fit means adjusting the dado head; the adjustment can be as easy to do as loosening an arbor nut and turning an adjustable dado head, or it can be as bothersome as grinding down a steel router bit. No matter how familiar you are with making fine adjustments in your own dadoing operation, it takes time. Furthermore, in traditional cabinetmaking practices, we use entirely different detail operations to fulfill the variety of purposes: mitres for fitting toe kicks to finished ends, rabbets for concealing the attachment of backs and nailers, and slots for inserting adjustable-shelf standards. If we use face frames, we also need to drill for dowel or screw insertion or cut fairly precise mortises and tenons.

The European detailing system is almost entirely based on drilling holes. Bit sizes and spacings between centers are rigidly standardized. Whereas a dado head requires fine adjustments in two dimensions (depth and width of cut), line boring requires only one (depth, or plunge). The standardized hole dimensions are totally unrelated to material thicknesses. Hole placement, in terms of locating the center of the horizontal hole line, is a factor of material thickness. Even here, though, finer adjustments are less troublesome. Some of the best European line-boring machines are designed to allow contemporary movement of the table and the head, meaning that a fine adjustment in vertical drilling (through the surface of the panel) will be compensated for automatically in horizontal drilling (into the end of a panel). In other words, you can rotate the drilling head from a vertical position to a horizontal position without in the least bit altering the drilling dimensions or locations. Such a machine has accuracy built in. (See Illus. 88.) Simpler and less expensive tools, designed for the custom shop, will also help ensure precision.

The 32-mm standard also does away with a good many setup changes and adjustments. With the center of the top hole in the vertical boring pattern accurately located, all the other holes in the pattern are also precisely placed. This is true with expensive stationary machinery as well as with very inexpensive tooling such as a "spacing bar." As we saw in Chapter 2, only one setup is needed for boring both front and rear vertical hole lines, and one horizontal hole pattern is all that is necessary for drilling along the top and bottom of the end panels.

It is quite clear that close tolerances are achievable in the European system with a minimum of skill and time invested. This naturally makes the line-boring method attractive to cabinet manufacturers because they need fewer skilled woodworkers.

Storage and Shipping. Another reason that line-boring technology can be so beneficial to some users is that cabinetry made this way is capable of being shipped flat, before assembly. Such cabinetry or furniture is sometimes called knock-down furniture if it has joints that can be taken apart and later reassembled.

Illus. 88. A multiple-spindle boring machine is capable of drilling horizontally and vertically. The unit shown here is in the horizontal position. (Courtesy of Busellato S.p.A.)

The users who derive the greatest benefit from this capability are the large-scale manufacturers who distribute their products to distant locations. Cabinet components are stacked flat and sent inside a box, together with the fasteners needed for assembly and installation. This kind of shipping will require only about one third as much space as the transportation of preassembled cabinets. (See Illus. 89.) Naturally, this kind of shipping is not very appropriate if staining and clear finishing are necessary after assembly.

Customers sometimes enjoy the benefits of knock-down furniture, too. Of course, few people are interested in taking their kitchen cab-

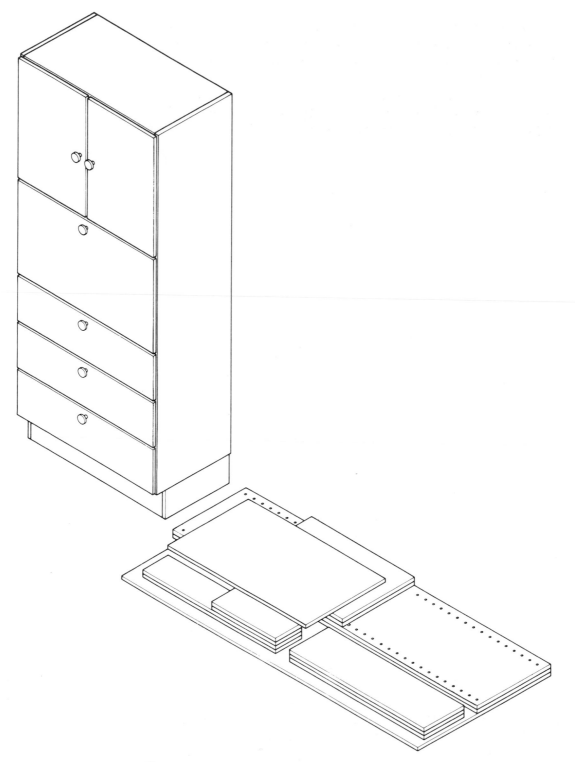

Illus. 89. The knock-down capability allows the furniture to be shipped or stored in less space. (Courtesy of Häfele America Co.)

inets with them when they move, but desks, wall units, and entertainment centers are often easier to move in disassembled condition. The consumer can disassemble and reassemble much knock-down furniture fairly easily with just a screwdriver.

Obviously, most of the advantages of line boring have to do with savings in time and a built-in kind of accuracy. When we look at the real how-to of line boring, this will be even more evident.

Disadvantages

Any realistic look at line boring must include an honest evaluation of the system's drawbacks as well as its advantages. The most encompassing of these difficulties is the mere notion of change itself. It is simply easier and temporarily less expensive to continue with the detailing and cabinet-assembly systems we are used to. On the other hand, people who are not interested in learning about the European system are not likely to buy this book in the first place. As we have observed earlier, and as we will doubtless observe again, the European cabinetmaking system is not likely to fully replace the traditional approach, but we should have the option to choose processes from either one.

Formaldehyde. A more specific disadvantage of line boring is the potential for release of free formaldehyde. Every hole that penetrates a panel's surface will allow some formaldehyde to escape into the interior of the cabinet box, where it can collect. Whenever the cabinet user opens a cabinet door, he or she is likely to get a concentrated dose of the formaldehyde. As some kind of safeguard, in the United States at least one state requires by law that every hole drilled in a panel be used for attachment or assembly, that it be treated with a tiny amount of finishing material, or that it be covered with a specially made plastic fitting. In general, it's best to drill only those holes that will be needed for cabinet assembly and attachment of accessories.

Appearance. There is nothing particularly attractive about a line of unnecessary holes in the end panel of a cabinet. I have heard people refer to line-boring patterns as the "Swiss cheese look," the "uzi approach" to cabinetmaking, and even the "St. Valentine's Day massacre." Many people, though, prefer the vertical hole line to several strips of shelf standard. Besides, drilling hole lines for the insertion of shelf supports is a very old idea, evidenced in many fine antiques. Therefore, the aesthetics of a vertical hole line may be largely a matter of individual taste. My own opinion is that a hole line for supporting adjustable shelves is a fine idea, as long as that is the real reason for the unfilled holes. There should not be any holes for an adjustable-shelf support at any height that would be ridiculous for a shelf location. We seldom need any shelf located within 32 mm of the cabinet bottom, or even within the first five multiples of 32 mm for that matter. Why, especially in the custom shop, should we drill even a single hole that is not essential?

Exceptions. Despite the apparent ease with which we can do most detailing within the line-boring operation, it does not take care of every milling or detail cut for European cabinetry. For example, end panels and cabinet bottoms must be slotted for back insertion, and wall cabinets have to be specially notched to fit around the fasteners that hold them on the wall.

* * * * *

We have seen some of the major pros and cons of using line boring as an assembly-detail methodology. Line boring is certainly a method that all cabinetmakers should be able to perform in their own shops—either as a routine operation or in occasional, as-needed situations. Let us next look at several tools and techniques that will accomplish this job for you.

MULTISPINDLE BORING MACHINERY

Some of the best boring equipment is capable of drilling two hole lines at the same time. (See Illus. 90.) Nearly all of these machines are equipped with pneumatic stock-clamping features and millimetrically scaled stops to be used for stock alignment. Each line may possess as many as 39 spindles or more.

The multispindle borer has a number of adjustments. First there is the matter of which bit sizes to use and which locations should be drilled. As we suggested, the "Swiss cheese look" is out, and bit life is further promoted by reducing the number of holes drilled.

Certain adjustments will allow the operator to set up for variations in panel thickness, drilling depth, and stop location (critical placement of the holes in relation to the end or edge of the panel). Handwheels, linked to digital readouts, are often used for these adjustments. (See Illus. 91.)

Of course, one edge or end of the panel is usually positioned against some type of rigid fence to control one of the critical dimensions such as the 37-mm backset. There can be flip-over stops, also, that can be used in positioning the secondary hole lines necessary for drawer rails and other variant applications.

With adjustments precisely set, the operator positions each panel to be drilled with the particular pattern that has been set up and then uses a foot pedal to engage. The pneumatic clamps assume their

Illus. 90. Two banks of multispindle borers will generate both vertical hole lines at the same time. (Courtesy of Holz-Her U.S. Inc.)

position first, to hold the panel firmly. Fractions of a second later, the drill bits are boring their way into the surface or edge of the panel, in exactly the right positions.

Line borers that are considered "economy versions" are capable of drilling only one line of holes at a time, though such equipment can still cost thousands of dollars. Each panel must be repositioned and drilled for a second hole pattern. This would obviously be easiest to accomplish if we could simply turn the panel end for end, position it against the same stops, and reengage the clamping and drilling machinery. This is one reason that it is important to have fully reversible components—it maintains simplicity of milling. In the vertical hole line recommended in Chapter 2, the top and bottom 5-mm holes in the line were both positioned exactly the same distance (40 mm) from the closest end. We do this not only to create a fully reversible end panel, but also to allow ease in machining.

Illus. 91. Convenient digital-readout hand control for exact adjustment of stops on a line-boring machine. (Courtesy of Holz-Her U.S. Inc.)

There is somewhat of a problem with using a single-line borer in this way, however. We probably do not want extra holes because they will generate the "uzi look" and because we should seal in formaldehyde. Yet, we will frequently drill many extra holes if we decide to drill fully reversible hole lines by merely flipping each panel over and redrilling.

In drilling the 5-mm holes for a base-cabinet end panel, we need drawer-guide mounting holes near the top of the panel, but we do not want holes this close to the bottom of the panel. Thus, if you are using a single-line borer (see Illus. 92), it is better to use a pair of matching stops to locate the hole line. One flip-over stop can be used when the front edge is set against the fence, and another can be used when the rear edge is placed against the fence.

The flip-over stops are also necessary when extending a hole line, even when using a two-line boring machine. There are not many boring machines that will allow the operator to punch all the holes that are necessary in a tall-cabinet end panel at one time. Even a machine with a capacity for 39 bits will only span a length of about 49 in.

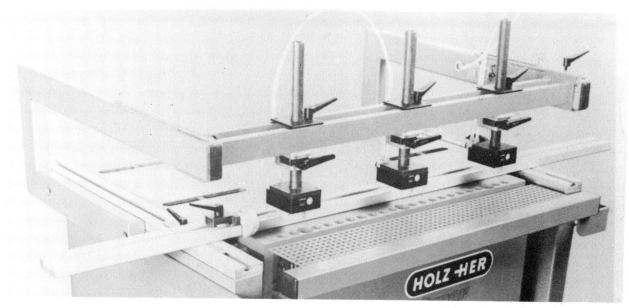

Illus. 92. *A single line-boring machine. Note the fence and flip-over stop.* (*Courtesy of Holz-Her U.S. Inc.*)

In a system designed for speed and versatility, there are a few factors that can limit the woodworker, especially the custom woodworker. Customizers, if they employ hole-line technology, do not want to invest in multiple-line borers; they also do not want to drill more holes than they need. Using one single-line borer for all the drilling in a European cabinetmaking operation can involve some setup changing. The customizer needs two entirely different hole lines for 8-mm dowels and 5-mm screws or fittings. Bit sizes are different; spacings (in terms of the number of multiples of 32 mm) are different. Stop locations and fence placement are different, too. Then there is the necessity for rotating the drilling heads back and forth between end-boring and surface-boring positions. Other variations also may present themselves. On the vertical hole line, the customizer will want to add holes for the lower drawers in a stack or for slide-out shelves. With all this setup changing, the labor-saving advantage of hand-tool line boring over conventional detailing methods decreases a bit. The main advantage of a stationary, single-line borer may be its built-in precision. For perfect hole-line patterns, nothing is better than a stationary boring machine, but at the present time, most low-volume producers are opting for hand-tool line boring.

In large-scale cabinetmaking operations, we can find several factors that create simplicity and time savings—factors that customizers are not willing to employ. Larger operations do not object to extra holes, for one thing. In addition, factories often possess more than one line-boring machine, allowing great specialization of each tool. For instance, there can be a two-line machine for generating the vertical pattern, and another machine for horizontal boring. Fairly high production volume can justify investing in this kind and amount of machinery.

Line-boring tooling that allows rapid, precise milling seems to be a necessity if we want to employ European assembly techniques. Unlike the edge-banding operation, though, there seems to be no "middle ground" tooling. If you want to accomplish Euro-style construction, you must either use some type of hand tooling, or you must avail yourself of a fairly expensive line-boring machine. As we shall see, however, the hand tooling can be very effective for the customizer.

HAND-TOOL LINE BORING

Woodworkers who use line-bored holes for an assembly system can do so in several different ways. But regardless of which system they choose, there are some general rules that must be followed so that accuracy can be maintained.

The most important line-boring rule has to do with clamping. It is vital to clamp panel stocks firmly. One of the ways that the European cabinetmaking system maintains accuracy is through clamping. In order to get the holes of mating parts to line up perfectly, it is vital that the panel not move as bits penetrate the surface or end. There are many negative results of a misaligned hole line: rocking adjustable shelves, unattractive facing joints, and improperly working drawers. Because a drill bit can vibrate somewhat as it bores, clamping also helps ensure proper hole diameter.

Another vital line-boring concern is making sure of consistent reference points. That is, we must make sure that matching hole locations are measured from the same place on the assembled cabinet. For instance, the 8-mm dowel hole drilled into the surface of an end panel must be exactly the same distance from the bottom of the assembled cabinet as is the matching hole in the end of the bottom panel. These holes must also have exactly the same backset. The main thing to remember about getting holes to match exactly is to use exactly the same setup for both. Thus, if you are using some type of jig to drill matching holes, then you must align the jig on both components in exactly the same way in relation to the same reference point. A jig must sit as squarely against the bottom and front of the end panel as it does against the undersurface and front of the bottom panel. Specks of dust must be prevented from interfering with proper alignment. And the jig itself must not be susceptible to flexing or shifting.

It's also vital to drill only those holes that are necessary. This has already been mentioned, but it is even more important if we are doing our line boring with hand tools because of the time factor. Every unnecessarily drilled hole involves a waste of time not only in drilling the hole but also later on when we decide to plug or seal the hole with a plastic plug or a few drops of lacquer.

Boring Gearbox

One possibility for the small shop is the boring gearbox. This is a tool that you can mount to virtually any good-quality drill press, converting it into a multispindle boring machine. (See Illus. 93.) Its case-hardened steel gears, spaced exactly 32 mm apart (oc), will turn up to five or six bits together. The gearbox has steel guide shafts to ensure proper alignment with the drill-press table and fence. This tool adaptation is an excellent way to extend the use of your drill press.

One obvious usage of such a multispindle gearbox is for drilling a vertical hole line. You can use a series of stops or marks to extend the vertical line as long as it needs to be. And remember that you have the option to drill only those holes that are actually *needed,* instead of an entire vertical hole line. For holes to support an adjustable shelf in a standard-sized base cabinet with a single drawer and door, you will certainly not have to operate the drill-press arm more than twice for each line. Five in-line gear centers means 10 holes, spaced 32 mm apart, in two plunges of the drill press. This is nine spacings, a span of 288 mm (~11⅜ in.). Since we hardly ever position a shelf within 8 in. of the top or bottom of a vertical space within a base cabinet, and since the height of most base door openings is usually in the neighborhood of 24 in., these 10 holes are adequate for the space. Even with a standard wall cabinet, we should only have to operate the

Illus. 93. A boring gearbox—turning a conventional drill press into a multispindle borer. (Courtesy of Häfele America Co.)

drill-press lever three times per hole line, since 15 holes translate into 14 spacings to span 448 mm (~17⅝ in.). Naturally, using the gearbox for other vertical line holes, such as the holes for mounting hinge plates and drawer-guide members, will require additional planning for hole locations, some alterations in setup, and more boring.

The boring gearbox may not be the best tool to use for drilling horizontal patterns, where we need perfectly mated holes on two members. It is not only somewhat unusual to set up a drill press for drilling into the ends of panels, but it can also be difficult to achieve the kind of perfect mating that we desire in European assembly.

As in any European style boring operation, it's important to clamp stocks firmly in place before each plunge of the drill press. Many cabinetmakers simply use a free hand to hold the panel firmly against the drill press and fence. This is probably adequate when using a good-quality drill press and boring box, but some woodworkers prefer to attach a mechanical or pneumatic clamp to their drill-press tables. In fact, air-assisted tools can be added to a drill press both for stock clamping and for operating the boring plunge. This is an extremely good arrangement, especially with foot-pedal controls, because it frees both hands for handling the panel.

Scales

Very useful in conjunction with the multiple-spindle boring gearbox just described is a precisely machined scale with fast-clamping flip-over stops. (See Illus. 94.) The fence assembly itself can be over 8 feet long, with very precisely marked gradations to be used in determining hole locations relevant to the ends of panels. The fence assembly can then be fitted with several of the flip-over stop devices, which can be moved and locked into position anywhere along the scale's length. These are naturally very helpful in drilling holes in repeat locations. For instance, in the example we gave earlier, drilling specific holes along the vertical hole line, the stop devices would be extremely useful. With four such devices, the detailer can carefully locate two on each side of the gearbox and achieve reliable positioning for all four plunges required in obtaining the 10 holes needed for the adjustable-shelf hole pattern. Each stop location would yield five of the required holes. The two stops to either side mean that we can turn each end panel end for end, place the front or rear edge against the fence, and always be measuring down from the top as we should.

Drilling Jigs

There are many manufacturers who market jigs designed to accurately locate the holes needed for the 32-mm system. The simplest type consists of a metal bar or wand fitted with hardened bushings exactly 32 mm apart. (See Illus. 95.) The edge and end of the wand are equipped with stops that automatically take care of the 37-mm

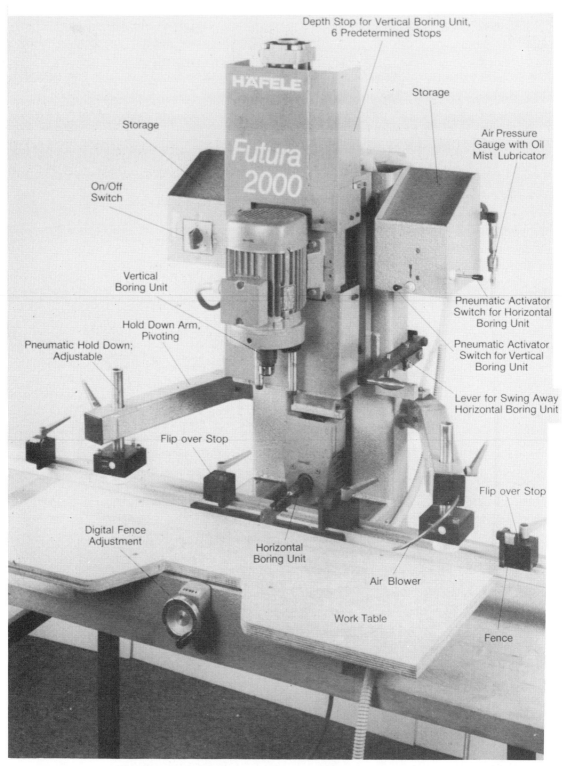

Depth Stop for Vertical Boring Unit,
6 Predetermined Stops

Storage

Storage

Air Pressure
Gauge with Oil
Mist Lubricator

On/Off
Switch

Vertical
Boring Unit

Pneumatic Activator
Switch for Horizontal
Boring Unit

Hold Down Arm,
Pivoting

Pneumatic Activator
Switch for Vertical
Boring Unit

Pneumatic Hold Down;
Adjustable

Lever for Swing Away
Horizontal Boring Unit

Flip over Stop

Flip over Stop

Digital Fence
Adjustment

Horizontal
Boring Unit

Air Blower

Work Table

Fence

Illus. 94. Scaled fence assembly with flip-over stops. (Courtesy of Häfele America Co.)

158

Illus. 95. Jig for locating holes in the 32-mm system. (Courtesy of Häfele America Co.)

backset and top-hole placement as well as spacing. When you have a need to move the jig down and locate holes without reference to the panel end, the end stop can be rotated upwards and out of the way. You then insert a "locating pin" through one of the bushings of the jig and into a hole already drilled.

Boring wands are available with bushings to allow drilling of both the horizontal and vertical boring pattern (5-mm and 8-mm holes). In fact, a few traditional tool manufacturers make and sell drilling guides for the type of drilling based on 32-mm line boring. (See Illus. 96.) Some also market traditional line-boring jigs based upon ¼-in.-

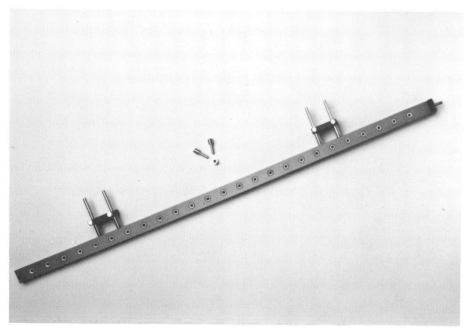

Illus. 96. American firms such as Align-Rite Tool Company are now offering a range of 32-mm-based tools. Note the adjustable edge stops, the locating pins, and the drill depth gauge. (Courtesy of Align-Rite Tool Company.)

or ⅜-in.-diameter holes and 1¼-in. spacings. Cabinetmakers who perform line boring with any regularity at all will truly benefit from using line-boring jigs. Jigs quite similar to the ones we have shown here can also be used for drilling the horizontal hole pattern of 8-mm holes (or 10-mm holes for the cabinetmaker who prefers larger dowels). (See Illus. 97.) Those who use line-bored holes for both assem-

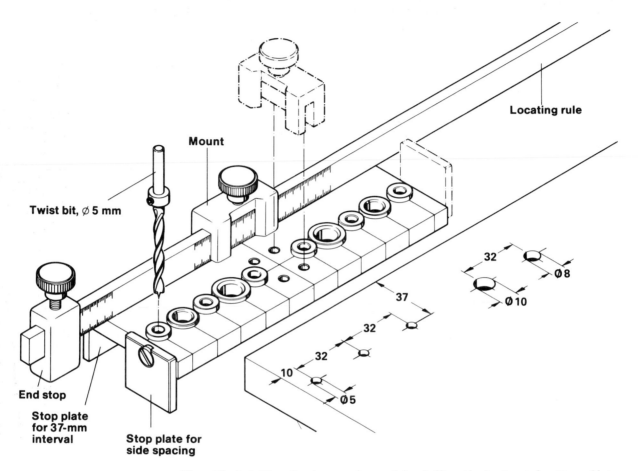

Illus. 97. A drilling jig that can be used for drilling the horizontal pattern. Note the locating rule and the variety of bushing sizes that allow the craftsman to choose backset, dowel diameter, and panel thickness. (Courtesy of Häfele America Co.)

bly and for attaching accessories will probably want two wands—one for drilling the vertical line, and the other for drilling the horizontal line. This saves many setup changes and also helps the customizer to achieve a useful level of standardization.

When using an alignment jig such as one of those we have described, boring is performed with a hand-held electric drill. Depth of holes is controlled by means of a depth stop fitted firmly upon the bit itself. Woodworkers who use this system must make every effort to ensure the accurate placement and effective drilling of holes. The following are several keys to successful jig-style line boring.

1. Hold the jig in place with one or two quickly engaged clamps, such as vinyl-protected spring clamps.
2. Use a sharp bit.
3. After drilling one hole in its proper location, insert the locating pin to make sure that the jig won't slip.
4. Make sure that the depth gauge has been placed properly and that it will not slip (drill into a practice piece).
5. Take the time necessary to perform each boring plunge steadily and vertically straight; speed will come from accuracy, not from being in a hurry.

Drilling into the ends of cabinet components, such as bottoms, tops, and rails, is fairly simple and reliable when using a drilling jig. The very same tools are used without changing setup. All you need to do is to position the drilling jig so that you will be boring into the ends of the stock rather than into the surfaces. The end stop is still set against the end of the panel, but the edge stops are now positioned against the panel's surface.

Line boring naturally takes more time with a jig or a boring gearbox than it does with a stationary machine, but investment levels are tremendously lower, and both systems are much faster than marking a + for each hole's center and then drilling the series.

Related Tooling

Other jigs and tools are also available to go with or complement the 32-mm assembly system. These tools are generally used for drilling the holes needed when mounting doors or using connectors other than dowels.

The companies that sell the European type of hardware, particularly connecting fittings, also usually tend to sell hand-tooling systems that are specially designed for installing their own brands of connection fittings.

We have already touched upon one of the advantages of glueless assembly techniques—its knock-down and reassembly capability for the manufacturer and the end user alike. Another is that knock-down fittings further simplify the cabinetmaking process. They do, after all, allow cabinetmakers to avoid incorporating a system for coating glue onto dowels and the insides of dowel holes. Knock-down fittings also eliminate their need for using clamp pressure as part of their assembly operation.

Most knock-down fittings require the drilling of slightly different hole configurations from the European standards previously listed.

Many of these fittings employ the concept of an eccentric that fits around the head of a metal dowel, or bolt. (See Illus. 98.)

Before going any further with the how-to of drilling for assembly fittings, it's important to mention that you may encounter a problem

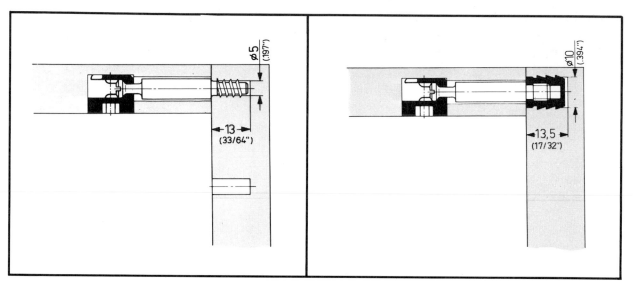

Illus. 98. Assembly fillings used to join panels. These consist of an eccentric and a bolt. (Courtesy of Hettich America Corporation.)

in terminology with your supplier. For example, I have referred to a tiny item called an "eccentric." But this very same item can be called something else—an "accessory," for example. What one company calls a bolt another calls a metal dowel. The terms are assigned by the hardware manufacturer. To make matters more difficult, there seems to be no generic name for some of the connectors, and so we have to depend on brand names. If you elect to use these kinds of connectors, make sure you know exactly what the fittings look like as well as the machining they will require. It is often helpful to look through a few European hardware catalogs before choosing connectors.

Preparing panels for this kind of assembly requires boring one more hole than those in the dowel assembly we have been suggesting as a standard.

The horizontal boring pattern remains very similar to that for wood-dowel assembly. You drill a series of holes into the surface of end panels near the top and bottom edges. These holes can have a diameter of 5 mm for affixing threaded bolts, or 8 mm or 10 mm for press-in plastic sockets. Of course, matching holes must be bored into the ends of the horizontal members to be joined, and these might sometimes have an unusual diameter.

The major difference in machining is that the horizontal members

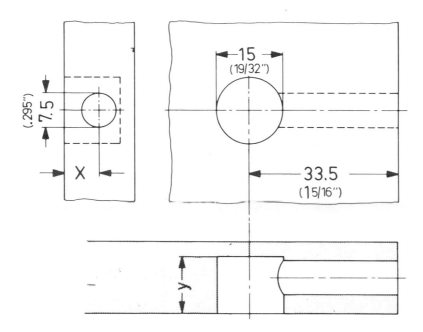

Illus. 99. The boring pattern in a horizontal panel for an eccentric assembly fitting. (Courtesy of Hettich America Corporation.)

require holes in their surfaces for locating the eccentric hardware. (See Illus. 99.) These are flat-bottomed holes, often 15 mm in diameter, that connect to the hole drilled into the end of the panel. The use of eccentric fittings requires special-sized bits and a jig designed to place and align these bits correctly. (See Illus. 100.)

Illus. 100. A jig used in the drilling for eccentric fittings. Left: shown in the setup for drilling the 15-mm hole for placement of the eccentric and the connecting 8-mm hole. Right: shown in the setup for boring the 5-mm hole for placement of the threaded bolt. (Courtesy of Häfele America Co.)

There are other connecting fittings available, as well. One type, requiring a 20-mm hole, is designed to eliminate the need for drilling connecting holes into the end of the horizontal panels. (See Illus. 101.) It, too, requires its own special jig.

In low-volume custom shops, drilling guides of the wand variety may be the best choice, especially if you plan to do line boring with some frequency. The wand-type jigs combine great accuracy with relatively low investment cost.

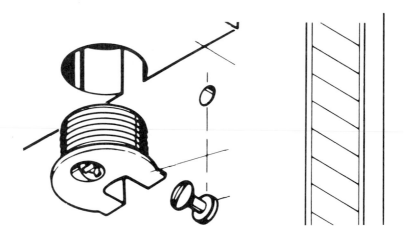

Illus. 101. Another type of knock-down connector. Positioning of the 20-mm hole in the surface of the horizontal panel like this means that it is not necessary to drill any connecting holes. (Courtesy of Häfele America Co.)

Assembly Boring

It is possible to assemble cabinets with European connectors and still do no actual line boring. This approach could be called assembly boring because it is possible to drill the necessary holes with a hand drill, as needed, while the cabinet panels are being assembled. This system makes use of connecting fittings, such as angle connectors or connecting screws.

Angle connectors are designed to fit exactly into the specifications of the 32-mm system, but they can be used to fasten any components that come together at right angles. They can be thought of as right-angle brackets. (See Illus. 102.) Although they are primarily intended for attachment of thick back panels, they are occasionally used as a means of assembling end panels and horizontal components (usually only in locations that are at least semiconcealed). As with other right-angle brackets, they can be set and screwed in place while the two panels are clamped into their exact joined position.

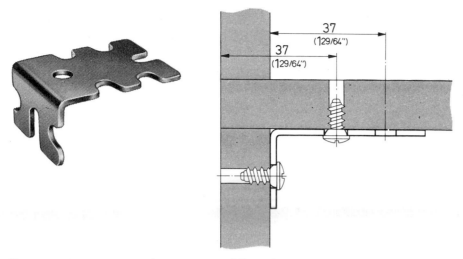

Illus. 102. Connecting angle. (Courtesy of Hettich America Corporation.)

You can follow a similar procedure when assembling with connecting screws. Panels, let us say a top rail and an end panel, are set together in exactly the arrangement desired. The top and front are perfectly flush; the panels are perpendicular. The cabinetmaker clamps the panels firmly into this arrangement and then uses a step drill to create a pilot hole in the rail and both a clearance hole and a countersinking hole in the end panel. (See Illus. 103.) While assembling, this sort of machining requires less exactness in locating holes. This extremely simplified milling-and-assembly system is a good alternative for the cabinetmaker who plans to work only rarely in the

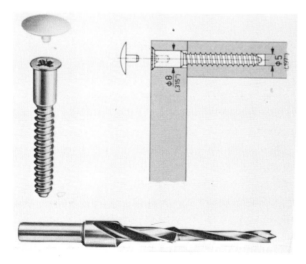

Illus. 103. Step drill used for installing the connecting screw. (Courtesy of Hettich America Corporation.)

European mode. Of course, these same connectors can just as easily be used with precisely drilled, horizontal hole lines made with a sophisticated boring machine or with the aid of a boring jig.

* * * * *

The technology for precise line boring is obviously readily available to shops of any size. Furniture and cabinet factories can utilize stationary multispindle equipment that is precise and fast. Even traditional tool manufacturers have begun to develop equipment that will bore lines of holes, spaced exactly 32 mm apart, into both surfaces and edges. Customizers can choose among a wide variety of boring and attachment systems that are reliable, easy to use, and inexpensive to set up. Perhaps the biggest problems are for cabinetmakers with medium-sized shops who may find the jigging hand-drilling operation too slow and horizontal borers too expensive.

TRADITIONAL DETAILING

Most traditional woodcrafters are already using a detailing system based on dadoing and rabbeting that is fairly effective and accurate. When we are working with European style materials, however, our old reliable dadoing and rabbeting does present some problems that must be solved. Let us have a look at some of them before moving on.

First of all, dadoes and rabbets are usually intended to be further solidified and supported by glue and nails or staples. One trouble with this approach is that it is not desirable to drive nails through a precovered surface. There is no good way of filling the nail holes—thus, creating a particular problem on finished ends. A few strong proponents of the European system also insist that dowel- or connector-type joining is stronger than a dado or rabbet together with glue and nails. This is so, they say, because rabbeting or dadoing removes the strongest part of a particleboard panel—the dense part near the surface. The glue and nails only have the weak inner core to work upon. I have to say that this argument is not totally accurate. It is basically irrelevant because most of the stress on a dado or rabbet joint is usually lateral—perpendicular to the surface penetrated by the dado or rabbet cut. The way that a dado or rabbet carries the load of a shelf or other horizontal component is very strong, indeed. Furthermore, there is little in the traditional system to encourage panel separation, whereas the European system calls for drilling into panel edges—in itself a practice that can contribute to a panel's splitting in thickness, especially if the connector is a bolt rather than a dowel.

As noted near the beginning of this chapter, dado and rabbet dimensions are more difficult to perfect than hole dimensions. And building frameless means that detail dimensions are even more important. Sloppy milling on dado and rabbet cuts is not attractive.

Rigidity is another matter to consider. If you are building frameless, then you must generally rely on a back for rigidity in the cabinet. Dadoes and rabbets do very little to generate rigidity, whereas European connection systems do contribute in this area.

Another problem encountered with traditional detailing of precovered materials is chip out or tear away. In the first chapter, we looked at this problem in connection with panel-cutting tools and procedures. Here, of course, we can have much the same type of difficulty, depending on the kind of detailing system we use. Cutting channels with a saw-type dado head will produce more tear away than will machining the dadoes and rabbets with a router bit.

Finally, remember that blending European style materials with traditional milling techniques can create the need for extra components: nailers, hold-downs, and sleepers. Building these components into the cabinet often requires additional milling.

Design Alterations

There are a number of techniques that cabinetmakers employ to overcome the problems of combining precovered materials with traditional detailing and building techniques. Some of these involve modifications in joint design.

Deep Rabbeting. Cutting deeper-than-usual rabbets into end panels can totally eliminate the need for the horizontal boring line. Rabbets are usually cut to allow one panel to set into another by approximately ¼ in. to ⅜ in. But deepening this amount of inset creates a very helpful situation. (See Illus. 104.) First, we still have wood-to-wood contact, as we would with any depth rabbet, where the raw wood fibres exposed by rabbeting contact the ends of horizontal members. Second, we can drive fasteners from the top and bottom, and through the surfaces of the top and bottom cabinet components, thus avoiding holes in the surfaces of finished ends. Third, it is easy to use the conventional fasteners we are used to—nails or screws—in this situation. If you choose screws, it is vital to drill pilot, clearance, and countersink holes. With their deep threads and straight shanks, the European style screws may be best in this usage.

Stop Dadoing. This is really a very old technique, but it can be especially effective in detailing European style panels for frameless construction. Stop dadoes are simply dadoes that are not cut across the entire width of a panel. They are intended to receive the ends of notched panels. (See Illus. 105.) It is very common to get this result by first cutting a through dado and then adding an edge band. Bottoms, rails, and other horizontal members are first edge-banded and

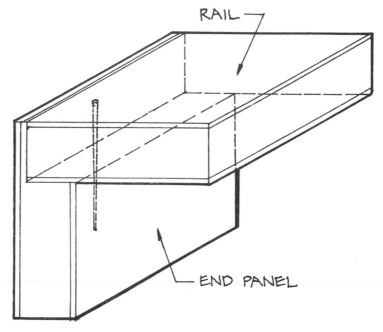

Illus. 104. Deep rabbets in end panels can eliminate the need for top and bottom horizontal boring patterns.

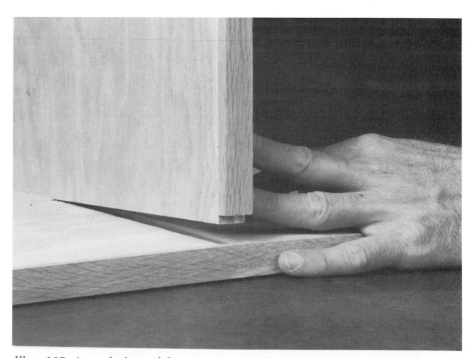

Illus. 105. A notched panel fitting into a stop-dadoed panel. Here, the stop dadoing was accomplished by running a through dado and then adding an edge band.

then notched to the depth of the dado with a dovetail saw or on a jointer.

Shelf Standard. It is not uncommon for cabinetmakers to use shelf standard when building conventional cabinetry. In fact, strips of shelf standard can also be used with preclad materials or in conjunction with other European design elements. When used with stop dadoing, deep rabbeting, or another European-American hybrid of techniques, shelf standard can eliminate the need for a vertical hole line. (See Illus. 106.)

Illus. 106. Shelf standard used with a "European" style bookcase. Note the absence of a face frame as well as the half-round facing.

It should be fairly obvious by now that we have the option of using some European design elements without using the entire 32-mm design system. Naturally, the more conventional techniques we use means the less we can refer to our products as European. Yet, as we have seen, European style can mean a number of different things: a simple and "clean" appearance, the presence of plastics-clad panels,

Illus. 107. An outside-saw-type dado head. (Courtesy of Freud in USA.)

the absence of a face frame, the vertical hole line, and so on. To say that European cabinetry must not be fabricated using any conventional techniques is ridiculous. Cabinetmakers, together with the people they build for, have the right to decide which European design elements to accept and which to modify or eliminate.

Table Saw Detailing

If you decide to use your table saw for cutting rabbets or dadoes in plastics-covered material such as melamine, there are a few techniques that will help to reduce tear away. Most important, whether you use the other techniques or not, is the principle of employing a sharp, high-quality carbide dado head. Generally, I have better success with the type that employs two outer saw blades and a series of chippers in between than I do with an adjustable dado head. This is probably because of a difference in chip load—the amount of wood and plastic material removed by each tooth, especially by the teeth that cut along the outer limits of the dado or rabbet because these teeth have the most to do with causing tear away. (See Illus. 107.) The "dial type" of adjustable dado can be used with effectiveness, however, because the newer models of these tools are vastly improved over the older ones.

Reverse feeding can be an extremely useful technique for cutting

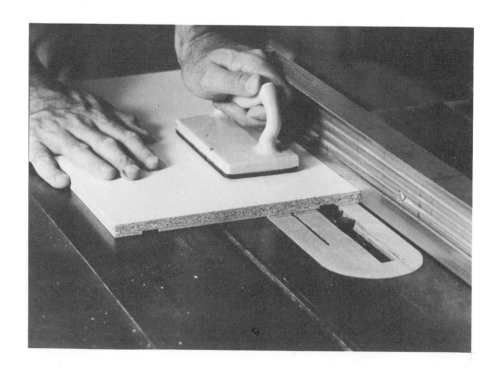

Illus. 108. Cutting a dado into a melamine-clad panel. Reverse feeding produces very clean cuts, and can be performed safely.

170

Illus. 109. An extended mitre-gauge face used for reverse feeding on a dado cut.

channels into preclad particleboard panels, but it should be used with great caution. (See Illus. 108.) It yields very little tear away, but there can be some safety pitfalls to avoid. It can be dangerous, for example, to try removing too much material at once. To overload the dado head's capacity to remove material or to cause a saw motor to lug down can mean loss of control on a feed, which in turn can result in a disastrous injury. A mitre gauge with a clamping feature is very helpful in this type of feeding. The clamping mitre gauge is a great asset in maintaining control while feeding, and it allows the detailer to keeps his hands away from the blades. Another help here is to extend the face of the mitre gauge. A long mitre-gauge face backing up the leading edge of the panel feed is also a good aid in control. (See Illus. 109.) I believe that reverse feeding can be a safe operation, or I would not have mentioned it here. I have performed low-load reverse dado feeds with my own table saw on dadoing cuts, such as the type needed for insetting a piece of adjustable-shelf standard. Yet, it is not a practice that I can recommend to other woodworkers, and I do know cabinetmakers who vow never to attempt it.

Another technique that can be helpful in yielding chip-free cuts is the slow feed. When cutting channels into particleboard, and when making such cuts with the grain in plywood components, it is possible to maintain a fairly fast rate of feed without much tear away. We tend to think of this feed rate as normal. But the same feed rate with melamine-clad panels (or cross grain on veneer) will produce a good many damaged surfaces adjacent to dadoes. The amount of such tear away can be lessened substantially by simply reducing the speed at which we guide a panel through the dado setup. In fact, this can be the simplest and safest way to attain good-quality rabbets and dadoes in preclad panels.

It is, of course, possible to cut dadoes and rabbets by kerfing repeatedly with a saw blade. In fact, we can reverse-feed these kerf cuts with a good degree of safety, since relatively small amounts of material are being removed. However, such a system obviously leaves much to be desired in terms of speed. The repetitious setups and feeds make this methodology ridiculous for most of us.

It is sometimes necessary to mitre-cut an edge of a preclad piece, and a table saw remains the best tool for this job. However, since plastics coverings can be brittle, and since the plastics are so unforgiving if they do get damaged in machining, it's usually best to set up for mitring on the saw so that the width of the panel passes between the blade and fence. This is also a safer approach than setting up

Illus. 110. Mitring a preclad panel on the table saw. Note that waste material falls harmlessly away.

172

with the blade tilted right into contact with the fence. The scrap piece can fall harmlessly away without becoming pinched or hurled by the saw blade. (See Illus. 110.)

Radial Arm Saw Detailing

With a radial arm saw, it is certainly possible to run channel cuts, especially dadoes and rabbets, in stock less than 15 in. wide. Chipping or tear away is not a problem because material is removed towards the panel's core. (See Illus. 111.) But if you are striving for

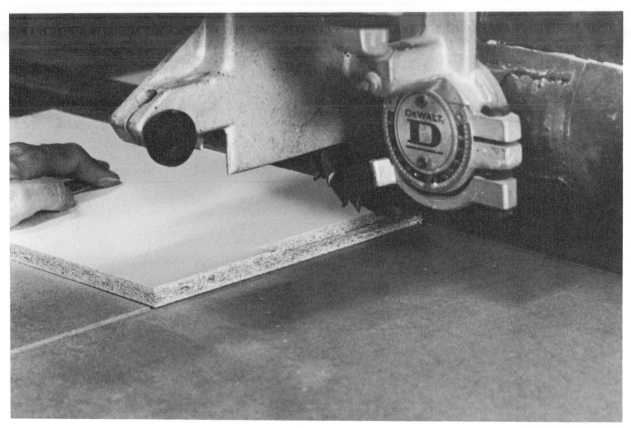

Illus. 111. Dadoing a wall-cabinet panel with a radial arm saw.

great accuracy in joining preclad panels, the radial arm saw can present some problems.

One difficulty can be channel depth. If the arm is not perfectly parallel to the table of the saw, then depth of cut will not be consistent from front to back. Slight differences in depth can be all right when building in the conventional style, because "face frames hide a multitude of sins." On the other hand, even small variations in channel depth can play havoc with the fit of doors, drawers, and backs when building frameless. Clearly, cabinetmakers who use a radial arm saw to dado and rabbet components must take extra care to ensure that the arm and table are kept perfectly parallel.

Another problem that you can encounter when using the radial arm saw for detailing preclad panels has to do with the quality and condition of the saw's bearings and guide. Any rough spot, even what might be considered a modest irregularity, in the guide action of the saw's bearings within the arm can have very negative effects in a plastics-covered component. Whenever the saw-and-motor assembly moves sidewards in the least, the blades will have a tendency to put an unsightly gash in the surface of the panel, or to tear out some chips. The problem is even worse when we are attempting to dado a wide panel because we have the added difficulty of trying to make two cuts meet perfectly in the middle. Obviously, dadoing European style materials with a radial arm saw requires a very reliable tool—a tool with extremely smooth-operating bearings and an arm that stays rigidly perpendicular to the saw's fence.

Router Detailing

For cutting dadoes and rabbets in prelaminated sheet goods, probably the best tool to use is a router. (See Illus. 112.) With a simple straight bit, it produces chip-free channel cuts of consistent depth. Furthermore, there is really no limitation on the width of stocks that can be dadoed with a router. When stock width is greater than the capacity of your jig (such as the type shown in Illus. 112), you have only to clamp a straightedge to the board to cut dadoes.

There are probably several reasons that the router is such a superior tool for dealing with preclad particleboard panels. For one thing, bit diameter is not much larger than shank diameter. This minimizes vibrations. Also, the cutting edges of the bit remove material parallel to the panel's surface. Contrast this to a blade-type dado head mounted in a table saw that has its cutting tips as far as 5 or 6 inches from the arbor, and that removes material perpendicular to the panel's surface. These factors are probably more significant than the router's speed. After all, a two-cutter bit rotating in a 20,000-rpm router means 40,000 cuts per minute, whereas a saw blade with 24 teeth (such as the outside cutters shown in Illus. 107) will generate 82,800 cuts per minute when mounted on an arbor that turns 3,450 rpm.

When using a routing jig of the kind shown in Illus. 112, it is generally best to draw the router towards you, with the guide fence on the right. This means that cutter rotation is towards the fence, which tends to draw the router up to the fence rather than letting it wander away. For each channel cut, the panel must be clamped in

Illus. 112. Dadoing with a router and jig can produce excellent results.

place. Since chip load is so heavy, and since plastics and particle-boards can put a heavy strain on bits and motors, woodworkers who intend to rout dadoes and rabbets should use a high-quality router and carbide-tipped cutters. There is one cutter design that virtually eliminates chipping when making any sort of channel cuts. This type of bit is a reverse-helix bit—a bit whose cutting angle creates a down-slice action to hold panel surface fibres down during the cut. (See Illus. 113.)

A router can easily be used to cut the channels or slots necessary for placing and fastening shelf standard. Cabinetmakers generally perform this operation with the aid of an edge guide that is mounted directly to the tool's base, and that rides along the edge of the panel being dadoed in this way. (See Illus. 113.)

Panel routers have become one of the most valuable tools for carrying out conventional techniques on preclad panels. (See Illus. 114.) Panel routers are very versatile in that they are useful in both large production shops and in smaller shops that are set up mainly for

Illus. 113. A reverse-helix or down-shearing cutter. (Courtesy of Safranek Enterprises, Inc.)

Illus. 114. A router with an edge guide can be used to cut channels parallel to one edge. (Courtesy of Porter-Cable Corp.)

custom projects. A good-quality panel router is not inexpensive, however.

A panel router's usefulness in the small shop has to do with its vertical orientation. This makes for savings in floor space and facilitates material feeding—and also makes it easier for the operator to see each workpiece clearly. (See Illus. 115.) The best machines are capable of both horizontal and vertical cutter movement, meaning that workpieces can be clamped firmly in place. Maybe most important is that panel routers allow us cabinetmakers to do all our channel cutting in all directions with one tool. We may have to change bits or

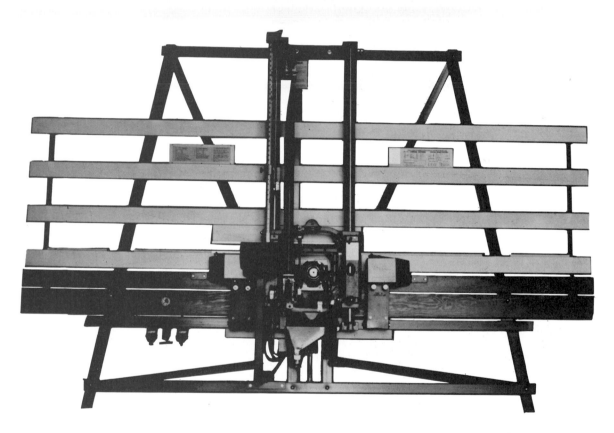

Illus. 115. Panel routers are designed to yield precise rabbets and dadoes. Their upright orientation saves space and facilitates feeding. (Courtesy of Safranek Enterprises, Inc.)

cutting depth on a single job, but these adjustments are very easy to make.

A panel router can make a great deal of sense in the large shop, too. One very effective technique involves the use of a template together with a panel router. The manufacturers of these tools really stress the advantages of templates when making repetitious cuts.

Some reports suggest that the proper use of a template can reduce milling time by 75 percent!

Traditional Detail Design

Cabinetmakers who want to use dadoes and rabbets as a system for milling and assembly to create European style products have two basic choices. One possibility is simply to build cabinets with face frames; the other involves neither the face frame nor the line-boring system but rather a substantial modification in design and assembly.

You can give cabinets built with face frames a "European" styling by using preclad materials such as melamine, and by mounting doors and drawers in such a way that the finished product has a clean, contemporary look. For example, accessories are mounted so that gaps between doors and drawer fronts are very small, and they are mounted with 32-mm-system hardware. With this type of construction, traditional cabinetmakers don't have to change their approach to layout and design at all, except for perhaps altering the width of face-frame stock so that it will work well with the overhangs called for by European hardware specifications. At most, they might have to invest in new tools for hinging and cutting. This is how most traditional builders first become involved with European cabinetry.

Some woodworkers consider this type of construction to be "imitation European" because of the presence of a face frame, but no one should really frown on this methodology. Even European style purists should look at it as a transition. As we shall see in the next chapter, cabinetmakers who attempt to build European in this way will need to do further detailing as they proceed with cabinet assembly.

The other way to build European with conventional channel-cutting techniques involves, as we've said, a great deal of modification in design and assembly, and employment of neither the face frame nor the line-boring system. On end panels, we cut blind rabbets for fitting top and bottom members as well as blind dadoes for placement of every fixed horizontal member. (See Illus. 116.) You can use the horizontal members for placement of drawer rails just as you would in the actual 32-mm system. There are a number of advantages to the blind dado approach: elimination of the face frame, an uninterrupted vertical line on the edge of the end panel through edge banding, elimination of the need for assembly fittings, and exposure of wood to wood for strong glue joints.

In the previous chapter, we looked at one way of accomplishing blind dadoes in conjunction with thick (at least ⅛-in.) solid edgings. The technique was simple: Run through dadoes and then add the edging material. You can also accomplish this type of cut by using a

Illus. 116. End panels milled with stop dadoes. On a panel router, this can be accomplished with templates. (Courtesy of Safranek Enterprises, Inc.)

template in conjunction with a router. This was the approach used to cut the virtually perfect stop cuts in Illus. 116. When using the router-jig approach, the kind shown in Illus. 112, most detailers simply pencil a stop mark right onto the panel, indicating where to end the dadoing cut. You can proceed in a similar way when using a radial arm saw for cutting blind dadoes. A table saw may be the most troublesome saw to use for this type of detailing, since you can't

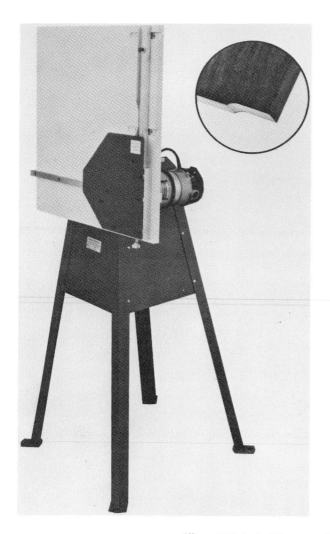
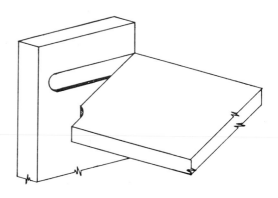

Illus. 117. Left: The growth of European style cabinetry has increased the demand for tools like this one. Right: Blind dadoes and notches must be a perfect match. (Courtesy of Safranek Enterprises, Inc.)

watch the channel cut developing because you have to feed with the panel face down. Furthermore, you have to depend on reference marks or stops that are positioned on the saw's fence or table. Regardless of the method chosen, the dado width should be the same measurement as the thickness of the stock used for the top, rail, or bottom.

The use of blind dadoes requires the milling of matching notches that are perfect. This can be accomplished with a partial feed on a jointer, a hand saw, or even a small, specially designed tool (see Illus. 117). Critical to proper machining of this notch cut is the depth of cut, which must be exactly the same as the depth of the blind dado into which it fits.

Naturally, when using the blind-dado-assembly approach, you can still drill a vertical hole line for insertion of peg-type shelf supports, or cut vertical channels for placing adjustable-shelf standards.

Anyone who has done a fair amount of cabinet work, or even someone who has looked carefully at fine old furniture, will recognize that the blind-dado system has been around for quite some time. Frameless design is not a new idea at all. Cabinetmakers have been joining "flat panels" via the blind-dado-and-matching-notch system for centuries. In today's trade, many cabinetmakers are proving that the old technique is still reliable, and that it is an effective alternative to the line-boring system when it comes to building European style cabinetry. If we intend to use the blind-dado system, perhaps we should also use other techniques that the old masters used for furniture detailing and assembly. Most important perhaps was their back-installation system. The back is, after all, the main source of strength and rigidity in any cabinet that is constructed without a face frame.

Of course, you have probably noticed that both the European cabinet and the antique make use of backs that are set into slots near the rear of the ends. This is tremendously effective. Try thinking of the cabinet as an oversized drawer box. The rigidity of a drawer box is established by a bottom that fits fairly tightly into slots in the front and sides. Some cabinetmakers also cut these slots into their drawer backs. In the same vein, a European mode cabinetmaker cuts slots into the bottom and end panels, in which to inset a thin back. Some also cut such a slot into the top or top-rear rail of their cabinets. If you look carefully at the back-attachment detail of any antique chest (or merely a fairly old chest), you will almost certainly see a thin back panel that has been installed into rabbets along the rear edge of the ends and perhaps the top and bottom. The European box is very rigid; the antique box is very rigid, providing that its back panel(s) did not shrink a great deal with age. What we can see from this examination is that inset backs yield great rigidity for the cabinet box. Any of the channel-cutting techniques that we have looked at are appropriate for cutting the slots. Again, a router generally yields the smoothest cuts. Note that an inset back is absolutely necessary in any cabinet or furniture piece that you build frameless. An overlaid back simply does not lend enough strength. Note also that the choice of a detailing system for cutting this slot is totally unrelated to whether or not the cabinetmaker is building within the 32-mm mode. In fact, slot cutting is more akin to the conventional system of dado-and-rabbet cutting than it is to the line-boring system.

It should be fairly obvious why the traditional detailing system, based on the use of rabbets and dadoes, has remained popular. Clearly, it can be just as effective and strong as the line-boring system, with results that are just as attractive. We have seen that there are ways to produce chip-free channel cuts in preclad particleboard panels, and that dadoing can work well even when you are using edge bands rather than face frames.

It must be noted, however, that precise fits are generally more difficult to achieve with the dado system than with the line-boring system. This is because most line-boring tools automatically account for minor variations in measuring and alignment, by virtue of allowing us to use exactly the same jig or machine setup to detail members to be joined. If the dowel holes drilled into the end of a bottom panel are a millimetre too low, so also are the holes drilled in the mating end panel. We still achieve an excellent alignment of components. In the dado system, mating parts must often be detailed with two entirely different setups or even different tools. Note, for example, that generating a perfect ¼-in.-deep blind dado does nothing to ensure that we will also generate a perfect fit with the matching notch on the end of a horizontal component. Cabinetmakers who choose the conventional methods must take extra care in setting up, especially when they won't be using a face frame.

SUMMARY

The European 32-mm system is a major development in cabinet-making—not just giving us faster ways of doing the same processes we have been doing for centuries, but truly giving us an entirely different method for joining components. To generate the simplest possible way of fastening pieces together, the Europeans developed a modularized-cabinetmaking system based upon drilling a series of holes. In order for the system to work effectively, though, the holes must be located very precisely. European technology has therefore focused on developing a generation of machines that will perform this drilling, called line boring, with great precision.

European line boring is so standardized that all hardware systems and other fittings are easily installed. Most accessory-attachment holes are 5 mm in diameter and spaced 32 mm apart in the vertical hole pattern. Most cabinet-assembly holes are 8 mm in diameter and located to align with the exact middle of the mating panels. Where this modularization and standardization is complete, as in cabinet factories that only use the 32-mm system, skilled woodworking employees are almost unnecessary. Some 32-mm-system cabinetry is so simple to put together that even end users are capable of breaking furniture units down into a stack of flat components. This type of furniture makes use of knock-down fasteners for attaching pieces to one another.

Line boring can be accomplished with whole-system machinery or with any of a variety of jigs that do an excellent job of aligning and spacing holes. Multispindle borers are very expensive stationary tools, but some can drill all the necessary holes in both vertical or both horizontal patterns at the same time. It is a mere rotation of the heads to drill matching holes in the ends of horizontal patterns. In the small shop, you can create hole lines with a drill-press attachment called a boring gearbox, or with a hand drill used in conjunction with a set of drilling guides, or jigs. Some of these jigs that control spacing, hole diameter, and backset, are even American made. When using a hand drill, hole depth is controlled by a depth gauge fastened directly onto the bit. When drilling this way with hand tools, it is important to make sure that the jig is firmly clamped in place and that reference points are consistent; furthermore, the woodworker should only drill those holes that are necessary. Another option is assembly boring, in which the cabinetmaker aligns and clamps parts together and then drills countersink, clearance, and pilot holes for the insertion of screws.

Another method of creating European looking cabinetry involves the use of traditional detailing techniques—such as cutting dadoes, matching notches, and rabbets. The most effective conventional tooling for dealing with European style materials is undoubtedly the router, especially a router equipped with a reverse-helix cutter to ensure chip-free channels. Cabinetmakers can use rabbets for the attachment of the top and bottom, and dadoes for the attachment of fixed shelves and drawer rails. This approach could replace all horizontal drilling. The vertical line can also be eliminated, by virtue of cutting a channel for the placement of shelf standard, and by using ordinary screws for the attachment of accessories. However, the cutting of dadoes and rabbets may require much more time and care in machine setup.

Very important to building without a face frame, both in the 32-mm system and within the traditional approach, is the method of back-panel attachment. The back should definitely fit snugly into slots or rabbets cut near the rear of the end and bottom panels. This establishes good rigidity for the frameless cabinet.

RECOMMENDATIONS

The modern cabinetmaker needs to have the ability to perform line boring with reasonable speed and great precision.

It is quite possible, perhaps even probable, that all large-scale cabinet manufacturers will eventually convert entirely to the 32-mm-detail-and-joining system. Many of them already have. For such manufacturers, the 32-mm system is simply better than trying to turn out a large volume of face-frame-type cabinets. Edge-banded flat panels, joined with dowels or other hole-line fasteners, are produced faster; can be constructed from start to finish by less skilled employees; and, probably most importantly, will be superior in quality to face-frame-type cabinets that are mass produced.

As small-scale producers, custom cabinetmakers have some choices, however. In the first place, we don't need to fling our old methods out the window. Rather, we can begin with a few sensible line-boring tools that require a minimal investment and see where they lead us.

The place to introduce yourself to line boring is along the vertical hole line. The best introductory line-boring tool to purchase is undoubtedly an aluminum jig with 5-mm bushings spaced 32 mm apart. With it, naturally, you will need a few 5-mm European style bits and a depth gauge. This tooling will give you the most immediate versatility because not only can you use it for drilling a vertical hole line for shelf supports but also for drilling mounting holes for a variety of accessories such as doors and drawers.

If you plan to use a hole line for assembly, nothing will beat the similar wand or jig made for locating larger holes near the top and bottom edges of end panels.

However, the usefulness of the vertical hole line is quite limited if you are building with a face frame. The holes cannot be used for accessory attachment. Their only use is for adjustable-shelf support. There is not really any need for line boring if you plan to continue building a face frame for every cabinet.

What makes a great deal of sense is for customizers to adopt some kind of traditional but frameless system when they opt for the European look. This means cutting blind dadoes and matching notch details for purposes of assembly, but it will yield a sturdy frameless cabinet box. With this approach, customizers can utilize the vertical hole line for accessory attachment, if they so desire. They also can employ familiar tooling, techniques, and fasteners for purposes of assembly. They don't need to stock one sort of fastener for traditional cabinetry and another for European cabinetry.

Naturally, it is quite feasible for small shop owners to make a complete conversion to a 32-mm-line-boring approach. All it would take is a set of drilling jigs, a few bits, and a drill. Still, many cabinetmakers prefer the traditional method of joining cabinet components. Good-quality dado and rabbet joints take a bit longer to produce than butt seams held together by dowels or other fasteners, but they are also stronger. Furthermore, most customizers are more interested in producing high-quality end products than they are in great speed. For channel-cutting preclad components, a router remains the superior tool.

5
EUROPEAN STYLE DOORS AND DRAWERS

FLAT PANEL DOORS

There are two distinctly different ways of identifying doors as European.

One approach is to refer to a door as European if it is mounted with 32-mm-type, fully concealed hinges. This would suggest that the cabinetmaker can choose any style of door, from the most traditional to the most contemporary, and still refer to his or her cabinet as European. Of course, most people would probably think that this definition is a bit too loose. After all, if you construct a cabinet with the hinges as the only European element, then the cabinet can be built of hardwoods and plywood; it can have a face frame; it can be constructed without a single 5-mm or 8-mm hole; its parts can, in fact, be joined with dadoes, glue, and nails; and, finally, the look of the doors and drawers can be utterly traditional—such as the look you get with raised-panel doors. In almost every sense, such a cabinet is a traditional American cabinet.

Perhaps a more legitimate way to define "European" is by identifying a look or style that is conveyed by the doors. Euro-style doors are generally flat doors. They are usually plain panels of preclad particleboard that have been edge-banded. When mounted upon the cabinet box, these doors are most often spaced only 6 mm ($\sim\frac{1}{4}$ in.) or so apart. This close positioning is, of course, a direct result of frameless construction. The doors are overlay type, and they nearly always overlay a facing that is only 16 mm to 19 mm wide. In keeping with the flat, contemporary look, the doors are naturally attached with fully concealed hinges. If this is an acceptable definition for European cabinetry, then what type of cabinet box the doors are attached to will actually matter very little. Doors can be spaced about ¼ in. apart just as easily when mounted to a face-frame-type cabinet as when mounted to a frameless 32-mm box. Even people who press for a complete conversion to the European system will admit this; although, when they do so, they are usually trying to make the converse point that traditional cabinetmakers can build totally European boxes and still give their customers a traditional look by attaching frame-type doors.

In this book, we shall accept that when doors are flat, overlaid, and spaced closely together, the cabinet can be defined as European. Ultimately, it is up to you to determine which design, construction, and appearance elements constitute an acceptable definition for your own furniture and cabinetry, but there are at least two reasons for accepting door style as one of the essential elements of European cabinetry. As pointed out earlier, most people outside the cabinet trade think of the European style, not in terms of hole lines or frameless construction, but rather in terms of the flat, contemporary look that comes from using preclad particleboard and from attaching flat doors. But probably the best reason to consider door appearance as an essential element of European design has to do with the way these doors are made. They are generally cut from preclad particleboard panels, to very exact tolerances, and then edge-banded. In other words, they are fabricated pretty much like any other European cabinet component. This is naturally by design. Manufacturers who build modular 32-mm-system cabinetry want the capability to make doors in exactly the same way that they make other cabinet parts.

There is probably no way to overemphasize the importance of the difference between traditional door making and "European" door making. When fabricating traditional doors, often we must go through a number of steps to create a single door, and these steps often involve the use of tools that are unnecessary in other stages of cabinet building. Consider making raised-panel, arch-topped doors, for example. (See Illus. 118.) We will probably need all solid stock for this kind of door. Thus, we start by selecting suitable boards. This can involve matching color and grain figure, as well as choosing the flattest boards available if you are using surfaced (S2S) stock that is already close to final-door thickness. If we are using oversized material, the next step is to flatten the boards and get them to the correct thickness by feeding them through the jointer and planer. This, along with surfacing face-frame stock, is the main function for a planer in the traditional cabinet shop. Next is the matter of edge-straightening the stock, an operation most easily performed on the jointer. Note that the primary function of a jointer in traditional shops is edge-straightening of face-frame material and other solid stocks.

The next series of steps has to do with preparing the raised panel. The boards are glued together to make an oversized panel. Then the panel is usually belt-sanded smooth and cut to size and finished shape. The straight cuts can be made with a table saw or radial arm saw, but we may have to change the blade. The arched cuts must be performed with a band saw or saber saw, and then only after being marked from a pattern.

Now, it's time to head for the shaper. (See Illus. 119.) We need to cut a combination slot-and-edge-form detail on the interior of all

Illus. 118. Raised-panel, arch-topped doors are traditional doors requiring a number of steps.

Illus. 119. A single-spindle shaper. (Courtesy of Delta International Machinery Corp.)

frame members. We need a coping cut on the ends of rails to create a type of mating tenon. Finally, we need the broad, deep cut all along the outside of the raised panel. Not only do these types of detailing require a number of setup changes (unless you are fortunate enough to have a multispindle shaper), but we are also using a very specialized tool. Traditional door making is the primary function of a shaper in most shops.

Finally, we have reached the assembly stage of our door—or, have we? Before getting out the glue and clamps again, it's a good idea to sand certain parts of the door—interior edge forms and both surfaces of the raised panel. When we do assemble, we need proper glue application where stile and rail come together, but we must be careful to glue the panel only to the rails, and then only near the middle. In fact, some cabinetmakers use a brad gun, and no glue at all, to secure the panel. Even with the door assembled, there is more sanding to do, and there may be more milling involved to yield a "lip," or an outer edge form.

In contrast to the involved process of making traditional doors is the great simplicity with which we can fabricate flat or contemporary doors—the type of doors we are calling European. First, we cut a door panel from precovered particleboard and then band its edges. If the panel has a veneer covering, we may have to do a bit of sanding. If we are using thick solid edging, the edging itself will probably require some sanding. An edge form such as a round over will require additional milling. Not only does this kind of door making call for fewer tools and operations than the traditional style, but it also allows European system cabinetmakers to use almost exactly the same tools that they use in building the rest of the cabinet.

FABRICATING EUROPEAN DOORS

The first point that you need to note in connection with the fabrication of flat doors is that flat drawer fronts can usually be made in exactly the same way. If the doors on a European style kitchen are going to be made by cutting panels from melamine-clad particleboard and then adding a ¼-in. solid-oak edge band along three edges and a length of solid-oak continuous pull along the fourth edge, then the drawer fronts can be made in exactly the same way. If the spacing between doors is intended to be approximately ¼ in., then the spacing between doors and drawer fronts, as well as the spacing between drawer fronts, should also be about ¼ in. Therefore, until we come to a discussion of techniques for hinging doors and for attaching drawer fronts to drawer boxes, much of what we say about doors will also pertain to drawer fronts.

European System Door Making

Although we have already covered most of the important aspects of European style door making, this is probably a good time to reemphasize some points.

Cut quality is extremely important on door panels because both sides of the door will have high visibility. But when cutting end panels to length, you don't need anywhere near the degree of chip-free cuts required for doors. Any minor surface chipping near the top or bottom of an end panel will be covered by a horizontal member or at least well hidden from view. If you select dado-rabbet-type construction, some surface chipping will be eliminated during the detailing operation. However, there is no way to hide chipped or splintered surfaces on a door. On the inside of a cabinet door, tear away is less objectionable than on its exterior (primary surface), but it is objectionable nonetheless. European saws, with their precise tolerances and their scoring blades, are specifically designed to eliminate tear away. Of course, good-quality traditional saws with sliding-table and scoring-blade features are also available now. (See Illus. 120.)

The edge banding of doors is carried out in exactly the same way as the edge banding of other components. As with door cutting, though, the quality of the bond must be virtually perfect along the door edges. Doors are not only more visible than other cabinet components but they also have a more rugged life due to continual openings and closings. There must be no dead spots in the bond because they will become even more evident with the passage of time.

One type of milling and assembly work that pertains to doors only is the addition of continuous bar-pull stock along one edge or end. Such continuous pull stock is usually milled with a projection, something like a continuous tenon, so that it can be fitted snugly into a matching slot, or mortise, milled into the edge of the door panel. (See Illus. 121.) The slot can naturally be cut in any convenient way (for instance, with a router or table saw), but this requires another setup. Most cabinetmakers fix the pull's protrusion into the door slot with a bit of glue, some pressure, and a few small-headed brads. I would caution you regarding brads, though. Any time you are attempting to drive a piece of hard steel through a brittle plastic surface, you are running a few risks. Safety can be an issue here because high-pressure plastics such as melamine can bend or even deflect a nail. Furthermore, such plastic has a tendency to chip or flake when we nail through it, especially close to an end, as we are talking about here. It is a problem not unlike the tear-away trouble generated by

Illus. 120. An American-made sliding-table dimension saw with a scoring blade. (Courtesy of Delta International Machinery Corp.)

Illus. 121. A continuous wood bar pull must usually be interlocked with a door panel's edge.

some saws. In fact, it can even be a worse problem to deal with because, in creating room for itself, the nail can displace wood and resin particles to the extent that they cause a bubble in the melamine. One way of circumventing this problem, possibly the most "European" way, is to cut a slot that will create a snug fit and then to use glue and no fasteners. (See Illus. 122.) In normal usage, this arrangement is certainly strong enough.

When applying any type of thick edging, the order of application may be important to you. For example, you may want to edge-band the top and bottom ends of each door before you apply edging to its vertical edges. Or, you may want to do these operations in exactly the opposite order. In either case, an orderly progression helps to establish unity in the cabinet job.

Door Layout

With general considerations determined, we can look at the matter of determining the overall door size as well as the cutting list for the various components.

As they do with any type of door, cabinetmakers begin door layout for European style doors by first determining overall door width and height. With most European style doors, this is simply a matter of establishing an overlay dimension. The amount of width overlay is based on several factors.

First is the matter of panel thickness. If the cabinet box is made of panels with a thickness of 16 mm (⅝ in.), the overlay must obviously be less than if the doors are to overlay panels that are 19 mm (¾ in.) thick.

Door-panel thickness is significant, too. Depending on the hinge used, of course, we sometimes need more reveal, or space, between

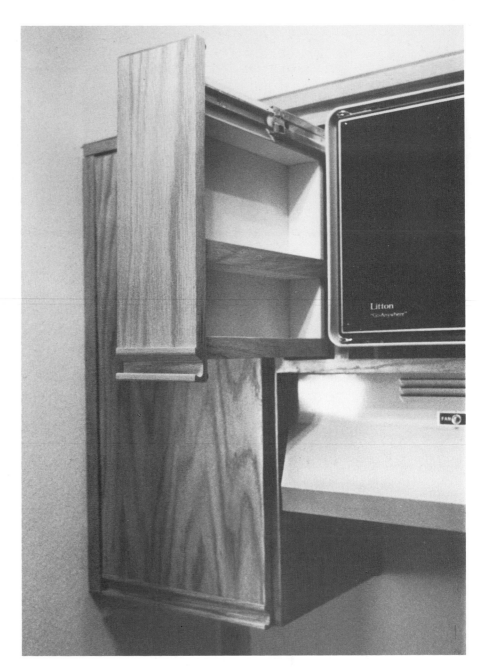

Illus. 122. Is it a door or a drawer? This spice rack is mounted in a wall cabinet. Note the continuous pull, which was attached without nails. Also note the thick moulding on the wall end, which maintains the 1/4-in.-door-gap spacing.

doors for thicker doors. The wider reveal is necessary to allow one door to open fully without contacting the neighboring door.

Another matter is location. If a door is to be mounted at the end of an entire length of cabinet, or in a corner, the application is referred to as corner or full overlay. If two doors are mounted on opposite sides of the same panel, as on a partition, the application is called half or twin overlay. (Remember that in a really modularized cabinetmaking situation, manufacturers tend to avoid using partitions; full-overlay application is thus much more common. (See Illus. 124.) In some instances, full-inset or flush application is desirable on the European cabinet, and this is also a possibility in determining width overlay.

One last factor in determining overlay is hinge model. There is a wide variety of hinges available to us, and each is designed to fulfill a particular function. For instance, some are designed to open only 100°, whereas other models allow an opening angle of 130°. Some are designed to rotate the door completely out of the opening to allow maximum slide-out width, and others will rotate the door farther into the opening for those times when you must use a thicker door panel. There are also hinges and mounting plates specially made for traditional cabinetmakers who still want to build some projects with face frames. (See Illus. 125.) Each type of hinge will specify a maximum overlay, but it is best not to make your doors as wide as this maximum overlay because that will take away all the lateral adjustment built into the hinge. Thus, for a hinge that specifies a maximum overlay of 19 mm (¾ in.), it is wise to plan for an overlay of only 16 mm (⅝ in.).

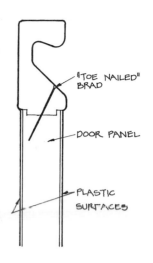

Illus. 123. A continuous bar pull can be attached with brads driven at toe-nail angles.

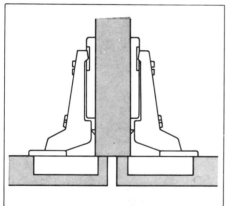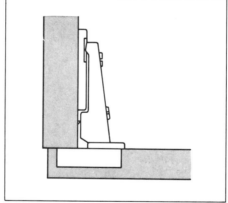

Illus. 124. Overlay applications. (Courtesy of Julius Blum Inc.)

All these factors can make the whole door-layout operation sound somewhat complicated, but it is not. For instance, I like to construct most of my cabinet boxes from ⅝-in. material. It is much lighter than ¾-in. stock, and yet it is still substantial enough for either dowel or dado construction. With frameless construction, I will have a consistent facing width of ⅝ in. I prefer a full overlay, but I think it is better to build long boxes with partitions than to build a bunch of short boxes to be joined together later; therefore, I will need half overlays wherever there is a partition. I also want about ⅛ in. (3 mm) of

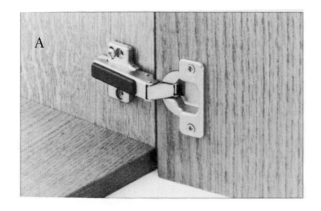
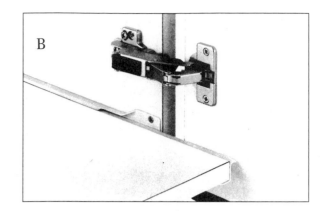

Illus. 125. European hinge varieties. A: 100° opening hinge. B: zero-protrusion hinge—165° opening to be used with slide-outs. C: 130° opening, thick-door hinge. D: 176° opening face-frame hinge. (Courtesy of Julius Blum, Inc.)

facing revealed wherever I have an end panel and a reveal of approximately ³⁄₁₆ in. (5 mm) between doors on a partition. Thus, I will choose ½ in. (13 mm) as my full-overlay measurement (⅝ in. minus ⅛ in.), and ⁷⁄₃₂ in. (6 mm) as my half-overlay measurement (⅝ in. minus ³⁄₁₆ in. divided by 2). Then I simply make sure that these overlay dimensions will be compatible with the hinges I have selected. If my doors are thicker than ¾ in., then I can make the reveal larger, or I can simply order some thick-door hinges. Where I need slide-out shelves to be mounted behind doors, zero-protrusion hinges are usually the answer. For an opening that is 14 in. (~356 mm) wide, I would need:

- a 15-in. (381-mm) door where both edges are full overlay,
- a 14⁷⁄₁₆-in. (~367-mm) door where both edges are half overlay, or
- a 14²³⁄₃₂-in. (~374-mm) door where one edge is full overlay and the other is half overlay.

In pair-door situations, we need to reduce the total door width by at least ⅛ in. (3 mm) to create some necessary clearance between the doors. Obviously, we also have to divide the width measurement in half. The most reliable procedure is first to add the overlay dimensions for both sides to the overall width as necessary, then to reduce the total by ⅛ in. or a bit more, and finally to divide in half. This yields the overall door-panel width on pair openings. Therefore, to cover a 30-in. (762-mm) door-opening width, we might consider the following overall door sizes (widths are maximums—doors will be easier to adjust if they are slightly narrower):

- two 15⁷⁄₁₆-in. (392 mm) doors where both doors are full overlay,
- two 15⁵⁄₃₂-in. (385-mm) doors where both doors are half overlay, or
- two 15⁹⁄₃₂-in. (388-mm) doors where one door is a full overlay and the other is a half overlay.

Length (height) dimensions are even simpler to determine because they are arrived at more arbitrarily. There are fewer factors involved because we need not be concerned with hinge operation. Our main concerns in determining overlay are facing width (box-stock thickness), desired reveal, and full- and half-overlay application.

In general, we consider facing thickness and reveal simultaneously, since these concerns are interrelated. If we desire a reveal of ³⁄₁₆ in. (5 mm), and the stock we are using for the cabinet box is ⅝ in. thick, then we will want to cover ⁷⁄₁₆ in. (~11 mm) of the facing. We can call this the total overlay dimension.

The full amount of the total overlay is added to the height of a door opening wherever we need a full overlay, such as along cabinet bottom panels. In half-overlay locations, such as where a drawer and door both strike against the same rail, we add half of the total overlay dimension (⁷⁄₃₂ in., or ~5 mm). We may want to reduce the overlay along the top panels of wall cabinets and tall cabinets if we plan to add a crown or other moulding. This creates a wider reveal, allowing us to attach mouldings more easily and with greater firmness. It is probably appropriate to think of this as a half-overlay location. Therefore, we would consider the following door heights for a door that is 24⁹⁄₁₆ in. (624 mm—a standard, as determined in Chapter 2) in height:

- a 25⁷⁄₁₆-in. (646-mm) door height where the top and bottom both have full overlay (probably a rare occurrence),
- a 25-in. (635-mm) door height where both the top and bottom both have half overlay, or

- a 25⁷/₃₂-in. (640-mm) door height where either the top or the bottom edge of the door has a full overlay while the other edge only has a half overlay (the most common situation).

Determining overall door sizes within the European system is much like doing the same operation conventionally. The major difference is probably working with critical, exact overlay and reveal dimensions rather than nominal ones.

European hinges can be used to mount flush doors as well as overlay doors, and here again, dimensions must be figured carefully. (See Illus. 126.) More importantly, each door must be made with the

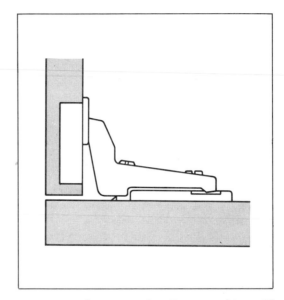

Illus. 126. Flush or inset application with a European hinge. (Courtesy of Julius Blum, Inc.)

utmost attention towards precision in order to achieve a good fit. In fact, the flush or inset application is where the door and opening must fit best, but this is nothing new to anyone who has mounted flush doors and drawer fronts. To arrive at the overall door size for flush doors, we simply subtract some predetermined gap measurement (perhaps ⁵/₃₂ in., or 4 mm) from the opening sizes for each door edge. Thus, for an opening that is 14 in. by 24⁹/₁₆ in., we need a finished door panel that is 13¹¹/₁₆ in. (348 mm) by 24¼ in. (616 mm).

Flush doors are less common than overlay doors in the European cabinetmaking system, but they can be used to create an unbroken look. Flush doors and drawers often have the same color and finish as the nearby facing for cabinet panels (edge banding). Such door panels tend to blend with the cabinet facings.

One final possibility to consider is mounting European style doors on cabinets with face frames. (Again, see Illus. 125.) When we do this, we proceed somewhat in the reverse from procedures suggested earlier. That is, we first decide on reveals and overlays; then we can determine the width of face-frame stiles, rails, and mullions. In fact, many cabinetmakers simply use their own standard face-frame-stock sizes as well as some consistent overlay measurement such as ⅝ in. Reveals, or door gaps, are wide—perhaps as wide as ¾ in. (19 mm) or more—giving the cabinetmaker these three clear advantages.

- The overlay measurements become nominal rather than critical measurements, allowing for less rigid precision.
- It is possible to use a finger-pull-cove detail instead of a knob or bar pull.
- Layout is simplified because we use the same overlay in all locations.

Thus, an opening that is 14 in. by 24½ in. might require a door panel that is 15¼ in. (387 mm) by 25¾ in. (654 mm). Whenever you use European hinges for a pair of doors, you will need to allow for the additional ⅛-in. clearance in width, mentioned earlier. Face frames do not change this. Therefore, for an opening that is 30 in. wide, we add the double overlay (1¼ in., or 32 mm), subtract the clearance amount (⅛ in., or 3 mm), and then divide by two, yielding two doors that are 15⁹⁄₁₆ in. (395 mm) wide.

Sometimes cabinetmakers will decide to employ the European door look and still build with a face frame. They accomplish this by using European style hinges and flat panel doors, and by establishing the narrow reveals that are so common in European design. They base the width of face-frame stocks on the door overlays and the specified reveals. If they are using a hinge that specifies ¾-in. overlays, for instance, and they desire a ¼-in. reveal spacing between doors, then they will obviously want 1-in. stiles because stiles only have doors covering their surface along one edge. Reveal measurement plus total overlays will be equal to stock width. This arrangement will necessitate 1¾-in. mullions because mullions are naturally covered by overlays along two edges. If there is a wall-to-wall situation, then the cabinetmaker can employ a moulding as thick as the doors. This moulding can be applied in such a way that it continues the motif of ¼-in. spacings while still fulfilling the function of most scribe mouldings—covering a gap between the wall and cabinet. (Again, see Illus. 122.)

The overlays and reveal are added together to yield stock widths for rails also. Specifying a ⅝-in. overlay, combined with our standard ¼-in. door gap will mean a 1½-in. width for the rails that separate a door and drawer front in the common over-and-under arrangement. A bottom rail might be ⅞ in.; a top rail might be 1⅝ in. if the countertop overlaps the facing by ¾ in.

Regardless of whether we are determining height or width measurements, the familiar rules apply: We need only add overlay amounts to opening sizes to list door sizes.

Once the overall door size has been determined, the only matter that remains is determining and listing the sizes of the various components that will be put together to make the door. Actually, most designers list the exact sizes of only the ply or particleboard panel. Customizers who plan to edge-band with lengths of solid edging or rigid laminate will also list these, but probably not by exact size. They may list by approximate length for individual pieces or by total length required. For a job on which you need a 12 in. × 20 in. door and two 15 in. × 24 in. doors, presume that you will be adding a solid edge band that is ⅝ in. thick to all edges. You would subtract for this edging thickness and list the exact sizes of the panels as follows:

¾-in. melamine-ply door panels

| Door A | 2 ea. | 13¾ in. × 22¾ in. |
| Door B | 1 ea. | 10¾ in. × 18¾ in. |

You could list approximate edge-band sizes for the same doors, either broken down as follows:

¾ in. × ⅝ in. solid edging

Door A	4 ea.	14 in.
	4 ea.	23 in.
Door B	2 ea.	11 in.
	2 ea.	19 in.

or as a total required length as follows:

¾ in. × ⅝ in. door edging—~20 ft.

In operations involving edge banding from continuous rolls, you don't need to determine approximate lengths of the edge-banding material, of course. Yet, it still remains absolutely necessary to determine the exact size of door panels. When planning for the thinnest edgings—such as foils, papers, and thin vinyls—you don't need to subtract any amount for the edgings. You can consider panel cutting sizes to be the same as overall door sizes. Subtract a half-millimetre, or 1/64 in., from the total door size if you desire, but this is probably unnecessary. When the planned-for edging is slightly thicker, such as with ordinary laminated plastics, it is necessary to subtract for the edging's thickness. This will help you to avoid fitting or mounting problems. To account for this thickness, the best approach is to put together two thicknesses of the edging materials and to actually measure it. A subtraction of $\frac{1}{16}$ in. (~ 1.5 mm) per door is often the result.

Blending

Earlier we looked at one type of blending: mounting simple flat doors on face-frame-type cabinets with European hinges to generate the "European look." Recall that what we mean by blending is using any combination of traditional and 32-mm-system techniques to create the intended European styling. Thus, we can consider any approach that combines a conventionally built box with European looking doors as blended. The goal here is the creation of a particular appearance. We can achieve this by using concealed hinges, by edge-banding prelaminated panels for our doors, and by incorporating such style elements as narrow reveals and unbroken, horizontal, linear motifs.

In some circumstances, it may be plausible to generate the European look by fabricating drawers and doors from solid stocks. Remember that the goal is to make flat doors, and edge lamination of solid planks will certainly achieve this.

High-volume cabinet manufacturers are naturally very interested in making flat doors with the least possible labor; more specifically, they want to avoid dependence on skilled labor. Therefore, they tend to select door materials that require no sanding or finishing—materials such as melamine-covered particleboard. They also don't want to see any time spent in gluing and clamping together door and drawer panels.

Low-volume customizers, such as ourselves, have some other choices, providing that we are willing to invest some additional time in door preparation. Of course, that is one reason we are customizers: We tend to think more in terms of the project itself than do high-level producers; we are willing to invest some additional time.

When high-volume manufacturers want to produce a door design with a wood grain, they generally select particleboard panels that are covered with wood-grain plastics. Then they usually band the edges with plastics. The result is a good-quality door panel that costs very little to produce.

On the other hand, when customizers set out to make wood-grain doors and drawers, they will generally choose veneer-covered panels or lumber as their raw material. When they choose veneer-covered panels, they are committing themselves to some additional sanding and to applying a finish. If they choose solid planks, they will also have to spend some time selecting boards with appropriate color and grain figure (usually with the goal of matching), gluing boards together, sanding panels flat, and cutting to finished size.

Veneer-Covered Door Panels. Some European cabinetmakers use veneer-covered panels for their 32-mm-based products, and doors of this type can be considered European in the strictest sense. Most producers of veneered doors use material with a particleboard core. Plywood-core panels can be warped a bit, and their thickness dimensions are not as reliable as those of particleboards. I actually prefer veneer-core plywood for doors, however, because it is so much lighter than the particleboard variety. This relative lightness makes plywood a more manageable panel to lift and cut. Besides, the reliability of door thickness is not often a concern. I still have to be concerned with warped panels, however, so that it probably takes me longer to select and cut door panels than it does the cabinetmaker who makes doors with particleboard. Another drawback is the presence of voids, particularly along edges where you plan to edge-band with any thin edging material. Of course, if you plan to use edgings with a thickness of ⅛ in. or more, voids are usually not a significant problem.

Selecting an appropriate edging for veneer-clad doors is largely a matter of choosing a thickness because most cabinetmakers usually prefer to use matching wood edgings to band the edges of veneered door panels. It is common to see a plastics-covered panel banded with wooden edging, but the converse is somewhat rare: We do not often see wood-veneer door panels edged with plastics. This is probably because plastic edgings are almost always thin stocks. The thickness of PVC tape (or even high-pressure plastic laminates) is not substantial enough to affect the look of a door panel's surface. Thus, for a red-oak door panel or drawer front, most cabinetmakers simply select red-oak edging with a thickness appropriate to fulfilling some particular need. (See Illus. 127.)

We have already identified the steps necessary for making most European doors—lay-out and list, cut with a minimum of tear away, and edge-band. When we are using a solid edging with veneer-faced door panels, however, it is necessary to consider the ways that sanding operations will affect door fabrication.

Woodworkers who cut their own edging for bending purposes should be in the habit of doing some sanding before application. Solid edge bands that are applied by conventional techniques, such as gluing and clamping or gluing and nailing, will generally have to be finish-sanded as one of the last steps in door making, but it is much easier to remove mill marks from the edging material before application. Cabinetmakers who have a good-quality thickness planer or access to a wide belt sander will want to cut edging stocks slightly oversized and then feed the long strips through one of these machines to get rid of mill marks. Yet, many small scale woodworkers do this sanding with a portable belt sander.

After the edging has been laminated to the edges of a veneer-faced door or drawer panel and the flush trimming has been performed, the door panel can be finish-sanded, by hand or with an oscillating sander. Some cabinetmakers like to use a router to get edging strips trimmed fairly close to the surface of a panel and then make the door panel perfectly flush by sanding. It is even fairly common to use a scraper or belt sander (with a 120-grit belt, perhaps) for this purpose. If a round over or another edge form is to be shaped into the solid edging, it is important to do this only after the edge and panel are flush. With joints made perfectly flush, finish sanding is performed with an oscillating sander as on any finished plywood panel. We want to remove any belt-sander scratches that may be present, and generally sand the door panel to an acceptable smoothness without endangering the veneer. Of course, only you can be the judge of how smooth to make this sanding job. I generally stop with 150-grit paper if I intend to use a clear finish. Some cabinetmakers prefer to sand finer than this, and they might continue sanding with 180-grit or even finer papers.

Illus. 127. A veneer-faced drawer front with a solid edge band.

Solid-Stock Door Panels. Fabricating doors and drawer fronts from solid stock is a practice that has been around for some time. The European designers avoid it because it is labor intensive, because it consumes a good deal of lumber, and because the material is not dimensionally stable—that is, basically because solid wood is not particleboard. These are fairly good reasons. In general, we might also avoid solid-stock doors in situations where they could create problems with warpage or shrinkage and expansion. The best times to use solid materials to build European styled door panels are when all the panels are relatively small. Solid panels do allow us to completely skip the edge-banding operation, after all. Furniture projects are usually an excellent choice for the use of solid panels. (See Illus. 128.)

Illus. 128. This European styled desk has solid-stock drawer fronts.

The first job in making solid-lumber door and drawer panels has to do with wood selection. This is like any other facet of cabinetmaking where you need solid stocks. It is not our purpose in this book to go over all the skills and the knowledge that are necessary for effective wood selection. Indeed, the subject of wood selection can be complex enough for an entire book. The matters of color and grain figure, including the issue of whether to strive for matching or contrast, are largely a matter of your own taste, however. Furthermore, your own taste may well change over a period of years, or even weeks. Matching is undoubtedly the fastest approach. In most bunks of solid lumber, there is already some consistency as to color and grain figure because the source trees were grown in the same location over the same general period of time. Besides, striving for contrasts is difficult because we usually want consistency in our contrasts. That is, we usually want our contrasts to appear planned rather than random,

especially on European style cabinetry. Since most European cabinetry is made from particleboard, the employment of wood is usually
for the sake of appearance. Thus, the designer may choose boards to
go into a panel based on how well they blend together or according
to some type of contrast that may be evident.

Of course, another factor involved in material selection is trying to
eliminate warpage. For fabrication of door and drawer panels, we
want to choose only the flat, straight boards from our supply. If a
panel is made from flat boards, it is much more likely to be flat after
it is glued up. Keep in mind that rift-sawn and quarter-sawn stocks
are less likely to warp than flat-sawn materials. Rift-sawn and
quarter-sawn lumber is sliced from the tree in such a way that both
surfaces are equally susceptible to moisture absorption and release;
this is not so with flat-sawn lumber. (See Illus. 129.) Single boards
should be kept somewhat narrow, perhaps 3 to 4 in., especially when
we wind up working with flat-sawn lumber. This allows us to equal-
ize expansion by alternating the outer- and inner-board surfaces
across the width of a panel. This is less important in drier regions,

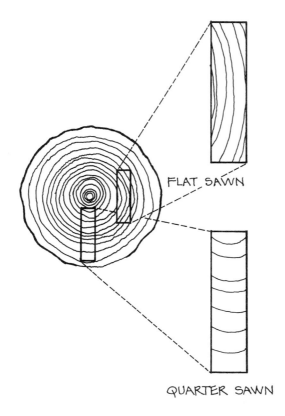

FLAT SAWN

QUARTER SAWN

*Illus. 129. Solid wood shrinks and expands more the farther the fibres are from
the tree's center. The effect is warpage on a flat-sawn board because the board's
outer surface is more subject to expansion than its inner surface.*

however, and when making drawer fronts. European drawer fronts are generally stiffened by a ply or particleboard subfront.

The next step in making solid-lumber panels is to cut the boards to approximate length. The pieces should be a couple of inches oversized in length. This will facilitate the easiest gluing and clamping, since we want to focus our attention on achieving tight, flat joints—not joints that are even on the end. We will cut to exact size later on.

Next, it is necessary to edge-straighten and cut boards to approximate width. Again, we want boards slightly oversized. If you are cutting to width with a good-quality circular saw that produces little vibration, you may be able to use sawn edges for lamination. Otherwise, it's back to the jointer with the boards to make every edge perfectly straight and smooth. Incidentally, in this kind of jointing operation, it is very important to make sure that your fence is perfectly perpendicular with the jointer bed. Although this probably seems obvious, I still see experienced woodworkers who do not take time to check this necessity. Even slight bevels on board edges can ruin the flatness of a door.

With all the edges straightened, it is finally time to glue up the panel. This should be a simple matter of spreading glue evenly, so that it will completely cover the surfaces to be bonded, and then applying pressure. If you are working with wood stock that is fairly close to final-panel thickness, it is wise to align the faces of individual boards to be as even as possible. Alternating bar clamps in an over-and-under arrangement can also help with flatness. You should use only your straightest clamps for this operation. Sometimes, after all, the pipe portion of a pipe-type bar clamp can be bent or twisted from a history of overtightening. Finally, it's important to allow the clamped panel to sit flat while the glue is curing.

After the glue has dried, it is time to cut the solid panel to exact size. Remember that solid panels will expand in width to a fairly large degree. It is thus very important that each panel be no wider than its listed size. (Naturally, the predetermined width dimension must be narrow enough to allow for this substantial expansion.) To cut panels square and to the correct dimensions, follow these steps.

1. Straighten one outside edge on the jointer.
2. Set the rip fence on the table saw according to the panel's exact width dimension and rip the panel to width.
3. On either the radial arm saw or the table saw, cut off ends perpendicular to the edges to get the panel to correct length.

Note that it is important to get the two edges straight and parallel before cross-cutting to length in order to achieve a square door or drawer panel. If the door or drawer panel is to receive an edge form such as a round over, then it also helps with dimension cutting to cut the panel upside down. That way, any splinters or tear away will be machined away when you run the edge-forming cut.

After it is cut out, the solid-stock door needs to be made perfectly flat, usually by coarse sanding. Shops with a stationary, wide belt sander can usually accomplish this very quickly. For the rest of us, though, this usually means a lot of extra sanding time with a portable belt sander. When perfectly flat, the solid door needs additional sanding—the same kind of finish sanding required on plywood door panels.

European cabinetry can include solid-stock doors. Still, when designing a European styled piece, cabinetmakers should have valid reasons for the additional cost and preparation time these doors require. Of course, in a shop equipped with a slow edge-banding system, the time saved by using particleboard doors is not so substantial, but solid doors will still be less reliable in terms of dimensional stability and warpage. I like to use solid stock for narrow panels such as drawer fronts, but I tend to prefer veneer-faced plywood for jobs requiring more than a couple of wide (over ten 12-in.) panels.

It is fairly clear that we can create a European look even when using real wood—veneer-faced sheet goods or solid-lumber stock. Another type of blending is to fabricate European style doors by cutting out panels from plastics-faced particleboard and then edge-banding the particleboard by some conventional means, such as adding a solid-stock edging with resin glue and pressure. In a way, conventional approaches to edge banding give us more freedom. The machinery does not dictate what type of door or drawer front we will make because the conventional approaches to adding edgings are all fairly slow compared to a unisystem edge bander. This is one area—customization—where low-volume producers still may have some advantage over manufacturers. Some of the unisystem machines are very versatile, of course; yet, most large-volume manufacturers only offer a few door styles to their customers. They feel that the key to profits is standardization and modularization, not customization. We have already looked at the techniques involved with this kind of blending in Chapter 3. In any case, a wide variety of European styled doors is possible in the small shop. (See Illus. 130.)

FABRICATING EUROPEAN DRAWER BOXES

In building European styled cabinetry, we can employ any of three types of drawer boxes, classified according to the sort of material used: plastics-clad particleboard, prefabricated-plastics components, or wood. The last of these, wood, includes plywood and is often used for the conventional drawer box. Each type is found with some fre-

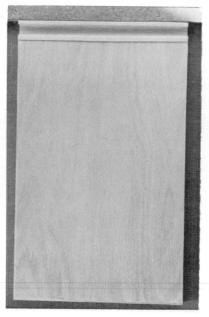

Illus. 130. We can produce European style doors in the custom shop, but the process takes longer.

quency in European style cabinets, and each has advantages as well as drawbacks.

Particleboard Components

Even though particleboard gained wide popularity as a secondary cabinet wood during the sixties and seventies, it was never used very widely as a drawer-box material. Not even medium-density fibreboard (MDF), which most cabinetmakers accepted unhesitatingly for cabinet interiors, was ever used with much regularity as a drawer-box material. This lack of acceptance probably had more to do with appearance and reputation than with anything else. These boards are certainly strong enough and possess enough machinability to be used for most drawers. But most cabinetmakers do not really consider the drawer box to be a secondary location as they do the inside of a finished end, the face of a cabinet back, or either surface of a shelf. The drawer box is more like the back side of a door—not a primary location, certainly, but also more subject to scrutiny than the secondary locations just listed. Thus, industrial grade particleboards have always been considered too large-flaked and too coarse-textured for drawer material. When MDF became readily available, most woodworkers still considered themselves too fastidious to use this smoother, finer material for drawer boxes.

Now that clad-particleboard sheets are available, many cabinetmakers use this material for drawer components. It seems especially appropriate to make drawer boxes from plastics-clad sheets when sheets with this same cladding are being used in secondary locations on a cabinet or furniture article. For instance, when you intend to make a cabinet's interior of almond melamine, then it makes sense to fabricate the drawer boxes from almond melamine as well. We may want to use ⅝-in. material for cabinet box parts but may prefer ½-in. sheets as cutting panels for drawer components. As with conventional materials, it is desirable, from the standpoint of reducing waste, to use the same material thickness for both cabinet back panels and drawer bottoms. This allows us to cut at least some of the drawer bottoms from the remainders of the sheets that we used for the cabinet backs.

The chief advantages in using plastics-clad particleboard for drawer parts are much the same as those cited earlier regarding such material for the cabinet box. Plastics-clad particleboard resists penetration of moisture, household cleaners, and alcohol, as well as many stain-producing substances; it requires no finishing, yet retains an attractive appearance over a long period of time; it is dimensionally stable, therefore remaining true and square for a long time; and it is fairly inexpensive, due both to initial cost and to little waste. Besides these advantages, with this material we usually have the option of matching the finish of the drawer box to that of the rest of the cabinet interior. We can also edge-band and otherwise treat the drawer components in much the same way that we do other parts of the cabinet.

There are a few disadvantages to using preclad particleboard for drawer components. One is that we have to take special measures to limit the release of free formaldehyde. Since the thinner sheets of the material that we use for drawer bottoms are often only clad on one side, this can be very important. The simplest approach can be to edge-band only the top edges of the box's subfront, back, and sides. (See Illus. 131.) Then, a coat of sealer, such as clear lacquer, can be applied to the entire underside of the drawer to seal both the underside of the drawer bottom and the bottom edges of the other drawer components. If all your components are plastics-covered on both sides, and you have a reasonably speedy edge-banding system, it may be faster to go ahead and edge-band both the top and bottom edges of the drawer's back, sides, and subfront. Of course, you may be striving for total elimination of the finishing process in your cabinetmaking operation, at least when you are building European styled articles.

For the traditionalist cabinetmaker, one of the biggest disadvantages of using preclad material for drawer boxes is the nonglueability of the plastic. With the introduction of staples and modern resin glues, many cabinetmakers recognized that it was not necessary to employ worked joints on drawer boxes. The new convention was to butt-join the drawer box. Aliphatic-resin glue (yellow glue) was spread along the ends of the subfront and back, and then staples were driven through the sides to fasten the components together. It is a fairly strong and effective system, especially with roller-type drawer glides or other drawer guiding systems that reduce friction. Reduced friction means less strain on drawer joints. The trouble is that the same assembly system will not work with plastics-clad materials. Neither resin glue nor any other conventional cabinetmaking glue will be much help when you are attempting to join a raw particleboard edge to a smooth plastic surface. Furthermore, attempting to staple through melamine or a similar material will almost surely cause some chipping or bubbling. The joint will be both ineffective and ugly.

Illus. 131. Drawer-box parts may only be edge-banded on the top edge, but the other edge must be sealed.

Mitring Technology. Tool makers have naturally developed new equipment to facilitate the manufacturing of plastics-clad drawers. As with all methodology involved in European cabinet construction, the system for manufacturing these drawers depends upon precisely planned and carefully executed milling.

One solution to the problem of gluing plastic components that may have occurred to you as you read the foregoing discussion is the use of mitre joints. If we use mitre cuts on both ends of the subfront, sides, and back, we will get wood fibres meeting wood fibres in all our drawer joints. Conventional glue can then be used. To further strengthen the joint, the cabinetmaker can drive brads instead of staples, thus reducing risks of chipping. This is a good solution that can be carried out with conventional tools and techniques, but notice that it will require good precision and much closer tolerances than any butt joining would require. In order for the drawer box to fit together properly, all of its components must be perfect: Each must be cut to exactly the correct dimensions, mitres must be precisely machined, and slots to receive the drawer bottom must be machined to the right depth. This is all certainly possible, but it will also take a fair amount of time on conventional equipment. The drawer making system that may be best suited to European cabinetmaking employs a router. This system begins with the mitre concept but requires even greater precision than that just described.

Imagine a single length of sheet material that "wraps around" the drawer bottom. This is made possible by cutting a double mitre, which is not quite a through cut, in three locations along the board. A tiny thickness of plastic material is left behind to fold over each corner as we do our "wrapping." At both ends, of course, a conventional mitre is needed. (See Illus. 132.) Not only must dimensions be determined exactly, but also depth of mitre cut. Naturally, machines have been developed to perform this specific milling operation, and their cost makes perfect sense to large-volume, modular producers. In fact, the machines also make good sense in mid-sized shops and in any shop where the operator intends to use both plastics-clad and other materials for drawer components. (See Illus. 133.)

With wrap-around-type mitred ends on the drawer back, sides, and subfront, putting the box together with conventional glue and nails is no problem. We simply apply glue along the raw mitred ends to be joined, fold the component around a fairly tight fitting bottom, and drive brads at the one corner where there is no wrapped-over plastic. A conventional brad gun can be used for this nailing, providing that the fasteners are fairly narrow. If some chipping does result, the damage is easily concealed by locating that particular corner at the rear of the cabinet. We have only to designate the opposite end as subfront and attach it to the drawer face.

Blending

With respect to fabrication of drawer boxes from plastics-covered material, blending will usually mean the use of machined details to allow the box to be assembled with conventional glue and fasteners. Of course, any milling that enables the woodworker to get wood fibres on the drawer sides into contact with the raw wood fibres on the ends of the subfront and back will do the job for us.

It is probably obvious that mitre cutting is among the easiest processes for milling drawer-box details that will fulfill this need. We simply run both ends of a drawer-box member through a precise

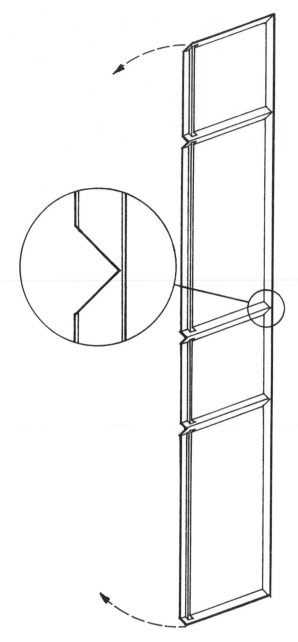

Illus. 132. Wrap-around drawer boxes are made with not-quite-through mitres. Obviously, locations of mitres must be exact.

mitring setup. After all, this can be exactly the same milling cut again and again. The trouble comes during assembly. First, each and every corner must be nailed, since this system of milling leaves no plastic to wrap over. Also, we need a firm, reliable means to hold each mitre joint while it is being nailed, meaning that we may very well

Illus. 133. A mitre-type drawer machine.

have to clamp each joint as the box is assembled—a rather time-consuming process. Wafer or spline joining is a solution to this alignment issue, but it requires cutting another set of precisely matching details.

Some conventional machinery will, of course, allow us to generate wrap-around-type mitres, most obviously the router. The router is fitted with a V-cutter. (See Illus. 134.) The bit can be set to project beyond the router base at exactly the correct depth to generate the type of cut desired. The trouble here is that setups can be time-consuming, particularly in custom shops where there can be a variety of different drawer widths and depths. Overall length dimensions and locations of the V-cut are different from drawer to drawer and must be determined and measured out independently and carefully. Therefore, it is most feasible to go through this type of drawer detailing either when time is of little concern or on a job where there are a number of drawer boxes with exactly the same widths and depths. When boxes have exactly the same width and depth, it is worthwhile to make a template for mitring all the boxes with a minimum of setups.

Milling details other than mitres may actually make better sense to the customizer. If all your drawer-box members are the same thickness, then possibly the simplest approach is to cut a rabbet on both ends of each drawer side to receive the back and subfront. The following are some of the advantages of this approach.

- All drawers can be milled for assembly on one setup, regardless of drawer width or depth.
- Only sides need milling.
- The necessary milling can be achieved by using a variety of equipment—such as a table or radial arm saw equipped with a dado head, router, or even hand tools.

Variations of the rabbeting method include the use of a dado for inserting the drawer back as well as the use of interlocking or semi-interlocking joints for building in the subfront. A dado joint in the rear and a double dado for the front (see Illus. 135) is one arrangement that can work fairly well. Some people argue that the loose particleboard core may have a tendency to crack between the front end of the drawer side and the dado cut into this piece. They are probably correct, but I have employed this system without any problem arising. Machining for a dado and a double dado will obviously take much longer than either rabbeting or mitring, but the parts fit together neatly, making a lovely drawer box. (See Illus. 136.)

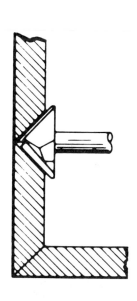
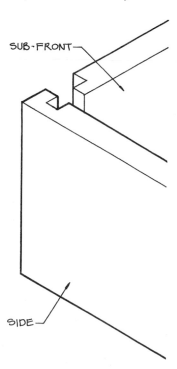

SUB-FRONT

SIDE

Illus. 134 (left). Wrap-around mitres can be milled with a router and V-cutter. (Courtesy of Safranek Enterprises.) Illus. 135 (right). Double dadoing can strengthen attachment of the front. There may be a tendency to crack at point A.

Illus. 136. Assembling a drawer box with dado and double-dado joints. Top: inserting the subfront. Middle: spreading glue to the side's exposed core. Bottom: nailing through plastic with a brad gun.

A semi-interlocking joint that can easily be used is the half French dovetail or bevelled rabbet. To create this joint, we can cut a reverse bevel into the ends of the subfront and then cut a matching bevel into the side's surface. (See Illus. 137.) Again, this works well with glue and brads.

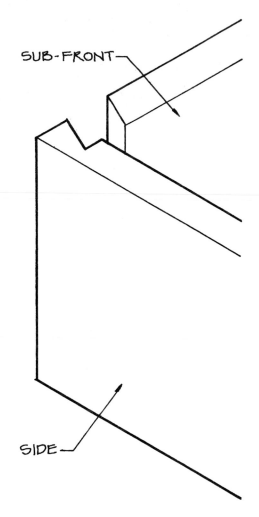

Illus. 137. The half French dovetail can be an effective box-joining detail, even with European-type materials.

Naturally, it is also possible to make old fashioned tail-and-pin dovetail joints with plastics-covered material, too, but that practice is getting pretty far removed from the notion of European cabinetry. In fact, some of the mill-work practices suggested here are not much in the spirit of modularized European furniture, but they are techniques that can allow traditionalists to incorporate plastics-covered sheet goods into their drawer making. If we really want to simplify the milling of plastics-covered drawer components, then maybe the best thing to do is nothing at all. In other words, one possibility is to butt components together and to join them with fasteners as we do elsewhere in the European cabinet. If the box components are held firmly together, as with clamps, then it is certainly feasible to drive either drywall screws or the deep-threaded European style screws to hold the box together. (See Illus. 138.) As when using screws to join

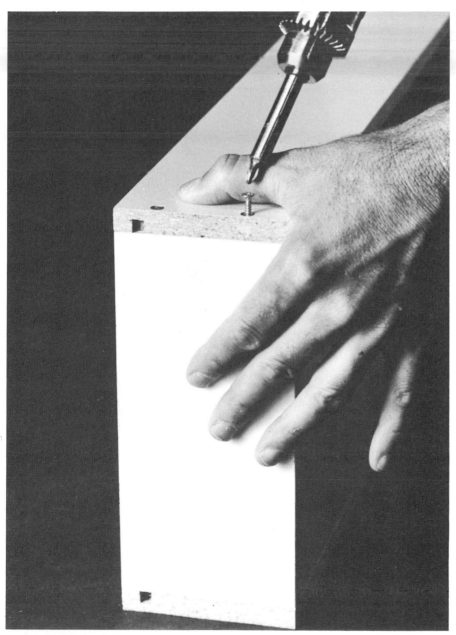

Illus. 138. European drawers can be assembled with screws.

box components, we need pilot, clearance, and countersink holes, accurately drilled, for this kind of fastening. (See Illus. 139.) A step drill is a great help. If you desire, you can even insert cover caps to hide screw heads and the large countersink holes. Screw-joined,

Illus. 139. Drilling the pilot hole for butt-joined, screw-reinforced drawers. Countersink and clearance holes were already drilled. For most reliable results, components should be clamped. For greater speed, a step drill could be used.

butted drawer components certainly have to be considered a real option for the builder of European styled pieces. This drawer-making system is simple and fast, as well as strong and accurate—and it can be used in any size shop. The all-rabbet system is also effective, especially for customizers and small shops.

Extruded-Plastic Components

In shops where drawer making is to be standardized around a modular system, drawers can be constructed from prefabricated lengths of extruded plastic. In fact, even the small shop operator can get involved with this type of drawer because it allows customization of drawer width while circumventing all the problems of dealing with preclad particleboard.

Extruded-plastic sides are paired. That is, they are produced as right-hand or left-hand sides. The sides have "fingers" that project inward to interlock with the drawer back. The sides are generally available in lengths close to 20 in. and heights around 3½ in., and thus not much customization is possible with these components in terms of drawer height or depth. The extruded back material comes in the same height dimensions as the sides, but it is available as a cut-to-length, 3-metre piece. This allows us to make our drawer boxes to virtually any desired width. The bottom is still usually cut independently, often from ⅛-in. prepainted hardboard.

With extruded-plastic drawers, there are usually no subfronts. Instead, the drawer fronts are affixed directly to the front of the drawer by means of small plastic clips or fixings. The clips are screwed directly onto the rear surface of the drawer front. The front ends of the drawer sides are designed specially to snap into position over these small plates. (See Illus. 140.) The drawer front itself must be slotted, of course, to receive the bottom panel—usually about 1 in.

Illus. 140.
Extruded-plastic drawer components. Note the fixings for attachment to the drawer front. (Courtesy of Hettich America Corporation.)

longer than the width of the bottom itself when the depth of the slot is approximately ¼ in. or slightly deeper. This depends partly upon the diameter of the blade you are using for slotting.

With prefabricated-plastic drawer parts such as this, it is often necessary to buy drawer glides that are specifically designed to work in conjunction with them. Be sure to check cost and availability of the whole system before you commit yourself to these components.

Wood and Plywood Components

Virtually any of the box construction techniques mentioned here will be effective when you are making drawer boxes from wood. In addition, you can butt-join your wood drawer boxes, simply using resin glue and nails or staples for a fastening system. Most cabinetmakers already have such systems in place in their own shops.

Perhaps what needs saying here is a word or two on when to use wood or plywood drawer parts in conjunction with a European cabinet. The answer is actually "whenever you want to," but I rather prefer some consistency in this regard. When I build or even see a European styled piece of furniture made out of wood-veneer-covered material, such as a desk or a bureau, I expect to see its drawers made from solid lumber or veneer-faced plywood. When the cabinet interior is made from melamine-faced material (or something similar), regardless of what the exterior is made from, I fully expect to see the same melamine-clad material (or extruded plastic) used for the drawer boxes.

EUROPEAN HARDWARE

Some of the greatest respect shown for European cabinetmaking is for its hardware systems. Probably the one thing that people like best about European drawer glides is their smooth, quiet operation. People also like the full concealment of European hinges; but perhaps woodworkers in particular enjoy them the most because they are so easy to adjust. (See Illus. 141.)

European Hinge Mounting

European hinges consist of three basic parts:

- the hinge cup—the part that secures the hinge to the door and that also creates space within the depth of the door for the mechanism itself to operate,
- the mounting plate—the part that secures the hinge to the cabinet box or face frame, and
- the hinge arm, or cranking—the part that links the cup to the mounting plate and that actually rotates the doors.

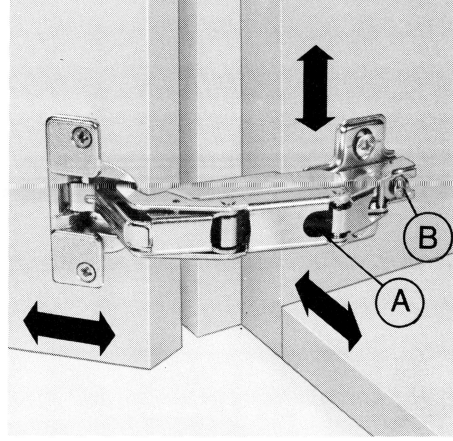

Illus. 141. By manipulation of four screws, the cabinetmaker is able to adjust a door up and down, in and out, and sideways. (Courtesy of Hettich America Corporation.)

As manufactured and shipped from the factory, the cranking and the cup are already joined together as they are to be used. The mounting plate is separate.

The first task in mounting European door hinges is to drill into the rear face of the door for placement of the hinge cup. This hole is always 35 mm (~1 ⅜ in.) in diameter, but its depth can vary somewhere between 10 mm and 13.5 mm or so, depending on the hinge model and manufacturer. There are other variables, too, particularly if you are using 32-mm-spaced holes of the case's vertical hole line to affix the mounting plates.

In order to locate the 35-mm hole in relation to the door's outside edge, you will generally have to consult the manufacturer's specifications. Again, this is a factor of door overlay, end-panel thickness, reveal, and application. For most Blum hinges, for example, this distance from the outer edge of the door to the closest point of the circular-cup mounting hole (called the drilling distance) is usually between 3 mm and 6 mm (⅛ in. to ¼ in.). (See Illus. 142.) Once you have determined the location, you can drill the 35-mm hole with a conventional drill press by making use of a special drill bit that generates a flat-bottomed hole. (See Illus. 143.)

There are basically two methods for securing the hinge cup to the door, either press-in or screw-on. With screw-on cups, drilling is complete as soon as you have drilled your 35-mm-diameter hole. The hinge cup is simply aligned properly and affixed with two screws. This is not so with the press-in variety. These require drilling two more holes, usually 8 mm or 10 mm in diameter, into which nylon fittings can be inserted. These nylon fittings have tiny ridges to prevent withdrawal, and they already have screws in them to allow the

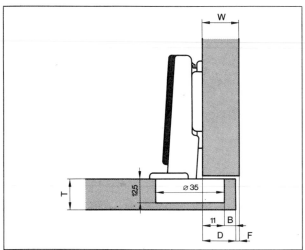 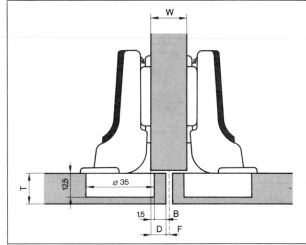

Door overlay D = 11 + Drilling distance B

Reveal F =
Side panel thickness W − Door overlay D

Door overlay D = 1,5 + Drilling distance B

Reveal F =
$\dfrac{\text{Side panel thickness W}}{2}$ − Door overlay D

Illus. 142. Variation in drilling distance is dictated by several factors. (Courtesy of Julius Blum Inc.)

mounting plate's removal, if necessary. With the three holes drilled, the hinge cup can be pressed in with an insertion machine or tapped in with a mallet.

Woodworkers who are using face-frame mounting plates or those not using a vertical hole line for mounting the door to the cabinet will find that placing the hinges vertically along the height of the door is really an arbitrary matter. These, also, are simply screwed in place when the door has been correctly aligned vertically. On the other hand, cabinetmakers who are using the vertical hole line for hinge attachment must take pains to make sure that they get a perfect match between the spacing of the hinges on the door and the spacing of the mounting plates on the cabinet. This calls for some very careful measuring.

European tooling specifically designed for precisely locating and drilling hinge-insertion holes will obviously be a real help in some shops—more than likely in medium-sized and larger shops where there is a fairly steady demand for this sort of hinging.

Perhaps the most important tool for hinging is a drilling jig. (See Illus. 144.) It is imperative to have such a jig in any size shop if you are attempting to use the entire hole system for hinge mounting. Such a jig, when used properly, allows for the accurate transfer of hinge-cup center location from case to door. A door drilling jig consists of a wand, fixed and moveable stops, locating pins, and marking or drilling plates. Naturally, in production shops where such locations are more standardized, such a concern becomes less vital.

The other important tool to possess is a boring-and-insertion machine. (See Illus. 145.) This machine will drill all three holes necessary for the installation of press-in hinges at once, and it will also

Illus. 143. A flat-bottomed boring bit. (Courtesy of Hettich America Corporation.)

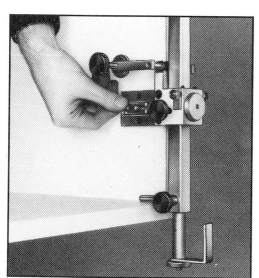
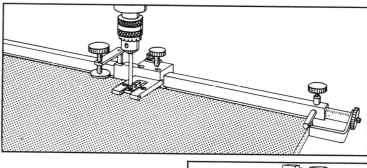
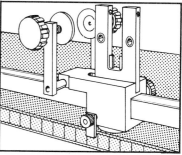

Illus. 144. A hinge-marking jig. (Courtesy of Häfele America Co.)

press them in snugly. Such a tool may not be terribly important in the small shop, where we have the option to screw on the hinges and mounting plates, but let us take a closer look at this issue. The

Illus. 145. A boring-and-insertion machine. (Courtesy of Häfele America Co.)

222

machine is obviously very similar to a drill press. By switching gear-boxes, the same drill press and boring-and-insertion machine may be able to fulfill a number of functions in the smaller wood shop. The right model, with the right accessories, can serve as a conventional drill press; it can drill horizontal and vertical hole lines, and even drill for hinges and insert them. It's best to buy such a tool, with its range of capabilities, if you are already in need of either a drill press or a European boring machine.

Blended Hinging Techniques

We have already noted that it is perfectly plausible to drill the large hinge-cup hole with an ordinary drill press. (See Illus. 146.) This is a valid approach to take if you are not installing large numbers of European concealed hinges. It would be ridiculous to drill holes for

Illus. 146. Even a small, inexpensive drill press can be used in the drilling of European hinges. Note the fence used to establish drilling distance and the reference mark used to line up the top end of this door.

the press-in nylon fittings unless you are able to accomplish in one plunge of the drill press the boring for all three holes required for nylon installation. You would not only have to change bits but also take special care to ensure that the three holes are perfectly placed in relation to each other. Most cabinetmakers, if they are using a conventional drill press for installing the hinge, also make the following adaptations in order to create a fairly functional system.

1. Drill only the hinge-cup holes for each hinge, using screws instead for the attachment of the hinge to the door.
2. Attach a fence to the rear of the drill-press table, as a means of controlling drilling distance.
3. Place marks on the fence to aid in hole positioning, lining up for each bore by aligning the top or bottom end of the door with a reference line. (See Illus. 146.)
4. Avoid using a vertical hole line for installing mounting plates—instead, use screws for the attachment to case and panels.
5. Attach the mounting plates to the cranking arm before attempting to fasten the plates to the cabinet end panels or face frame; this allows the door itself to be used as a measuring tool for transferring hinge location.

Of course, many cabinetmakers who use the drill press in this way soon invest in a gearbox and press-in attachment that will allow them to use the nylon fittings to attach the hinge cup to the door. They can naturally continue attaching the mounting plate with screws, as just described.

There are not many options to a drill press or boring machine for the mounting of European hinge cups, but one that can work well is the router. Of course, woodworkers who have a drill press will prefer to use one of the European 35-mm drill bits, but not every small shop is so equipped. When I did my first job requiring European hinges, I had no drill press and no money to buy one. Of course, my solution was to make a jig that would allow the straight bit in a router to do the job.

Such a jig is accurate as well as easy and inexpensive to make. It consists of a flat board (approximately 7 to 10 in. wide) with a round hole cut through it. The diameter of this hole must be somewhat larger than 35 mm because the router will follow its course by virtue of a template guide. In fact, the hole in the template should be larger than 35 mm by exactly the difference between the diameters of the router bit and the template guide in your router. For example, if your template guide has an outside diameter of ¾ in. and your straight bit cuts a ½-in. swath, then the difference in diameters is ¼ in. (~6.4 mm). Thus, you would need to cut a hole in your template that is

41.4 mm (~1 ⅝ in.) in diameter. A hardwood strip is fastened to the bottom as a fence to establish drilling distance. (See Illus. 147.)

To use the jig, you only have to measure out the location of each hole, clamp the jig into the door in the correct place, and guide the router around the hole in your jig by means of the template guide.

Still, both setting up and milling the holes go faster with a drill press and a 35-mm bit, faster yet with the boring-and-insertion machine.

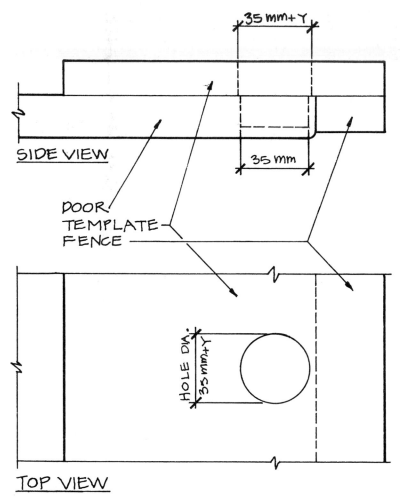

Illus. 147. A jig for routing hinge-cup holes. Y is equal to the difference between the diameter of the bit you are using and the diameter of your template guide.

European Drawer Mounting

Most European drawer guides are manufactured with features to improve the smoothness and quietness of their operation. Most are epoxy coated and have what is called a "captive profile" on one side.

Captive profile refers to the shape of one of the case-mounted drawer runners that wraps around and more or less locks in the matching roller on one side. (See Illus. 148.) Guide members that are mounted on the box can be attached to drawer side surfaces, embedded into the box's surface (groove mounted), or fastened beneath the sides. Full-extension options and rear-mount sockets for face-frame con-

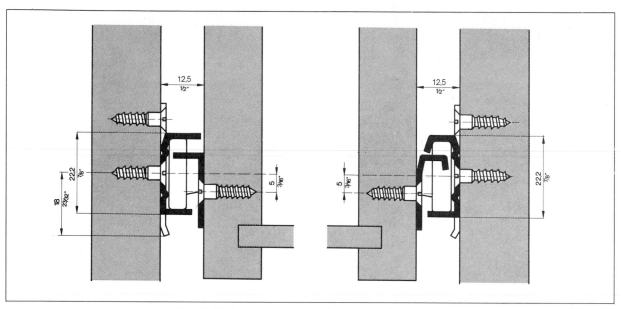

Illus. 148. A side-mounting drawer guide with a captive profile on right. (Courtesy of Julius Blum, Inc.)

struction are also available. (See Illus. 149.) As with traditional guides, each has specific applications.

Most European guides are made with case members that are spaced 2 mm ($\sim\frac{1}{16}$ in.) back from the face of the cabinet. (See Illus. 150.) Their mounting holes are located so that they can be attached by use of the vertical hole line. For example, there is one hole near the front that is exactly 35 mm (OC) back from the front of the guide. If we add the 2-mm spacing that is supposed to be employed between the front end of the guide member and the face of the cabinet, we have 37 mm—the exact amount of backset for the vertical hole line. Other mounting holes are spaced to the rear of this front hole, often in predictable spacings, such as 64 mm, 96 mm, or other 32-mm-based measurements. In production shops, overall depths of base cabinets can be determined in conjunction with these dimensions. In other words, an end panel's width can be calculated so that the 37-mm backsets at the front and rear will match the hole spacings of a particular drawer guide.

In most shops, even the larger ones, the drawer guide's case mem-

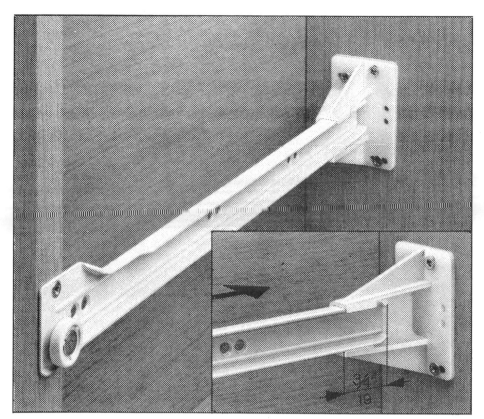

Illus. 149. European drawer guides can be attached directly to face frames and fastened into a socket at the rear. (Courtesy of Julius Blum, Inc.)

ber is attached with screws. When using the 37-mm backset vertical hole line for attachment, it is necessary either to insert 5-mm-diameter nylon expansion sockets into the holes prior to driving conventional wood screws, or else to employ the deep-threaded, fatter European screws made specifically for applications like this one.

In terms of drawer-guide mounting, many cabinetmakers do not see any great advantage in making use of the vertical hole line. We are still driving screws, after all. Of course, if we are driving fasteners into predrilled 5-mm holes, then accurate vertical alignment is already established, but you may already be aware of fast and accurate ways to achieve this. As we shall see, there are a number of such methods.

The primary means of attaching guide members to the drawer box itself is with wood screws. The process of attaching the side-mounting type of guide is a very conventional one for the traditional woodworker: It's a simple matter of driving screws directly through the holes provided in the guide-box member and into the drawer side. For attaching bottom-mount guides, we can either drive the screws through the bottom or through the side of the profile. (See Illus. 151.) However, driving wood screws through the bottom of the profile and into the edge of the drawer side will necessitate some variations in procedure.

If we attempt to drive screws into the side's bottom edge on a conventionally made drawer box, two problems will usually develop due to the way that the bottom was installed into slots. One problem is splitting. Since there is so little material between the slot and the drawer side's bottom edge, and since the material is the loosest particles in the core of the particleboard, it would be extraordinary if there were no splitting. The other problem with the conventionally fit bottom is that the bottom-driven screw will generally align with the exact place where the edge of the bottom meets the bottom of the slot into which it has been fit. There will be a strong tendency for the screw to force the components apart. The result is an unsquare

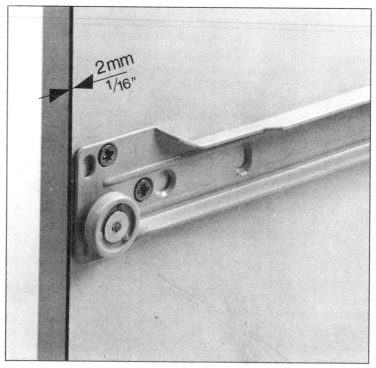

Illus. 150. Left-hand case-mounted member of a drawer guide. (Courtesy of Julius Blum, Inc.)

drawer box. The Europeans avoid this entire problem by constructing their drawer box differently when they plan to use the bottom-mounting-type hardware. They use no slots in the sides at all, but instead use a drawer bottom that overlays the drawer's sides. Screws can be driven through the profile, through the drawer bottom, and into the side's edge. (See Illus. 152.)

Illus. 151. With a drawer profile that wraps the bottom, we can drive screws into the sides' surfaces or their bottom edges.

Groove-mounted guides can be attached without alterations in box assembly, but we obviously have to mill a channel to accept the box profile itself. Since so little thickness of the material is left after cutting the channel, other means must be used to secure the member to the box. For example, a special tool can be used to expand prongs that lock the member into place. (See Illus. 153.)

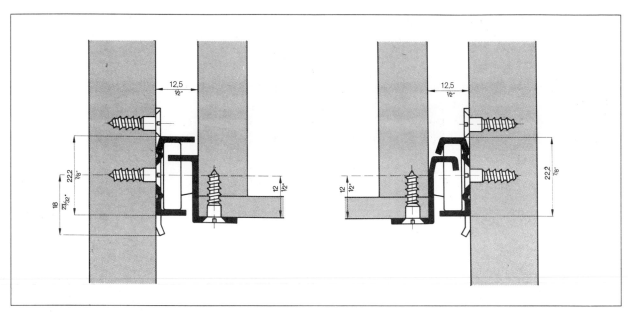

Illus. 152. A bottom-mounted drawer-guide system. Note the overlaid bottom. (Courtesy of Julius Blum, Inc.)

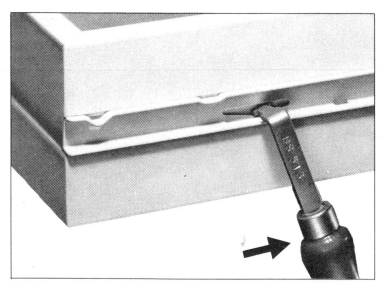

Illus. 153. A groove-mounted drawer profile. Note the special mounting tool used to expand the prongs. (Courtesy of Julius Blum, Inc.)

Blended Drawer Mounting

In exporting their fine hardware systems to America, the Europeans knew that the popularity of their products partly depended on making it easy for traditionalist woodworkers to install components using conventional tooling and fasteners.

A special profile mounting tool really simplifies the installation of drawers into the cabinet box. Several European hardware producers make such tools available in conjunction with their own drawer-guiding hardware. With this method, we simply insert the case-mount member of the drawer guide into the tool, hold the tool against the facing of the cabinet in the desired location, and attach the hardware with screws. (See Illus. 154.) The tool will do a good job of aligning hardware perfectly square in relation to the front edge of the

Illus. 154. Mounting a drawer-guide case member by using a mounting tool. (Courtesy of Julius Blum, Inc.)

cabinet. Again, the importance of precise, square-cut components should be clear.

Drawer-guide case members can also be attached to the end panels of a particular cabinet with the aid of a framing square or by simple measuring. This technique is easier before assembling the cabinet box. (See Illus. 155.)

Illus. 155. Epoxy-coated European drawer guides being attached with a framing square. Note the other blended techniques, such as dadoes.

If you decide to use European guides that wrap around the bottom and you want to use a conventional box, you can do so successfully by clamping the box across its bottom near each hole location, drilling a pilot hole for the full depth of the screw, and then driving the screw. (See Illus. 156.)

Illus. 156. Drilling a pilot hole with the bottom profile clamped in place.

It's important to note that when using a European drawer guide, we will often have to allow for more vertical clearance than we ordinarily do for conventional side-mount drawer guides. This is because the roller configuration on the European guides may necessitate lifting one roller over another.

If you want to incorporate European drawer guiding into your cabinet project, you can do so without making any major adaptations or buying any really expensive equipment.

SUMMARY

Doors can be called European based upon their hinging or their flat appearance. Generally though, we should probably accept the contemporary look as a necessary element in any definition of European doors.

Most often, European doors are made by cutting flat panels of clad particleboard and then edge-banding these panels. Some European styling includes flush inset doors, but most are overlaid.

Overall door dimensions are based on several factors, including material thicknesses, hinge type, overlay, and reveal. When a face frame is used in conjunction with European hinges, we usually based the width dimensions of stiles, rails, and mullions on our predetermined reveals and door overlays. To achieve a cutting-panel size, we simply subtract the thickness of the banding material for each edge.

In some shops, it may be plausible to generate the European look with solid-stock drawer fronts, but this can be very time-consuming. Veneer-core plywood can also be used with good effect. Both of these materials may create some difficulty with warpage; solid stock can also give us problems with shrinkage and expansion.

The three types of drawer boxes that can be used on the European cabinet are clad particleboard, extruded plastic, and (conventional) wood or plywood. Clad particleboard is functional and rather popular in cabinetry that is made from the same material, but it does require special treatment. Plastics-clad particleboard can be assembled via several techniques. The most modular, most standardized, and perhaps most truly European is the wrap-around mitring method. Others are the rabbet, the double dado, the bevel rabbet, and the screw-assembled butt joint. Equally European but offering fewer opportunities for customization is the extruded-plastic system, in which we buy drawer sides of predetermined length and fit them to our own drawer fronts and cut-to-length sections of fabricated back material. On a European style cabinet made of wood, we may want to include conventional wood drawer boxes.

In order to make use of European mounting hardware, we do not really need any special equipment. Yet with the doors in particular, some machinery or tooling can save a substantial amount of time for the production-oriented cabinetmaker. This is particularly true for door mounting, where a boring-and-insertion machine can reap some real benefits even in the medium-size shop.

RECOMMENDATIONS

Medium-sized cabinet shops need to offer a line of contemporary European styled doors if they want to compete with the larger companies. The style is here to stay. But for such cabinet shops, it may be wisest to order prefabricated doors from a door-making factory. This is probably a reality that is hard to get around. If they want to make their own Euro-style doors, the mid-sized cabinet firms will either have to restrict their product line and put some money into a good edge bander, or develop markets that allow them to customize.

In the small shop, especially where customization is respected, the woodworker should not hesitate to experiment with new contemporary styles as well as variations of the styles that already exist. Of course, when making doors with plastics cladding, it is necessary to use material with a particleboard core. But when making doors with a veneer face, veneer-core plywood is probably superior. The thickness of veneer-core plywood is not a critical issue for doors. Its minimal warpage is easy to compensate for by virtue of the adjustability of European hinges, and its light weight makes it a pleasure to work with. When generating a European look on a project, though, solid stocks should only be used when the entire job consists of fairly narrow components.

For an edge-banding process, customizers ought to focus on thick edgings, although a hot-air edge bander can allow them to produce doors with rolled edgings very quickly. The thicker edgings may allow some aesthetic expression. They are also less likely to be reproduced somewhere else with an automatic edge bander.

I love the notion of the wrap-around drawer box, too, and the tool can pay for itself fairly quickly in many shops. I have used the dado-double-dado system with success, but I prefer the simplicity of the all-rabbet approach. The virtues of plastics-clad materials for drawer boxes are fairly obvious.

In terms of tooling, you shouldn't overlook the value of a drawer-mounting jig. If you want to use the vertical hole line for mounting doors, it will be pretty hard to do without a hole-location jig for purposes of exact hole placement.

Finally, with the growing popularity of European hinges, it is probably best to improve drill-press technology in every small shop. The most versatile purchase you can make is a boring machine that allows you to do conventional drilling, system line boring, as well as hinge drilling and insertion, by merely changing the boring gearboxes.

6
ASSEMBLING THE CABINET

A NEW METHODOLOGY

Cabinetmakers who are committed to the 32-mm cabinet-construction system base the entire assembly stage of their operation on hole lines. They do not need to stock great supplies of glue, nails, or sandpaper; they do not need a wide variety of tools, as traditional woodworkers do. In fact, 32-mm modular manufacturers do not even need to depend on highly skilled labor for assembling their products. With precisely cut and bored cabinet components, the cabinet assembler only needs to follow very simple instructions to put together a cabinet box, attach its accessories and levellers, and have it completely ready for shipping. European assembly methodology, after all, is simply a matter of installing a series of fasteners. This is a radical departure from traditional cabinetmaking in which the cabinet assembler must have a wide range of skills as well as some good judgment.

The line-boring system can be used in conjunction with several types of connectors, but they fall into two broad categories: dowels and assembly fittings. The assembly fittings can either be two-piece or one-piece connectors.

If we define European cabinetry as line-boring-based assembly, then the system is truly different from the traditional method for building the box. Still, dowel construction has a very long history, and so does one-piece fastener construction—the sort based on simply driving screws to attach one part to another. Perhaps instead of looking for differences between the traditional and the European systems, we should be focusing on those factors that they both hold in common.

Assembly, in both the traditional and the European systems, is the step that takes longest to complete. If you have ever worked in or visited a medium-sized traditional shop, you undoubtedly noticed that more workers were involved in cabinet assembly than in any other phase of the operation. This is probably true in the smallest shops, too. A cabinet project that takes a ½ hour to design and 2 hours to cut out and machine can take 5 or 6 hours to assemble and send. A similar situation exists with 32-mm construction. The assembly step can be the bottleneck in the preparation of European cabinets. Some owners of modular 32-mm shops report that the flow of production must be matched specifically to the shop's assembling operations. This is a good idea not only because assembly takes a bit longer than the other steps in production, but also because storage can be a problem. In high-volume shops, it is important that cabinets not be assembled too soon. There must not be a mountain of cabinetry to contend with in the shop. Large shops deal with this potential problem in two ways. First, they ship some cabinetry RTA (ready to assemble), packed flat in boxes. Second, they make it a goal to assemble cabinetry just before sending it out to the job site for installation.

Obviously, hobbyists and operators of small shops do not have the same assembly problems to deal with as do modular producers. Nevertheless, these customizers, these lower-volume producers, still have to spend a substantial amount of time in assembly. However, depending on certain variables, such as the available tooling and the materials used, they may spend less time in assembly than in other phases of their own "European" cabinetmaking.

When cabinetmakers reach the assembly stage of their European operation, they will generally be following these steps:

1. joining the box components,
2. attaching the back,
3. mounting accessories such as doors and drawers (as described in Chapter 5), and
4. attaching levellers or another base, if necessary.

Of course, if we are using solid wood or veneer in any primary surfaces, we may have to interrupt this process at certain points for sanding. Natural wood and wood veneer also require finishing after assembly is completed.

In this chapter, we will first look at the purest European methods: dowel assembly and fitting assembly. Then, of course, we will examine some alternatives.

DOWEL ASSEMBLY

To join flat panels with 8-mm dowels, there are two key considerations beyond the proper milling of the components. Proper spreading of a measured amount of glue is important. To make full use of the entire adhering surface of each dowel, glue should coat the entire dowel. There is no other way to get an effective dowel joint. We also do not want too much glue because it will slow curing and seep out where we do not want it. The other important matter is pressure. All cabinetmakers who use dowels for the joining of flat panels will attest to the need for clamping while the joint sets. There is some expensive machinery capable of fulfilling these two important functions, of course.

Think of a nail gun. Then imagine that your nail gun shoots dowels instead of nails. That is exactly the notion put into practice for the most rapid insertion of dowels. Such a "dowel gun" is pneumatically driven and receives a continuous feed of both glue and dowels. The gun can be activated to dispense a carefully metred film of resin glue into each hole being used for assembly. It can be triggered in a different way to actually inject the 8-mm dowel. In minutes, the operator can apply glue and inject dowels in all the holes in the ends of every horizontal member of a cabinet, then inject glue into the holes in the horizontal boring patterns, and thereby have a case that is ready to be put together.

Of course, you don't need to have a dowel gun such as this to distribute glue and insert dowels for the European cabinet. With accurately cut and drilled pieces, many smaller shops use the dowel-insertion methods, anyway. It is certainly viable to inject glue into holes with a glue bottle, but you should make a special effort to distribute the glue evenly inside the hole. A small brush can be used to apply the glue, or the glue can simply be "dumped" into each hole and then stirred about with a thin strip of wood. A 6-in. length of ¼-in. dowel serves well for a stirrer. The glue can also be applied to the dowel itself before insertion. Dowels can be tapped into their respective holes with a plastic mallet or small hammer.

With glue and dowels injected, it's now time to join the components and apply pressure for curing. Since the case will be square only if it is sitting perfectly square under pressure, you must make sure that pressures are applied perfectly flat and evenly.

In the large shop, clamping is by means of a large stationary case clamp. (See Illus. 157.) This is a large tool into which an entire assembled cabinet can be placed for curing under pressure. Stationary case clamps are large and heavy, but their heavy steel frames mean precision and long service. Most are pneumatically operated and quite expensive.

A more realistic investment for all but the largest shops is a set of bar-type case clamps. These are similar to the bar clamps you are used to. In fact, it is possible to use conventional bar clamps as case clamps so long as the case sits flat and square as it cures.

The case will generally need to sit under pressure for a matter of minutes. At normal room temperature, which is the proper working

Illus. 157. A stationary case clamp for modular cabinetry. Cabinetry cured in such a clamp will come out perfectly square. (Courtesy of Altendorf America.)

temperature of the glue, the dowel joints should be cured within a half hour. When curing is complete, the cabinet is ready for the back attachment and installation of accessories.

Preattachments

In practice, the installation of a back and even the mounting of accessory hardware can be accomplished prior to the gluing and clamping procedures. Such priorities are really design decisions. In many shops, the back is inserted into its slots as the other box components are being glued and attached. When the case gets clamped, the back panel is already in place. This procedure allows all four of the back's edges to fit into slots and helps in ensuring that the cabinet box turns out square. Other shops prefer to slide the back into place after the rest of the box components have been dowelled together, usually from the top. The back panel fits into slots on three edges and can be attached to the rear edge of the cabinet's top panel. Some cabinetmakers believe that this method helps to simplify the actual dowel-assembly operation. It also allows the assembler to reach in easily from the rear and make minor adjustments to drawer and slide-out hardware.

It may also be easier to attach some door and drawer hardware to the end panels prior to assembly, especially if you are making full use of the vertical hole pattern for accessory attachment. The standardized spacing allows this technique to work. Modular 32-mm manufacturers almost always follow this procedure. The advantage is that it is so much easier to attach the drawer case profiles and mounting plates to panels that are lying flat on the workbench. Besides that, the location of the hardware has to be predetermined, and the assembler needs only to count holes to determine correct placement. Measuring is not necessary at all.

If hardware is mounted in 5-mm holes prior to assembly, careful planning is essential so that accessories will match properly. The centers of hinge cups fixed into the doors must be exactly the same distance apart as the centers of corresponding mounting plates attached to the end panel. Keep in mind that, although the mounting plates will be exactly the same distance from the center of the door opening, the hinge cups may not measure the same from the door's center. This is because overlays may not be the same at the top and bottom of the door opening.

For example, consider a base cabinet with the ordinary drawer-over-door arrangement as base unit 1 from Illus. 36. (Refer back to Illus. 36.) The door opening is 624 mm high; we are using 16-mm stock. If we attach the mounting plate by use of the second and third holes (from top to bottom), then the center of the top mounting plate is 72 mm below the drawer rail and the bottom mounting plate is centered 72 mm above the cabinet bottom. Center to center, the plates are 480 mm apart $(624 - 72 - 72)$. To determine hinge-cup positioning, we have to consider overlays. Presume we are designing towards a 3-mm reveal. This will mean a 13-mm overlay (full overlay) at the bottom and a 6.5-mm overlay (half overlap) at the top. Suppose we elect to increase the reveal between the door and drawer to 4 mm and do away with our half-millimetre measurements. (Larger reveals are a help in adjustment.) Thus, we will have an overall door height of 643 mm $(624 + 6 + 13)$. The bottom hinge cup will be centered 85 mm $(72 + 13)$ from the door's bottom end, while the top hinge cup must be centered 78 mm $(72 + 6)$ from the door's top end. The cups will be exactly 480 mm apart $(643 - 85 - 78)$, just as the mounting plates are.

Similar figuring must be performed in order to position the drawer front. Assume we have a conventional-style countertop that covers the top 19 mm of the cabinet front (refer back to Illus. 31, B). Thus, we need to add a 6-mm overlay for the bottom of the drawer opening, but in fact we have to subtract 6 mm at the top of the drawer to allow for the top that projects 3 mm $(19 - 16)$ into the drawer opening, as well as for a 3-mm gap. Overall dresser-front height is therefore exactly the same as opening height—112 mm. (Refer back to Illus. 34.) Presume we are using bottom-mounting drawer guides that raise the drawer's bottom approximately 6 mm above the drawer rail, and that we make the box 90 mm in height to make sure that it can be tilted into its space. When we mount the box to the subfront, we need to allow for the 6-mm overlay of the drawer front and the 6-mm "raise" created by our chosen drawer guides. In other words, the bottom edge of the drawer must be exactly 12 mm above the front's bottom edge. This will leave 10 mm from the top of the box to the top of the drawer front.

Naturally, to make this full use of the vertical hole line, you must plan out all these factors as part of your general designing before you cut or drill anything. A proper fit is taken care of by correct dimen-

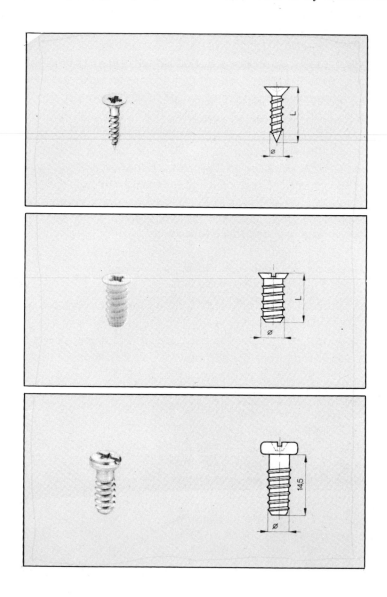

Illus. 158. A wood screw (at top) and two types of Euro-screws for mounting accessories. O is #6 or 7 for the wood screws, but equals 5 mm for the Euro-screws. (Courtesy of Julius Blum, Inc.)

sioning, and correct dimensioning is accomplished in the layout stage.

In any case, if you decide to attach case-mounted hardware before assembly, the process is extremely simple. The assembler first lays both end panels down flat on a workbench and then counts holes for positioning. In the base-cabinet example we have been using, presume that 8-mm dowel holes have been bored for attachment of the bottom, the two front rails, and the rear rail. Hinge mounting plates will be attached with screws going into the second and third holes above the bottom dowel holes, and the second and third holes below the drawer-rail dowel holes. Drawer members will be secured into the hole immediately above the drawer rail as well as the other 5-mm holes that line up with it horizontally. (Refer back to Illus. 27.) Then screws will be driven—either the 5-mm shanked Euro screws, or narrower wood screws, for which ribbed-nylon expansion sockets must first be driven in with a hammer, just as explained in the previous chapter. (See Illus. 158.)

If the back was not inset during the gluing of the other case members, it should be slid into its slots immediately after the curved case comes out of the clamps. Staples or a few screws should be driven through the rear surface of the back panel and into the rear edge of the top or top rail. This adds rigidity.

Attaching Levellers and Cabinet Hangers

With the basic box put together and the back inserted, the next step is to install levellers in the base or tall cabinet—or cabinet hangers in the wall cabinet.

There are several different types of base-levelling units that can be used in a base or tall cabinet. Some can be adjusted from the inside of the cabinet. (See Illus. 159.) Others must be adjusted by removal of the clip-on toe kick, but they have the advantage of invisibility. The fixing hole does not break a primary or secondary surface. (See Illus. 160.)

Base levellers are attached by virtue of holes, bored at a diameter somewhere between 10 mm and 15 mm. Since the toe kick will be mounted directly to the base levellers with clips, careful placement of the holes is important. If you use this type of toe-kick attachment, be sure to plan your boring pattern on hardware specifications that will control the location of your toe-kick boards. Hole diameter and depth are also those specified by the particular manufacturer. Boring can be performed as a part of the total line-boring operation, or with jigs, as an interruption in the assembly process.

Levellers actually consist of several parts, as indicated in Illus.

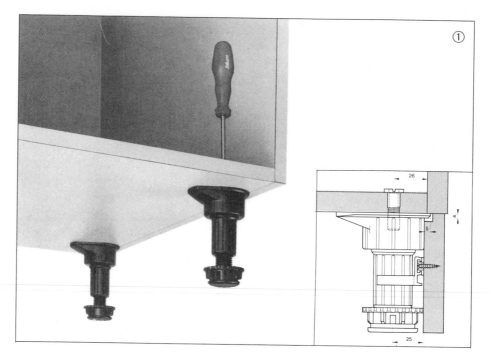

Illus. 159. Base levellers such as this one can be adjusted from inside the cabinet. Note the asymmetrical section of the fixing block, the flange, which can be turned to support an adjacent cabinet. (Courtesy of Julius Blum, Inc.)

160. The portion at the top of the fixture—called variously a dowel plate, mounting plate, or fixing block—is securely mounted to the bottom panel of the cabinet. To attach the type requiring a through hole, follow these steps.

1. Insert the fixing screw from the top side of the cabinet bottom.
2. Finger-tighten the mounting plate onto the fixing screw where it protrudes below the bottom panel.
3. Tighten the fixture from above with a screwdriver and install a cover cap to cover the screw where it is visible inside the cabinet.

The type of mounting plate that affixes in a stopped hole (as in Illus. 160) is simply pressed or tapped into place. Then a locking screw is often driven. With either type of fixture, the actual leg or elevating support should be left unattached until installation.

You can prepare for the plinth, or toe kick, for modular cabinetry such as this in a couple of ways. One way is to prepare a toe-kick section for each individual piece of cabinetry. This is usually an effective approach only when entire levellers are secured to the cabinet. The advantage is in production sorts of shops. Toe kicks can be fitted precisely, and there is no likelihood of a mixup in terms of forgetting components. Further, there is less on-site labor involved because the kickboards do not have to be cut to length or fitted with mounting clips. All this work is taken care of by the assembler. Of course, the drawback is that there will be a seam between each segment of kick panel. In fact, adjacent sections of pattern material may not even match.

Of course, the other method is to send lengths of toe-kick material to the job site for cutting to length. A continuous panel can be used to cover the open space beneath two or more base units. This undoubtedly looks better, but it involves a bit more on-site work.

Toe-kick clips are installed by insertion into a slot cut into the rear face of the toe-kick material, or they are simply attached with screws to the kick panel.

Wall cabinets, if they are to be attached according to European methodology, must be fitted with hanger hardware. To prevent detrimental forces from being exerted on frameless European cabinetry, wall cabinets are not actually fastened to the wall at all. Instead, wall cabinets are more or less hooked onto a steel rail that is mounted to the wall. (See Illus. 161.)

The hanging fixture should be installed in the European wall cabinet just after the back has been inserted. It is necessary to cut a notch in the back panel before affixing the hanger, and it's probably slightly easier to do this notching before the back has been put in place. It is also necessary to cut a notch into the end panel so that it will clear the hanging rail, but this can be done at the time of installation.

The hanger fitting is attached to the upper-back portion of the end panel after its "hook" portion has been passed through the notch in the back panel. Many of the fittings are designed to be fastened into holes of the vertical boring pattern; others can simply be attached with wood screws driven directly into the end panel's surface, as indicated in Illus. 161.

With the case assembled, the back in place, and the hanger or

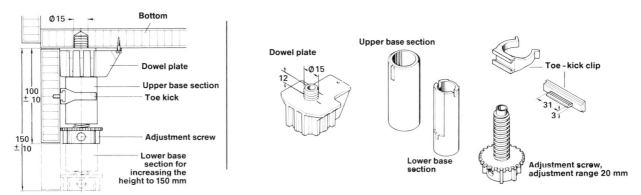

Illus. 160. This base leveller is not visible inside the cabinet; it must be adjusted from below. (Courtesy of Häfele America Co.)

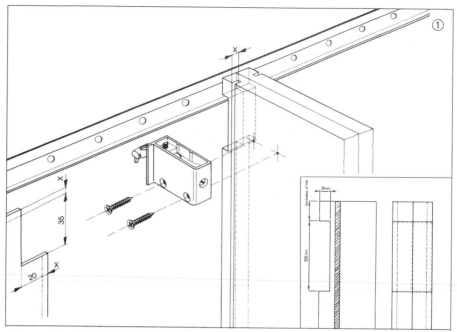

Illus. 161. European rail-and-hanger system for installing wall cabinetry. Note the notches that must be cut in the back panel and the end panel. (Courtesy of Julius Blum, Inc.)

leveller hardware in place, basic cabinet construction is complete, except for placement of the doors, drawers, and other accessories. In the previous chapter, we pointed out the techniques and the tooling required for attaching doors and drawers. In the European hole-line system, doors—with their hinge cups in place—and drawers—with their guide components attached—should actually fit right into their designated spots, needing only the least amount of adjustment.

The assembler may also need to attach other minor components—such as door and drawer bumpers, cover caps, perhaps even adjustable shelves held in place by shelf supports from beneath and plastic hold-downs from above. (See Illus. 162.) There may be other hardware called for as well, but all of it should be compatible with the 32-mm-spaced, 5-mm-diameter, 37-mm backset vertical hole line.

FITTINGS ASSEMBLY

There can be several reasons to assemble your European cabinetry with assembly fittings or connectors rather than with dowels. For one thing, they can completely eliminate the need for glue in the assembly operation. What may be more significant is that they can free the cabinetmaker from having to perform clamping operations. Woodworkers may also want to build certain cabinet units with releasable

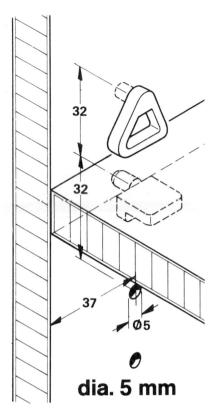

32

32

37

Ø5

dia. 5 mm

Illus. 162. Even shelf hold-down devices are based on the 32-mm system. (Courtesy of Häfele America Co.)

joints, or, for the sake of compact shipping, they may want to pack and send RTA (ready-to-assemble) furniture units. We shall also see that assembly with certain types of metal fittings can make the cabinetmaker less dependent on true hole lines. In fact, the small scale shop can easily incorporate some of these connectors with a minimal investment in new tooling and still build cabinets that are entirely "European."

Two-Piece-Connector Systems

In the chapter on line boring, we already noted the basis upon which the two-piece-connector system works, but perhaps it would serve us well to review it here briefly.

Two-piece-connector systems are nearly all based on the operation of an eccentric mechanism that locks components together. The eccentric portion of the fitting is designed to fit into round holes drilled into the surface of the horizontal members. The location of this hole, almost always close to the end of the horizontal panel, is dictated by the length of the bolt portion of the fitting. Another hole must sometimes be drilled into the horizontal piece, a hole bored into the end of the panel and deep enough to reach the hole drilled for the eccentric. (Refer again to Illus. 99.) With some of the fittings, it is only necessary to drill one hole into the horizontal members for each fitting; the large-diameter surface hole is located close enough to the end of the panel so that the boring bit actually overhangs the end of the panel by a small amount. This is what creates the entry for the fixing bolts. And, of course, there must be a matching hole bored into the surface of the end panel, one of the holes in the horizontal pattern. This matching hole is usually 5 mm in diameter, although it is possible to use one of the larger 8-mm or 10-mm dowel holes for this type of fitting, too.

Most European hardware producers market a line of eccentrics designed to fit a 15-mm hole drilled into the surface of the horizontal member. Others will fit a hole with a diameter of 20 mm, 25 mm, or even 28 mm. Since they are precisely machined to line up exactly with a fixing bolt that passes through the exact center of the horizontal member's thickness, the eccentrics are available for several different panel thicknesses. (See Illus. 163.)

Illus. 163. Shown here are 15-mm-diameter eccentrics, fixing bolts, nylon inserts, and cover caps. This is Häfele's "Minifix 15" series. (Courtesy of Häfele America Co.)

Most of the 15-mm and 20-mm eccentrics can be inserted into their surface hole with mere finger pressure. When horizontal and vertical cabinet components are set together, the assembler can turn the whole eccentric to lock the parts together. Tightening can be done with a slotted or Phillips screwdriver or with an Allen key. (See Illus. 164.)

Many of the eccentric fittings that are installed right at the end of a horizontal member have a flat side and make use of a slightly different eccentric tightening system. Since the fixture itself does not rotate, it is often held firmly in place by virtue of nylon ribbing. Most such fittings must be installed by tapping in with a hammer or with a press-in insertion machine. Where great resistance to lateral movement is required, some of these hardware fixtures fit into a secondary attachment hole. This type, too, is usually fastened by nylon ribs and must be inserted with firm pressure.

Illus. 164. Full, round eccentric fillings are easy to tighten with conventional tools. The plastic type can even be tightened with a coin. (Courtesy of Hettich America Corporation.)

With the eccentric portion of the fitting in place, the assembler must next install the fixing bolts into the surface of the end panels. Again, this is extremely simple. Most of the bolts have a slotted or cross-point head on one end and threads on the other so that they can be easily driven. Threads may be wood-screw style or Euro-screw style. Of course, the wood-screw style can make a lot of sense to customizers who want to minimize the amount of boring they do because these screws can be driven with a mere pilot hole, but they are more reliably driven into nylon expansion fittings or bushings that are first tapped into 5-mm holes. The Euro-style threads are for driving the bolt directly into 5-mm holes. Naturally, there are also ribbed models designed for insertion into the larger nylon bushings. There are even some bolts made for the attachment of two horizontal panels to the same end panel, actually allowing the end panel to be used as a partition. These have no threads but rather a head at each end to fit into eccentric fittings in both horizontal patterns. Other specialty bolts are available also.

The assembler simply drives each fixing bolt into the vertical panel with a screwdriver as far as possible. Most fixing bolts are made so that the threaded portion ends at a flange or at a thicker portion of metal. When the bolt is tightened all the way to the flange, it protrudes exactly the right amount to reach the eccentric properly. If not tightened far enough, the eccentric may not achieve enough "pull" against the bolt head. Because of the flange, it is almost impossible to overtighten.

With all bolts and all eccentric fixtures in place, the cabinet can be assembled. I think it best to lay one of the end panels down on the workbench with the fixing bolts sticking up perpendicular. Then each horizontal component can be attached, one at a time, by aligning the holes in the ends of each piece to slip down over the matching fixing bolts and dropping into place. Of course, before you attempt to lift, align, and drop each piece, you should make sure that each eccentric fitting is turned with its open side, the entry side of the fitting, facing out towards the end panel. This will allow penetration of the bolt head that it will be embracing. By stabilizing the horizontal member (sitting vertically atop the end panel) with one hand, you can still very easily use the other hand to tighten the eccentric fitting with your chosen tool. If the components were drilled with the kind of accuracy that is expected in the European system, they should align perfectly.

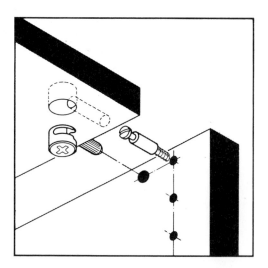

Illus. 165. Eccentric operation here first makes the bolt head captive and then exerts pressure on it. (Courtesy of Hettich America Corporation.)

Once all horizontal parts have been attached to one end, the assembler may want to insert the back if it is the type to be set into slots on all four edges. Then the other end panel can be fastened. Make sure that the open portion of all the eccentrics is turned outward again, and then lower the end panel into place by guiding the protruding bolts into their respective holes. Once the eccentric fittings have been turned to hold the components together, the cabinet is virtually assembled. If the back was not inserted earlier, then this is the time to slip it in and fasten it.

The type of eccentric fitting with one flat end, the type that is inserted right at the end of the horizontal member, involves only a slightly different technique. First, there are no end holes through which to guide a bolt. The horizontal components can be positioned by simply slipping the open U-shaped part of the fitting down around the protruding bolt head. Since the fitting itself does not turn, the eccentric is operated by turning an angularly arranged screw. The mechanism closes off the open end of the U-shape, making the bolt head captive, and then exerts force against the bolt head. (See Illus. 165.)

Other aspects of assembly, such as mounting accessories and attaching levellers or hangers, can then proceed much as described in the previous section on dowel-type cabinet assembly.

There are a few other styles of the two-piece-connector system that we should look at because they call for changes in the assembly system just described.

One different style involves the drilling for and inserting of the cam fixture into the end panel. Fixing bolts can then be driven into the ends of the horizontal cabinet members. The eccentric is operated again by means of an angularly positioned screw. (See Illus. 166.) Variations include the replacement of the metal fixing bolt with a plastic fitting. (See Illus. 167.)

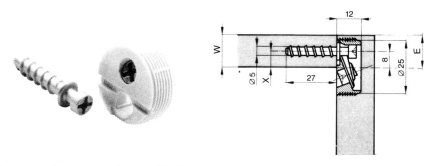

Illus. 166. This style of assembly fitting involves drilling the surface of the end panel with a large hole. The fixing bolt is simply screwed into the end of the horizontal panel. (Courtesy of Julius Blum, Inc.)

Illus. 167. In the application, the cam will be tightened around a plastic "dowel."

Still another type of two-piece assembly fitting is the surface-mounted variety. Of course, the fittings are more in the way than flush types of fittings, but they ensure high stability. They can be screwed in place or press-fitted into predrilled holes. (See Illus. 168.)

Once the cabinet box members, including the back, have been put together, assembly can continue with the mounting of doors and drawers along with the attachment of levellers and cabinet hangers. This process can proceed just as described in the earlier dowel-assembly section of our discussion.

Two-piece connectors are an excellent idea for cabinetmakers who want to make use of the hole lines for purposes of assembly. They allow us to construct real European 32-mm-based cabinetry without glue and wood dowels and without clamps. The fittings are not visible outside the cabinet, and most are functionally out of the way on the interior of the cabinet. They are extremely simple to install with only a minimum of training and tools. This assembly system also makes good sense for users who want to assemble their own furniture or for those who want to be able to tear down furniture for shipping.

One-Piece-Connector Systems

One-piece connectors are probably the easiest and fastest connectors that can be used to assemble the European cabinet. They are actually simple screws with some special design elements. The threads are

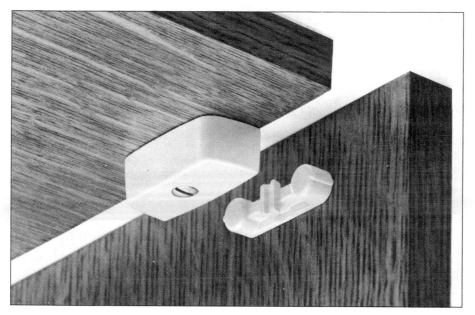

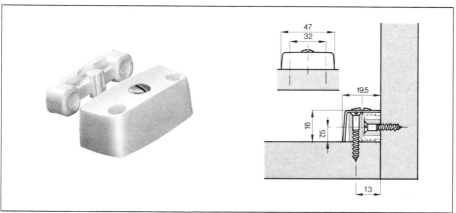

Illus. 168. A surface-mounted, two-piece corner fitting. This model is attached with screws. (Courtesy of Julius Blum, Inc.)

straight and especially deep cut to yield maximum holding power. (Refer again to Illus. 103.)

As noted in Chapter 4, we actually do not need to perform line boring at all to make these connectors work. Instead, we do assembly boring. In other words, we perform the boring operations as the cabinet is being put together. Basically, we set the cabinet components together as they are to be joined, clamp them firmly, drill, and finally drive the fasteners from the cabinet's exterior. The joints are still releasable, and the components can be taken apart and reassembled a number of times using the same holes and fasteners.

To assemble the cabinet box with one-piece connectors, we usually work with the back edges against the workbench rather than the way we would work with two-piece fittings. The system is similar to the usual assembly approach for traditional cabinetry, but the reasons are different. With traditional cabinetry, the assembler works with the front edge up so that it will be easy to even up the front edges of the components, and so that the face frame can go on right after the box is assembled. With most of the cabinet pieces exactly the same width resting edgewise on a flat table, there should not be any alignment problems with our European cabinet. The reason to assemble the European cabinet face up is so that it can be properly clamped in each corner.

The best way to clamp the box as a prerequisite step to drilling is all corners at once, which can involve the simultaneous use of a number of clamps. For example, a narrow cabinet—such as a wall unit, consisting of two ends, a top, and a bottom—would call for placement of four clamps prior to boring, one in each front corner. For a deeper cabinet, we might want to clamp rear corners as well for the sake of proper alignment during drilling.

The clamps that are easiest to use are universal-type corner clamps. These have perpendicular jaws and are operated with one crank. They are marketed by the same companies that sell other European style hardware and tools, and, since they save the cabinetmaker so much time and trouble, they are well worth their cost.

With the entire cabinet unit clamped together, the assembler uses a portable electric drill equipped with a step drill bit to do the necessary boring. Although exact placement of the holes and connectors is not necessary, we would probably want to place the connectors in about the same locations that we might place dowels or two-piece connectors. It is a good idea to use a jig for this boring so that the bit enters perpendicular to the drilling surface. With the holes drilled, it is a simple matter to drive the connectors with a Phillips bit or a hexagonal-shaped driver. A variable speed drill makes this part of the operation very easy.

One-piece connectors will show on the cabinet's exterior, obviously, but there are few installed cabinet locations where this matters anyway. For finished ends, the cabinetmaker will want to cover the fastener heads and holes with color-coordinated cover caps.

Again, if the back seat was not placed during the boring and fastening process, it should be installed now. Then it is naturally time to attach accessories, hangers, and levellers, as described earlier.

It should be obvious why the assembly of European cabinets and furniture does not take a great deal of skill. The assembly techniques, by dowel or connector, are excellent for modular systems and for RTA furniture. The key to good-quality assembly and good-quality products within the 32-mm system has a lot more to do with careful planning, precise cutting, and accurate milling than it does with high-quality assembly.

CONVENTIONAL ALTERNATIVES

There are a number of cabinetmakers, especially hobbyists, who are interested in building European styled cabinetry without employing every element of hole-line technology. Their products may not be completely European in every sense, but as we have noted elsewhere, European cabinetry can be defined in several different ways, and there is no absolute criteria of what constitutes the European style except that determined by the woodworkers themselves.

In this section, let us assume that the assembler is using traditional assembly methods, fastener systems, and tools to build cabinets or furniture that either look European or are fabricated from Euro-type materials, such as preclad particleboard. We shall mainly be concerned with the adaptations that must be made in these common assembly methodologies to build the kind of product desired.

Preparing Components for Assembly

If you are working with preclad particleboard, you will not have to sand any of the box components in preparation for assembly. Still, there are some preparations that may be necessary, depending on your assembly routine.

One necessity may be the sealing of raw particleboard. If you are using conventional metal shelf-standard strips for your adjustable shelves, then it is a good idea to apply a coat of lacquer or another clear finish to the raw particleboard that is exposed when you cut your channel for placement of the shelf standards. (See Illus. 169.) If you use dado/rabbet-type assembly, there may be other locations in need of treatment as well, such as the bottom and top ends of finished end panels.

Traditional cabinetmaking often involves the installation of hold-downs at the top of base-cabinet ends and partitions. These are strips of wood, usually about ¾ in. thick and 2 in. wide, that will later be used for attaching countertops. The countertop installer simply drives 1¼-in. screws through the hold-downs and into the underside of the top to fasten it in place. Ordinarily, a cabinet assembler attaches these to the inside of the partition or end with resin glue and nails, but this will not be very effective with European materials. Remember that conventional glue does not adhere to plastic cladding.

One solution is to remove the plastic cladding wherever you intend to attach a hold-down. You can cut a full-scale ¼ in. × ¾ in. rabbet, or you can simply perform a cut that removes only the cladding. One rapid technique is to feed the top end of each component through the table saw. The fence is adjusted so as to control the depth of cut. The distance between the inside tip of the blade and the fence should be slightly less than the material thickness—but enough to remove the

Illus. 169. This melamine-clad wall-cabinet box has channels for placement of shelf standard. The assembler is treating the exposed particleboard with clear lacquer.

plastics cladding. Blade height should be no greater than the thickness of the hold-down, probably ¾ in. (See Illus. 170.) The exposure of raw particleboard allows for conventional attachment with glue and nails.

Another preparation is the attachment of sleepers—the feet that raise base cabinetry off the floor and to which toe kicks are attached. Sleepers are generally mounted to the undersurface of the cabinet bottom by means of glue and nails. Not only does the resin glue not adhere to the cladding on the cabinet's bottom surface, but nails driven through the bottom's interior surface are another problem, not the most desirable situation if you want to preserve the integrity of the cladding on the cabinet's interior surface.

For a two-part problem, we need a two-part solution. One helpful measure is to use an alternative type of "glue." Construction adhesive is a good choice here since it attaches reasonably well to many plastics-clad surfaces. Available in caulking-gun cartridges, it is also easy to apply. To avoid the necessity of driving fasteners through the bottom's clad surface, it is best to first attach a hold-down strip to each sleeper so that screws can be driven from beneath to fasten. (See Illus. 171.)

Traditionally operating custom cabinetmakers do not generally have the aversion to partitions that modular builders have. Partitions will mean cutting notches for the placement of nailers, unless you "hide" the nailer behind the back panel or use another method for installation. Notching is a routine operation, and you can probably accomplish it with your usual technique. Saber saws are suitable, but you might want to use a fine blade to limit chipping.

Box Assembly

The main thing to keep in mind about using conventional assembly techniques with plastics-clad materials is undoubtedly the "unforgiving" nature of this material. The emphasis here is on avoiding accidental penetrations of the melamine or other cladding. With dadoes and rabbets cut, it is a fairly simple matter to apply glue and to drive fasteners by any of the ordinary methods, including a nail gun.

Illus. 170. Removing plastics cladding along the top end of a partition. A hold-down can now be attached with glue and nails.

Illus. 171. Attaching sleepers to clad surfaces.

(See Illus. 172.) But take extra care not to miss. Even though you are driving fasteners through a section of material that has been reduced in depth because of a dado or rabbet, a brittle surface remains present on the entry side of the component. This plastic, through which we have to nail, can act as a deflector; it can change the angle of the nail's entry. In addition, swells and breaks in the surface of the cladding are very easy to see, and nearly impossible to repair.

Illus. 172. Nails can be driven into clad particleboard with a nail gun.

Also, because of the unforgiving nature of precladding material, you need to take some additional care in attaching a face frame and toe kick. Alignment at finished ends should be nearly perfect. (See Illus. 173.)

With this guiding principle in mind, you can proceed with assembly much as with the traditional box. In putting together the basic box parts, begin in the middle and work your way outward. Then attach the face frame and kick as usual. Just remember the "unforgiving" factor.

Illus. 173. The edge of a face-frame stile should align perfectly with a finished end. The cabinet interior here is clad with melamine. Note the notch that is about to be cut.

Back and Nailer Attachment

Some traditionalist cabinetmakers have always made it their practice to fit cabinet backs into slots or rabbets that are milled into the cabinet's bottom and finished ends. They also place nailers behind the backs so that they are not visible after the unit has been installed. Cabinetmakers who are used to building like this will find very few difficulties in adapting to the plastics-clad materials. Nailers can be guided onto the unclad face on the rear side of the back panel. Conventional nailing is possible; from the rear, nails can be driven through the nailer and back and into partitions, ends, tops, and hold-downs.

When nailers are located inside the back panel, and when there is no rabbet or slot cut into the bottom and end for placement of the back, several difficulties may arise related to the nonglueability of plastic.

If you use plastics-clad material on the cabinet's interior, you may also want to make any visible nailer from the same material. For example, if your cabinet boxes are made from ⅝-in. (16-mm) panels that are covered in almond melamine, you may decide to use exactly the same stock for nailers. This makes a good deal of sense for a couple of reasons. You will get color coordination, and you will be salvaging some material that would otherwise go into the trash. (See Illus. 174.) You may encounter some difficulties, though, or at least some matters that will slow you down. First, it is important to band

Illus. 174. Base cabinet with a melamine interior. Note the melamine-clad nailer. Its raw edges were lacquered.

the edges if they will be seen. If the nailer's edge will not be seen but also will not be set against another component such as a countertop or cabinet panel, it should be sealed against formaldehyde emissions. Strength may be the second issue. If you are used to using 2-in. pine nailers, you will probably find that this width of particleboard does not yield enough reliable strength. Third, since its face is plastic, we need to find a better method for attachment to panel edges and hold-downs than simply gluing and nailing. Finally, we also need a more effective method for attachment to end panels because their surfaces are also covered with plastic.

The emissions problem can be solved with color-matched rolled vinyl or lacquer, depending on the visibility level. A nailer width of at least 3 in. will generally yield enough strength for the mounting of the cabinet to a wall, unless the cabinet unit will have no back. The best method for firmly attaching the nailers is screws. The deep-threaded Euro screws are probably best, but drywall screws or wood screws are suitable, too. The most important matter is probably pilot-hole drilling. Without a pilot hole, the narrow panel used for a nailer can split fairly easily. (See Illus. 175.) Of course, sometimes you may

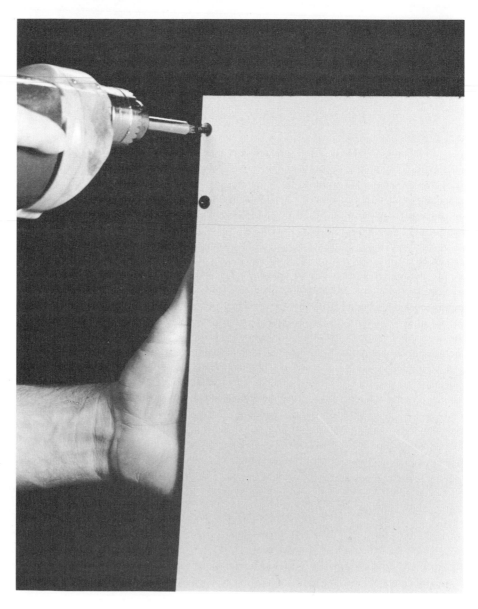

Illus. 175. Driving screws for nailer attachment.

prefer not to drive screws from the exterior of the cabinet—through a finished end, for example. In such locations, right-angle brackets mounted on the inside are a good solution. The European connecting angles will work very well in this application (refer again to Illus. 102), but so also will ordinary right-angle brackets available in almost any hardware store.

Some cabinetmakers like to attach cabinet backs with staples and a bit of glue. In fact, this is the conventional technique, whether the woodworker is fitting the back into slots or not. The only problem here again is the nonglueability of the back panel's inner surface, but the solution is simple. All we need to do is apply beads of construction adhesive to the rear edges of the top, bottom, and end panels, as well as to the rear surfaces of nailers, prior to positioning and stapling on the back. (See Illus. 176.)

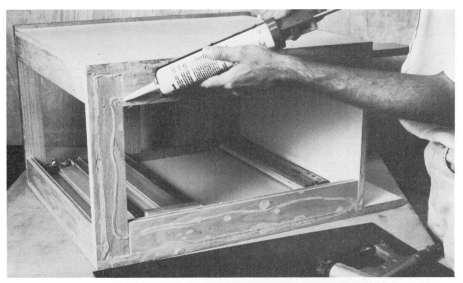

Illus. 176. A conventional back attachment is possible with a plastics-clad back.

Accessories

There is one main difference between mounting European accessories and the traditional methodology: the hardware is different. If you are building a European styled cabinet that has doors, it will be quite hard to get around the use of European hinges. And, as we have observed elsewhere, some styles of European drawer guides are very different from traditional box-guiding systems.

Doors. Hardware manufacturers have made it easy for us to mount doors on traditional cabinetry with fully concealed hinges. They have provided us with mounting plates that allow the use of these hinges on face-frame cabinetry, and in other situations, as well.

With any conventionally assembled cabinetry, it is a good idea to level the entire cabinet before attempting to mount and adjust the doors and drawers. Some cabinetmakers like to lay the cabinet unit on its back for mounting because each door can be set in place rather than held in place; others prefer the cabinet sitting upright on their benches because this arrangement is almost exactly the same as when the cabinet is installed. A perfectly flat, level table is a great benefit in any shop, but during this operation, especially.

European hinges in a traditional setting usually mean face-frame mounting. And usually this means employment of the same hinge-cup-and-cranking assembly used when mounting doors to end panels. Special mounting plates allow attachment to face frames. (See Illus. 177.) The assembler attaches doors to face frames by first

Illus. 177. Most European hinges can be attached with face frames by means of special mounting plates. (Courtesy of Julius Blum, Inc.)

262

affixing the appropriate mounting plate to the cranking unit that has already been attached to the door. Hinges are fully closed, and the door is positioned as desired on its face opening. Then the assembler reaches inside the cabinet and marks the location of the screws that will be driven to fasten the mounting plate to the frame. Although European hinges allow adjustment in all directions (see Illus. 178),

Illus. 178. All European hinges have excellent adjustment features built in. Locking-screw B is for lateral movement, A is for in-out movement, and C is for vertical movement. (Courtesy of Julius Blum, Inc.)

we should be careful to locate the mounting plate as close as possible to its perfect location. One misalignment that can be easy to create in mounting with this type of hinge is in the in-out location of the screws that attach to the face frame. Most of the mounting plates have built-in location guides—prongs that hook onto one face of the frame to locate it properly. (See Illus. 179.) The screws used for this type of mounting plate are often rather thick. They need to be, due to the great torque placed on them. Pilot holes are essential.

One advantage of this type of door mounting over true 32-mm-

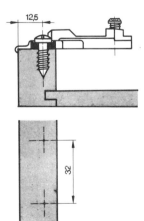

Illus. 179. A face-frame mounting plate. Note the prongs to lap over the frame's front surface. (Courtesy of Julius Blum, Inc.)

based mounting is that there are fewer critical attributes. That is, it is not vital for any holes on door and end panels to line up perfectly. In fact, many traditionalists use European hinges and drill only one hole—the one for the hinge cup. Vertical hinge placement can thus be rather arbitrary.

Drawers. European drawer guides—with their vinyl coating, captive tracking system, and cam-action-lateral-adjustment option—can be superior to conventional side guides. In this, you will have to judge for yourself. Regardless of your decision, it should be clear that, European or not, virtually any guide can be used with almost any box, providing the designer knows ahead of time which guide unit is to be used and develops the drawer plan accordingly.

Since European side-mounted and bottom-mounted guides require approximately ½ in. on both sides of the drawer box, it should be fairly obvious that we have the option to use conventional American side-mounted guides with European drawer boxes. (See Illus. 180.) Most conventional side guides also require exactly ½ in. of space on both sides of the drawer box. There is at least one advantage to conventional drawer guides: They allow the box to be up to ⅝ in. taller because they make a direct, full-front entry rather than needing to be tilted into place as do many European guides.

There are several ways to attach side-mounting guides to a face-frame-type case. One is the European profile socket. (Refer back to Illus. 149.) To mount a drawer with one of the European style drawer runners and sockets, follow these steps.

1. Select a drawer guide and socket to combine and achieve the correct length (the socket should engage at least ¾ in. of the mounted drawer profile).
2. Attach the front end of the case-mounted profile to the inside edge of the face frame with a screw, making sure that it is positioned about ¹⁄₁₆ in. behind the face.
3. With profiles attached to the box, insert the drawer into its opening.
4. Make sure that the drawer front's rear face fully contacts the face frame; clamp it in this position, if you desire.
5. Move case-mounted profiles to support the drawer in this closed position and attach sockets to the rear of the cabinet with staples or screws.

Drawers installed in this way should need little adjustment.

You can follow the same mounting procedure with certain conventional side guides. Manufacturers market sockets for their own hardware systems, and they also make wrap-around drawer profiles available for rear mounting. (See Illus. 181 and 182.)

Another method that can be applied very easily with any type of side-mounted guides involves the use of particleboard profile mounts. These are strips up to 3 in. wide that are cut from the same sheet-good material as the rest of the cabinet box. They are attached front to rear, flush with the inside edge of the face frame, thus providing a side-mounting surface for our guides. (See Illus. 183.)

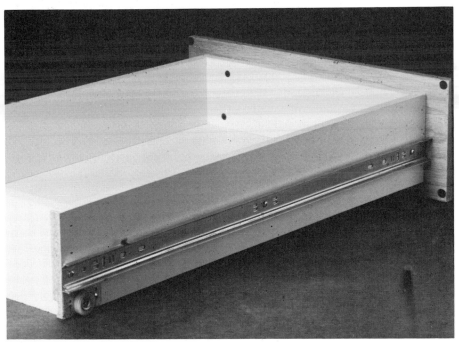

Illus. 180. Conventional American guides can naturally be used on European cabinetry.

We can use wooden profile mounts to install drawers somewhat similarly to the way we use sockets. We attach the guide's case member to the mounting strip with the correct front-to-back positioning. The case member is then fastened to the inner edge of the face frame with a screw. The drawer is inserted and aligned so that the front strikes the face flat. Finally, the profile mounts are moved into proper position to support the drawer, and fasteners are drawn to hold them in this exact position. This method works best before a cabinet back is attached.

In general, slide-out shelves are mounted in much the same way as drawers, with two substantial differences. Since slide-out shelves must disappear completely behind doors, the amount of backset for the case-mounted profiles must be increased. In addition, some care must be taken to ensure that the hinge and the drawer guides are not placed in the same vertical position. Otherwise, they will interfere with each other. (See Illus. 184.)

Regardless of whether you assemble with a traditional approach or

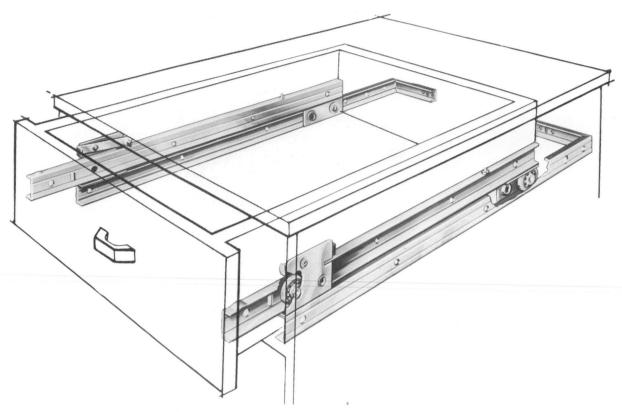

Illus. 181. A wrap-around case profile can be easily used with face frames and other rear-mount applications. (Courtesy of Knape & Vogt Mfg. Co.)

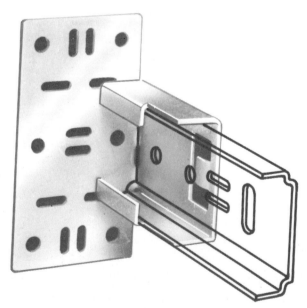

Illus. 182. Rear-mount sockets for conventional side guides. (Courtesy of Knape & Vogt Mfg. Co.)

Illus. 183 (top and bottom). Profile mounts made from particleboard. These are for slide-out shelves.

Illus. 184. Slide-out shelves behind European hinge-mounted doors. The vertical hinging location was raised so as not to interfere with the bottom slide-out or its guides.

completely within the context of the hole lines, the placement of accessories means that the cabinet is ready for whatever finishing it might require, and installation.

SUMMARY

The new methodology of hole-line-based assembly is advantageous because it doesn't require assemblers who are very knowledgeable or experienced at their job. It is based on the ability to achieve very precisely line-bored holes. Assembly of 32-mm-based cabinetry is therefore simply the installation of a series of fittings that will hold the cabinet together. Within the new methodology, though, assembly is still the slowest of the operations required to construct a cabinet.

European connectors are dowels, two-piece fittings, or one-piece fittings.

Dowel assembly of the flat cabinet components is very common in the European system. It involves spreading resin glue thoroughly and evenly, dowel insertion, and clamping. It obviously creates joints that are intended to be permanent. There is some very expensive equipment designed for high-volume manufacturers who do this kind of assembly—notably the dowel gun and the case clamp. Low-volume builders also have effective methods for achieving this type of assembly. For them, the process is very similar, just slower, since they have to spread the glue manually, and generally do clamping with portable case clamps or ordinary bar clamps.

Connector assembly can require drilling some larger holes. Two-piece connectors usually employ an eccentric device to lock components together. Usually, one of the parts to be joined is fitted with such an eccentric, while the other part is fitted with a fixing bolt. When the cabinet components are brought together, these two pieces of the connector interconnect. Locking is then activated by turning the eccentric.

One-piece connectors can be thought of basically as screws. Cabinet parts are joined by clamping them together; then by drilling pilot, clearance, and countersink holes; and finally by driving the screw-type fastener.

Connector-type assembly creates joints that can be released and rejoined.

With the basic European box put together, there is little sanding to do, and you can proceed directly to accessory mounting.

The back panel can be inserted into slots while the rest of the box is being put together, or it can be attached later. Also, door and drawer hardware can be mounted as a preparatory step, or after the box is assembled. Some special tooling is available for postassembly drawer attachment.

European installation includes the placement of the levelling-hardware base segments. These, too, are attached via boring, either by insertion or by more or less bolting them in place. Toe kicks are clipped onto the leveller legs, on the job site.

Hanger hardware must be attached to wall cabinetry by the assembler. Part of the hanger has to project through the cabinet's back panel, and a notch must be cut for this.

Accessories, chiefly doors and drawers, are also attached by the assembler, in conjunction with the hole line or as screw-on items.

You can also make a product with the European look by using conventional techniques, but it is necessary to take some measures to accommodate the most common European cabinetmaking material—preclad particleboard. Mainly, this means extra care in nailing to avoid chipping the plastic, the use of screws in certain locations instead of nails, some fastener-concealing techniques, and the use of construction adhesive where plastic surfaces must be glued.

RECOMMENDATIONS

The owner of a small shop can learn to make cabinets with basic line-boring assembly very rapidly, and there is really no reason to create extra work to avoid it. If you can put together a decent conventional cabinet, you can assemble an outstanding 32-mm-based cabinet. This is extremely important to understand. Whereas conventional cabinetmaking emphasizes assembly skills, 32-mm-based cabinetmaking emphasizes precise cutting and milling.

Most traditionalists love their system, and it is a good system. But the reasons for face-frame-type construction may be disappearing. Rigid backs, reliable fasteners, and good-quality particleboard have all combined to allow us the option to get away from face frames. What makes the most sense is probably to build European styles with the hole-line-assembly method and to use more conventional techniques to assemble traditional cabinets. After all, it is probably just as simple for hobbyists and small shop owners to incorporate the new technology as it is for them to continue modifying their old methods to fit the new materials. Remember that customizers have many options that modular builders may not. Most important, customizers are in close contact with their products and their end use. We can drill only those holes that need drilling and edge-band only those edges that are necessary to band. Indeed, if we are setting out to create products with a European look, why not build them in the European way?

There is really no new European assembly tooling needed except for clamps. If you elect to use dowel assembly, it is certainly feasible to use ordinary bar clamps for the required clamping during curing. And, of the 32-mm-based systems, dowel assembly is often aesthetically superior to connector assembly.

Connector assembly is undoubtedly faster. If you choose connector assembly in the small shop though, I would think you would prefer the one-piece system. It is clearly the simplest and fastest because it saves us from so much boring and bit changing. Many projects can go from the table saw to the edge bander to the assembly table, especially if you are not stuck on the vertical hole line.

The vertical hole line is really a different matter altogether. For many small shop owners, there is no real advantage to the vertical hole line. Considering that they have to use a jig for drilling the holes, screw attachment of most accessories is probably just as fast.

The choice of an assembly method really must be done in the planning stages of a cabinet project. It may be a general rule of thumb to build European projects with European techniques and to build traditional projects with traditional techniques, but we should not be afraid to blend the styles when it is appropriate and fulfills a function.

7
FINISHING
AND
INSTALLATION

POSTASSEMBLY OPERATIONS

Now what? We have assembled our European styled cabinetry, and all that remains for us to do is to deliver it, set it in place, and attach it to the building. Right? Well, perhaps not.

If you are committed to building an unadulterated version of the European cabinet, then you might want to skip the next two sections on sanding and finishing. One definition of European cabinetry, after all, is cabinetry that needs less sanding and finishing because of the use of preclad materials.

Much 32-mm modular cabinetry and ready-to-assemble furniture is designed with the elimination of sanding and finishing as a major goal. We have suggested earlier that this is one of the main reasons to use the European 32-mm system of cabinet construction. Since it is possible to fabricate an entire cabinet project from materials that are preclad with plastic laminates, PVC, or a similar substance, there may be no need for sanding or finishing it at all. This could be a tremendous advantage in the modular shop because it reduces requirements for skilled labor, tooling, inventory, and space.

On the other hand, the demand for real wood continues. And most real-wood components still need some sanding as well as protective finishing. In the next two major sections of this chapter, we will look at the need for sanding and finishing as it relates to the European cabinet as well as "blended" cabinet styles.

Another way of defining European cabinetry has to do with the way it is installed. Cabinetry that is built via the 32-mm system should be installed with wall-cabinet hangers and leveller legs—hardware that never seemed necessary within traditional cabinetmaking. In the last section of this chapter, we will take a closer look at this definition as well as European installation methods and their alternatives.

SANDING

We have said that European cabinetry can be defined as cabinetry that needs less sanding because of its component materials. Consider the word "less." What exactly is meant by "less" sanding? Very likely, that is intended to mean sanding fewer components or less total area on each cabinet. But we really need to consider whether either will mean less work.

Of course, wherever sanding has been completely eliminated, this distinction is totally irrelevant. "Less" means none. However, in smaller shops, the definition of "less" can be very significant, indeed.

Suppose that we have decided to make edge-banded doors in our conventionally equipped shop. We desire melamine-faced doors with a rounded-over, oak edge band. Not only is it very likely that the oak-edging material will need sanding, but also the sanding operation is made more difficult because the wood components are immediately adjacent to and flush with material that must not be sanded (the melamine cladding). The amount of sanding required may be less in terms of surface area to be sanded; in fact, we will only want to sand about 10 percent or less of the door's total surface area. However, if we proceed as we usually would with all-wood doors—by attaching oversized edging, trimming flush and rounding over with a router, and then sanding—it may take just as long or longer to sand these doors as it would take to sand all-wood doors.

There are two types of problems that can be associated with sanding the cabinet. The first, just described, has to do with the juxtaposition of components that require sanding (wooden parts) with those that must not be sanded (preclad parts). The other type of sanding-related problems we might encounter can arise from blending European and traditional assembly practices. This includes matters such as glue squeezing out where we do not want it, unintentionally produced clamp marks, and spots where we used a filler paste such as at nail holes and seams between components. (See Illus. 185.) These are seldom major issues in either European or conventional cabinetmaking. The difficulty comes when we blend the approaches. But low-volume cabinetmakers have to blend approaches if they want to produce cabinets with European styling. Most of us who work in small shops are not going to buy a $50,000 edge bander just so we can add ¾ in. × ¾ in. strips of wood to 19-mm-thick panels of preclad particleboard. Even mid-sized shops that are in transition towards unisystem edge-bander capability must blend systems when they construct cabinets with the European look.

Illus. 185. The seam between a bottom face rail and a melamine-clad bottom panel. If this cabinet were all wood, the assembler would probably fill the gap with plastic filler paste and sand.

Conventional Sanding Principles

There are really two reasons for sanding in the traditional shop. One reason is to achieve general smoothness. Everyone appreciates the fine appearance and texture of properly sanded wood. Sanding for smoothness includes sanding in order to remove marks and minor indentations. The other reason that traditional cabinetmakers sand is that sanding can be helpful in achieving flat joints. It is common, for example, to attach a face frame so that its edge extends beyond the surface of a finished end by a tiny amount, perhaps $\frac{1}{32}$ in. Clamps can be used to ensure that the stile of the face frame and the finished end meet with the narrowest possible seam. The assembler then sands the entire finished end, perhaps with a belt sander—thus flattening the joint. Continued sanding then generates the smoothness desired.

Proper grit is partly a matter of choice. In general, you should begin with a paper that is coarse enough to accomplish your job in a reasonable amount of time but no coarser than necessary. For smoothing the joint between the face frame and finished end, you should usually choose a 100-grit belt on your belt sander. You could begin with a coarser belt, depending on the quality of the joint before you begin sanding, but you will almost never need a belt coarser than

80-grit. After you've sanded the entire surface fairly evenly, it's time to use finer grit paper and to switch tools. An oscillating finishing sander usually follows the belt sander. However, some cabinetmakers prefer to do more hand sanding.

Some woodworkers continue working through grits until they have sanded the wood with 180-grit or 200-grit paper. Others feel that they have gotten their product smooth enough with 120-grit paper. This is really up to you. The most important rule is not to skip intervening grits. That is, do not expect to achieve a nicely sanded article if you belt-sand with 80-grit paper and then finish-sand with 150-grit paper. Each subsequent step in the progression of sandpaper fineness must be coarse enough to remove the scratches left behind by the prior-used sandpaper. Never jump more than 20 grits in your sanding (advance from 80 to 100, 100 to 120, and so on).

Remember, too, that sanding is a job that actually interrupts the assembly process in several stages. When following traditional practices, the assembler can neither do all the sanding before putting the cabinet together nor perform all the sanding after the components are joined. We do some sanding on the edges of the face frame before it is ever put together. After the face frame is doweled, tenoned, or screwed together, we usually sand its front and rear surfaces enough to make them flat. After the face frame is nailed onto the cabinet box and the nail holes have perhaps been filled with wood putty, we do more sanding, this time for smoothness.

Sanding the European Cabinet

When building cabinets with the European system, much of the need for sanding is simply eliminated. First of all, there is less exposed wood and wood veneer on the cabinet. And the premium placed on excellent, smooth cutting further reduces the need for sanding because this level of cutting produces quickly made, perfect joints. Also, with perfectly smooth, straight cuts, we do not need to depend on the gap-filling properties of glue to keep the seams as small as possible; components simply make good contact. Therefore, there's no glue that needs to be cleaned off or sanded.

The best unisystem edge banders have solutions to potential sanding problems built right into them. They precisely trim excess edging materials with circular saw blades so that no sanding is necessary to achieve flat joints. And their sanding and buffing subsystems can be set up not only to ease edges and "dress up" joints, but also to fine-sand the surface of the edging itself.

When building cabinets with a blending of 32-mm and traditional methodologies, the small shop woodworker can employ various techniques to get around the problems of sanding.

Eliminate Wood. Of course, the most obvious solution to the overall problem of sanding is to do as the European designers intended: If we merely eliminate the wooden parts that must be sanded, there is no sanding to do and thus no sanding problem. However, your design plan may call for some particular components to be made of wood, or you may want to showcase some wood on your project. No real wood means no real wood. What we really want to do is introduce wood elements into European cabinet design, not eliminate them altogether. Still, we can perhaps look for opportunities to eliminate particular wooden pieces if it will be helpful in solving the sanding problem.

Join Only Sandable Components. In using wood components, it is very helpful to avoid flush joints between sandable and nonsandable components. Therefore, you should try to carefully plan your project so that any flush joining involves only wood components.

If you are building cabinetry with a face frame, you will probably want it to be flush with the cabinet's end panel. It is best for the face frame and end panel to be made from wood of the same species. For example, if your face frame is made from solid birch lumber, you would probably cut the end panel from A-2 plywood with a birch face. When the seam is made, you can sand both the edge of the face and the surface of the plywood panel. In fact, as you will recall, such adjacent components can be treated in exactly the same way at exactly the same time. This is what most custom builders do. (See Illus. 186.) You might apply this principle when fabricating doors, too. The

Illus. 186. Most face-frame cabinetry is constructed so that the end panel meets the stile in a flush joint.

notion is simple: If you will be adding a thick-wood edge band, the panel itself should also be wood faced. Thus, whatever sanding is necessary after assembly can be done to an entire surface.

Presand. Making only wood-to-wood flush joints is obviously not the answer to all our needs in constructing European cabinetry. Whenever you must flush-join a wood component with a plastics-clad component, one of the methods that can be a big help is presanding. For instance, sanding the wooden component before assembly can be helpful with a wood edge band on a plastic door panel, a wood edge band or frame stile covering the edge of a plastic end panel, and a face frame's bottom rail covering the edge of a plastic bottom panel.

Preparing the wood component as completely as possible before assembly is an excellent notion, but there are a few pitfalls. First, we need to be careful not to produce too many nicks, dents, glue marks, or other flaws in the presanded component as we work with it to attach it to the panel. For instance, to attach the wooden stile of a face frame to a plastic end panel, we need to take special care not to do anything to damage the stile's edge, or we will wind up having to sand it after assembly anyway. Second is the matter of fitting and alignment. Remember that one reason for sanding is to achieve flat joints. When we attach a wood component to a plastics-clad component, though, we cannot very well do sanding to achieve a flat joint. Therefore, when we presand, we have to make sure that the components go together perfectly flush.

Some cabinetmakers use an alternate fastening system when they attach a face frame flush with plastics-clad components, and it usually does not require glue. The European assembly fittings can be very effective in this application, especially the eccentric type (refer back to Illus. 164) and the surface-mounted, screw-in type (refer back to Illus. 168). Of course, this involves some additional work with your drilling jig and portable electric drill, but there are some important benefits related to the sanding issue currently under discussion. Since this fastening system does not depend on glue, there will be no glue squeezing out of the seam as a screw or cam is tightened to lock the parts together, and thus no glue to be cleaned off or sanded. Also, because no glue is needed, you can do some trial assembly for the purpose of fitting the parts together perfectly. In other words, you can bore for and insert the assembly fittings, attach the face frame, and then release the joint and remove the face frame for additional trimming or sanding, if necessary. Finally, since the jigs, the bits, and the fittings are so precise, there will probably be no additional trimming or sanding to do anyway.

It is also possible to make glueless, releasable joints with conventional fasteners, such as wood screws or drywall screws. You simply attach a cleat to the inside surface of the finished end along the front edge so that screws can be driven from the rear for attachment of the stile. (See Illus. 187.) Again, glueless attachment allows release for perfect trimming.

If you are going to presand certain portions of a face frame to eliminate the need for postassembly sanding, releasable joints are a great help. Of course, you can use ordinary glue and fasteners in locations where flush joining is not necessary, such as where a mullion covers a partition or where a stile covers a wall end. Naturally, the time to spread the glue is after you are completely happy with the releasable, flush joints you are making. One last time, take the joint apart by removing screws or turning back the eccentric, spread glue wherever the cabinet box is to be contacted by the face frame's rear surface; then replace the frame, retighten the stile-end connection, and attach the rest of the face with finishing nails, aligning overhangs as you go.

Presanding can be helpful in making flush wood-and-plastic doors as well. However, we will generally have the same two problems here that we had in conjunction with the flush attachment of the face frame: We may produce some flaws during assembly, and we cannot

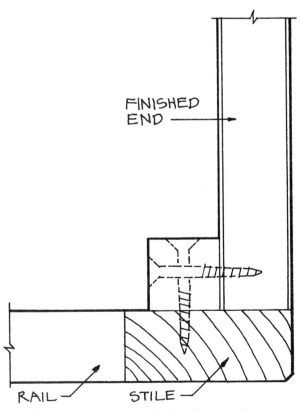

Illus. 187. Cleat-and-screw attachment of a face-frame stile.

use sanding to achieve flatness. But, there are additional problems we will encounter: Here, we also cannot use cleats and screws, nor will it be too likely that we will want to use eccentrics for attaching the wood endings, and we will probably need to apply glue. Indeed, it will certainly be a challenge to find a procedure that will allow us to attach presanded parts so that no further sanding will be necessary.

Many cabinetmakers perform some additional milling operations to help with the attachment of flush, presanded wood door edgings. Dowel pins, wafers, or splines are all options for this kind of door making. We could also cut a continuous mortise in the edges of the panel, and then shape the edging with a continuous tenon to fit into it.

The trouble with all these approaches is that they require perfect milling in several different setups. Do not underestimate the difficulty involved with this. We are striving for perfectly flat joints, after all, not joints that are simply fairly flat. Most of the tooling found in the conventionally equipped small shop is not up to this kind of perfection. Even if you are extremely careful in setting up, even if you have excellent techniques, it is not going to be easy to achieve the kind of perfect machining required in this type of application, especially in terms of reliability. With only slight imperfections on the detail work of only 10 percent of your panel feeds (and, remember, there are four feeds to make per panel) and 10 percent of your edging feeds, they are probably enough to double the cost of your door production. Actually, door panels and other cabinet joinery can be accomplished with milled parts. In all likelihood, however, some postassembly sanding will be necessary.

Of the several milling procedures to choose from, perhaps the most reliable is dowelling, at least if you are working with a good-quality jig and bit. The reference side of such a jig must be placed against the front surface of both components when you are preparing to drill. This ensures that the matching dowel holes will be located at the same distance from the surface of both pieces. Dowel pins are then coated with glue and inserted before the pieces are put together. (See Illus. 188.) The result can be a reasonably flat joint. Still, for whatever reasons, joints may not be perfect. Perhaps the drill bit entered at slightly different angles into the two matching holes. Perhaps the dowel pins were a bit too slender and thus failed to align the two faces you were trying so hard to match. In addition to misalignment troubles, you can produce a certain amount of glue squeeze-out. Dry assembly, performed to make sure that parts align properly, can be a helpful measure here. Of the machined-joining systems, dowelling is probably the best, since it is fairly fast and reasonably accurate—but it still will not produce the perfect results we are seeking.

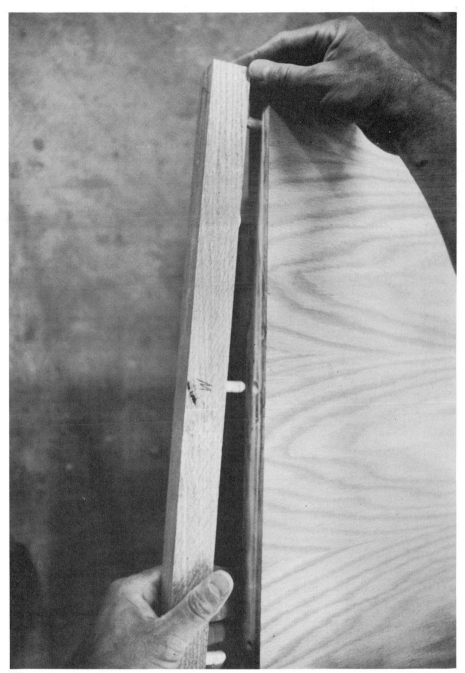

Illus. 188. Dowelling can be used to join components that must be fairly flush. Here, a thick and wide edge band is being attached to a top panel.

If simplicity is a virtue, and we still need to accomplish flush joints involving presanded wood parts, perhaps we ought to make some of these joints with glue, setting pressure, and no other fasteners whatsoever. This will depend on the circumstances. We already looked at an acceptable means for attaching a wooden face frame flush to a plastic-finished end. But it seems as if attempting worked joints introduces as many problems as it solves.

Simple butt joints are acceptable for adding flush wood edges to door panels and in other similar circumstances. Dowel joints or other worked joints are not necessary for strength in a door panel; they are needed only for alignment. What we do here is apply glue to the panel's edge and then attempt to achieve perfect alignment as we place the clamps. Masking tape can be helpful in this process. After the glue and edging are in place, the cabinetmaker uses several lengths of tape to wrap the joint and keep its parts from sliding around. Clamp pressure should be applied gradually to further help in this regard. This method will certainly proceed faster than worked joining, but we will undoubtedly wind up with squeezed-out glue, and perfect alignment will still be difficult to achieve.

There is one other way of processing sanded wood and plastic together to achieve fairly flat joints for components such as door panels. It may be the best technique involving conventional tools and techniques. As you shall see, we need the panel thickness to be less than the thickness of the solid material. Basically, this method consists of making a frame with the solid stock that is supposed to "edge" our panel, sanding it flat, and then cutting a rabbet around the inner edge of the frame for insertion of the plastics-clad panel. We can fasten by driving screws from the rear. (See Illus. 189.)

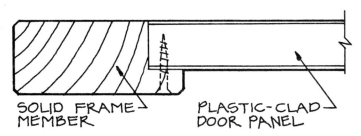

SOLID FRAME MEMBER PLASTIC-CLAD DOOR PANEL

Illus. 189. The perfect joint can be achieved with a solid-frame and thinner door panel. All sanding can be presanding.

All solid stocks must be wide enough to be legitimate frame members—at least ¾ in. The frame stock on the hinged side of the door must be wide enough to allow for drilling the 35-mm-diameter-cup hole—at least 1¹¹⁄₁₆ in. in total. The advantages of this approach should be fairly self-evident, but they are important enough to be listed anyway.

- Frames can be joined firmly with conventional techniques, such as using glue and dowels.
- Frame members can be butted or mitred.

- Frames can be sanded for flatness after assembly.
- Milling is accomplished in one setup, and none of the dimensions of the setup has to be critical.
- Fine adjustment is possible to achieve a good fit.
- We can do fine sanding to the wood frame before finally attaching the plastics-clad panel.

For the low-volume cabinetmaker, or any cabinetmaking shop that does not have state-of-the-art edge-banding equipment, this is an excellent solution to many problems that have to do with joining plastic panels to solid stocks. There are only two real pitfalls, and these can be dealt with by simply taking a bit of extra care.

One potential problem area is the corner. Since we are guiding a square frame around a router bit by virtue of a round pilot (see Illus. 190), our rabbet intended for panel placement will have round corners while the panel itself will have square corners. The obvious thing to do is to square out the rabbet cuts with a chisel and mallet, and this is the method I prefer. Other woodworkers like to round the corners of the panel itself, with a band saw, saber saw, or edge sander. The rounding approach can be a bit easier, I must confess, but your own decision probably should be based on appearance. It is generally a good idea to use round corners when there are other rounded-over elements in the design; when not, the square approach will look better.

Illus. 190. A carbide-tipped rabbeting bit. (Courtesy of Freud in USA.)

The other possible difficulty has to do with seaming or contact between the outside edges of the panel and the inside edges of the frame. This is a visible seam, and we do not want large gaps here. Of course, the quality of seaming goes back to the accuracy employed in cutting and milling. If you have great confidence in your own cutting/frame-assembly/rabbeting tools and techniques, you should simply go ahead. If you are not so sure, then you can do two things to help with accuracy: First, cut the panels only after the frames have been put together and rabbeted; and second, cut the panels oversized and fit them perfectly with the aid of a jointer or edge sander.

The fastest and most reliable way to make use of the notion of presanding is to perform it on components that will not need any touch-up sanding. And for most customizers, this means planning and carrying out joints that will need no finished sanding after the plastic and wood parts have been permanently assembled. With face frames, this can mean attachment by eccentric assembly fitting or by screws and cleats. With some panels, such as door panels, this will mean installing the plastics-clad panel into a prefabricated frame.

Eliminate Flush Joints. As we have already noted, one obvious way of dealing with sanding problems is to eliminate sanding altogether. We also observed that, though a lot of sanding can be eliminated by taking wood components out of our planned project, this is not really our intention. Rather than eliminating wood, another way of reducing the amount of necessary sanding is to eliminate flush joints instead. If we never set out to achieve flush joints, we can use presanded parts and may never have to do any postassembly sanding. Or, if sanding is necessary after assembly, the protruding component (usually the solid one) can be easily sanded.

When we decide to employ some nonflush joints on a cabinet project, there are only a few steps we can take to enhance appearance. These methods usually involve bevelling or rounding over the solid component.

Factory cabinet producers have used the nonflush approach for years, on thousands of cabinets. Custom cabinetmakers could do the same when their objective is to avoid sanding. Locations where this is advisable are those we have already noted—wherever a wood component meets a plastics-clad component. (See Illus. 191.) Again, the overhanging solid stock is easily sanded after the parts have been assembled.

For reducing dependence on skilled milling and sanding, this is an effective method. However, most custom cabinetmakers tend to avoid

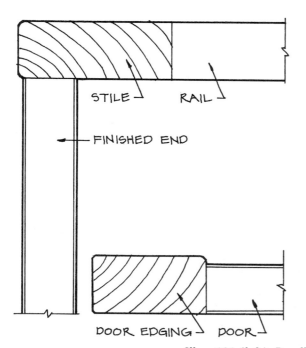

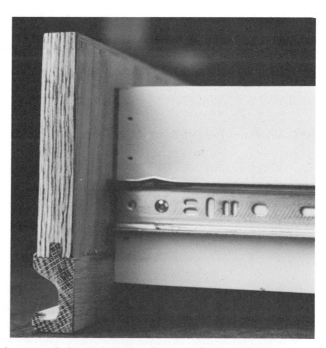

Illus. 191 (left). Bevelled or rounded-over corners allow overhanging solid components. This arrangement makes postassembly sanding easier. Illus. 192 (right). Door profile. Note the portion of continuous pull that overhangs the door's face. The detail means that we do not have to do anything to achieve a flush joint.

the arrangement, at least for face frames, since they think that it looks unprofessional. On doors and drawer fronts, the nonflush look is probably more acceptable. Even European continuous pull profile stock has a protrusion that overhangs the face of the panel to which it is attached. (See Illus. 192.)

If you are using a wood face frame with a melamine interior, you may encounter a joining problem in another area of your cabinetry—where the bottom rail is supposed to meet the bottom panel in a flush joint. This is a spot where almost no one would accept the nonflush arrangement, but since it is a secondary location, many cabinetmakers do not expect of themselves a perfectly flat joint here. They generally presand the top edge of the bottom rail, attach it so that it is fairly flush with the bottom panel, and move on.

Seam tightness is also less significant here because of the secondary location. This is important because we obviously cannot fill the crack and sand it flush as we could if both members were wood. Of course, as cabinetmakers, we want every seam as tight as possible, but let us remember that seam quality is a relative matter. Clearly, seams in a primary location must be close to perfect, but secondary means less visible and less visually important. If you have chosen face-frame construction, and you don't have access to a wide, automatic-feed belt sander, you probably have to prepare the rear face of your frames with a portable belt sander, and some slight imperfections in the frame's flatness may result. When the face frame is attached, the seam may be imperfect because of this. Seam quality can be improved by clamping, but perhaps we do not need the near-perfect seam here that we expect of ourselves in primary locations.

There is one more option to consider regarding the joint for the bottom rail and the bottom panel: We can eliminate the bottom rail altogether. This is an excellent option, even if you favor face-frame construction. You will still have the frame design you are comfortable with, but you will not have to deal with a joint or seam along the bottom. The bottom panel's front edge can be edge-banded instead of covered with a rail.

Alter the Sanding Tools. The assembled cabinet with adjacent wood and plastics-clad components will usually require some sanding, even if presanding was performed fairly well. We need tools and techniques that will accomplish this type of sanding. We may have this sort of work to do on end panels, on doors and drawer fronts, and along any flush seam. The object here is to remove material from the wood and to avoid removing any from the adjacent plastic.

Scrapers, especially flat scrapers, are useful for this sort of finishing work. Getting away from abrasives will, first of all, give us more control. Several characteristics of a hardened-steel scraper make this so.

There is only one entry point with a scraper, whereas there are hundreds or even thousands on a piece of sandpaper. When you perform the scraping operation, you can thus apply pressure on a certain portion of the tool (where it touches wood) and allow the rest of the scraper to "float" along (where it contacts plastic).

A flat scraper can be sharpened quickly and easily. Since a wood surface is cut and abraded more easily than an adjacent high-pressure plastic-laminate surface, it is possible to prepare an edge sharp enough for removing wood but not quite sharp enough to cut into plastic. When I sharpen my scraper, I set it firmly into the vise, draw my file across it 10 times with the coarser side, and then ten more times with the finer side. What I usually do after that to create the sharpest of cutting edges is to use a rounded piece of tool steel to force down the cutting edge. (See Illus. 193.) However, when I am

Illus. 193. Knurling half of a scraper's edge.

preparing to scrape along a seam where wood and plastics come together, I only force down half of the scraper. I use the sharper, forced-down part on the wood and let the scraper's other portion float along the plastic.

Masking tape can also help in sanding, particularly when you are using sandpaper or a scraper adjacent to a highly visible plastic surface. Masking tape cannot really stand up to the abrasion of sandpaper or the knife action of a scraper, but it can be used when you are trying to sand a wood section all the way up to an adjacent plastic surface. We mask over the plastic that is along the seam and then sand. Of course, we try not to contact the masking tape with our sandpaper anyway, but it will protect the plastic if we should slip.

Some types of shaded sanding blocks are helpful in this type of sanding because they are somewhat self-guided. For example, if you are sanding a round over along the edge of a plastic door panel, you might shape a covered sanding block to fit the rounded edge. Because the block "hooks on" the edge to be sanded, we have very good control. With a bit of care, it is possible to sand right up to a seam with such a tool. (See Illus. 194.)

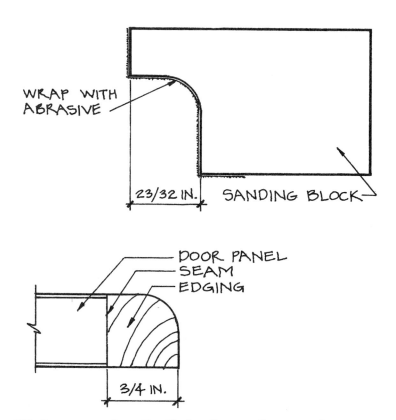

Illus. 194. Some types of sanding blocks allow excellent control.

Use Wood-Grain Plastic. If you desire the look of wood, but texture is relatively unimportant, you can use thin wood-grain plastics for edgings. These can be applied as ordinary edge bands and they create no sanding problems.

* * * * *

As you can see, there are methods the shop with conventional tools can employ to bring together a sanded wooden component and a plastics-covered one. Most are rather labor intensive, but they are examples of the versatility that allows custom woodworkers to continue competing in a modularized furniture world.

FINISHING

As with sanding operations, the amount of finishing required on a European cabinet is rather limited. We really do not need to introduce many new techniques into our finishing system to put a finish on our European cabinetry.

Let us first take a look at some of the most basic principles of finishing. Then we will look at those procedures that can be followed to finish portions of the European cabinet.

Conventional Finishing Principles

Today there are a myriad of cabinet/furniture finishing materials and systems for applying them. Each has its drawbacks as well as its advantages. Entire books have been written on the subject of furniture finishing, and it is not my purpose here to try to supplant them. But I do think it's appropriate for us to remind ourselves about finishing information that can have a bearing on European designed cabinetry.

Finishing Materials. In the most general terms, wood-finishing materials can be classified in one of three groups: materials that add color (stains), penetrating protective materials (oils), or surface-coating protective materials (lacquers or varnishes).

The primary purpose for staining is to alter the natural color of wood. Most stains are oil based, and they work by penetrating wood fibres and actually altering their color. Such wood coloration can be performed for a number of reasons. Woodworkers may want to even out the coloration of an entire job; they may want to create a tint that will enhance the total look of an entire room; or they may want to enhance the grain figure of a particular species of wood.

For most stains, the application procedure is simply a matter of flooding wood fibres with the material, allowing some time for penetration, and then wiping away the excess. It is also fairly easy to create your own colors by mixing different stains together or by adding concentrated tints. Once you have determined the right hue and darkness of a stain, it's rather difficult to make a mistake. About the only procedure that can create any problem is allowing the material to stand so long that it hardens and becomes difficult to wipe. You can use a brush, a cloth, or a spray gun for flooding the wood surfaces. A soft cloth should be used for wiping.

Staining does not really afford much protection for wood. As we have said, its real purpose is coloration. After an oil stain has cured for about 12 hours, a protective material can be added.

Some surface-coating protective material is what is usually applied over stain, although such a material is often applied to wood that has not been stained. It is a clear material that is usually applied in several coats. Lacquers, varnishes, and urethanes can all be considered to fall into this classification. The main purpose of such coatings is to lock moisture and other wood-damaging materials out of the wood fibres, but these finishes can also beautify the wood with glossy, semiglossy, or satin sheens.

Unlike using stains, it is possible to misapply clear finishes. Tooling is very important. Since they dry so fast, lacquers should be applied as a spray. Most varnishes wind up looking better if they are brushed on. Urethane finishes can generally be applied in either way. Naturally, there are exceptions in each case.

In the small shop, lacquers have been the most popular finish for years. This is because its rapid drying prevents many problems. Since it can be sprayed on with a suction-feed sprayer, lacquer can also produce the smoothest finishes. To apply clear coating, you should basically follow these steps.

1. Fine-sand the project with 300-grit paper, and remove dust.
2. Apply a coat of sealer (this is usually the same as the chosen clear-coating material, thinned by half).
3. After the sealer is dry, fine-sand, remove dust, and apply a full, wet, unthinned coat of clear material.
4. Repeat Step 3.

The sealer plus two full-strength coats are generally sufficient to afford protection from moisture and such. Naturally, every additional coat is another layer of protection. Depending on the intended use of a particular article, lacquer-finished pieces can usually benefit from additional applications because lacquers go on in such thin coats.

Penetrating clear finishes (oils) are, in many ways, the best finishes that can be applied to wood. Oils are almost impossible to misapply. They add luster to wood and accent its grain figure, they are formidable protectors of wood fibres, and they require only a soft cloth for application.

Oils are not as popular as the surface finishes, though, probably because oils must be allowed a good deal of drying time and because many of them do not start to build any sheen until we reach the fourth coat or so. Oils create exquisite finishes, but they may not be the best finish for you if you are in hurry.

To apply a penetrating oil as a finish, you should generally follow these steps.

1. Fine-sand the project and remove dust.

2. Flood the wood surfaces with oil and allow penetration for several minutes.
3. Wipe off excess oil with a soft dry cloth, and allow curing as per instructions.
4. Sand with a very fine grit abrasive and remove dust.
5. Repeat Steps 3 and 4 until you are happy with the finish.

Oil finishes protect by penetration and build very slowly on the wood's surface. You must be patient to apply oil finishes.

In terms of finishing techniques that can be used on the European cabinet, generally the sprayed-on lacquer is preferred over other clear finishes. At times in our discussion, we will refer to brushing techniques, where we will assume that the finisher would use a fast-drying, brushable, lacquer-type product, such as Deft. The fast-drying nature of lacquer makes it appropriate in both the small and the European shop, where speed and efficiency are so important. The other clear finishes can certainly be applied to wood surfaces on European cabinetry, however.

Finishing the European Cabinet

As is the case with sanding the assembled cabinet, the chief concerns we cabinetmakers have in the finishing of a European cabinet piece have to do with the juxtaposition of wood and plastics-covered components. In terms of finishing, however, the solutions are much easier to describe and carry out.

Again, the simplest solution is to eliminate the need for finishing. We can do this by avoiding the use of wood, either by incorporating plastic wood look-alikes or by simply committing ourselves to grainless cabinets and furniture. However, since most people still prefer wood elements in much of their cabinetry, let us move on to other solutions.

Prefinish. Prefinishing can make a good deal of sense, depending on the type of construction you are using. The more traditional or involved your assembly process, the less likely that you will do a lot of prefinishing. We do not want to be using glue or construction adhesive in proximity with our prefinished surfaces, for example. And, whereas we can lay plastics-clad panels down on a workbench and even slide them around quite a bit, this sort of treatment will have some very harmful effects on prefinishing wood panels. Perhaps the worst part of the whole notion of prefinishing is that we wind up repeating labor on damaged components, while the whole purpose of prefinishing is to economize labor. Thus, we should probably only perform prefinishing when we can reasonably expect not to scratch, knick, or otherwise damage our finished wooden components. There are a few such situations, of course.

Releasable joints allow us some opportunities to prefinish. Earlier, we pointed out that we could design a cabinet that incorporated eccentric fasteners as a means of attaching the face frame. This system allows presanding because the assembler can remove the frame, fit it perfectly to a finished end, and then reattach it. If you make releasable joints on the entire face frame, you certainly have the opportunity to stain, seal, and lacquer it before final attachment. This method may work out all right for small and very basic boxes—those with square frames, for instance—but it does not seem like such a good idea for more complex cabinets. The work saved by prefinishing is probably not sufficient compensation for the additional work involved in making the frame fully releasable. In general, we would need too many fasteners.

If flush joints are not necessary, prefinishing the components becomes more viable. This is because we can often reduce the number of fasteners or fittings.

A variation of these releasable approaches is to use only enough reverse-driven screws or releasable fasteners to effect good fits and seams. Glue blocks can be placed for reinforcement after the frame is perfectly fitted, sanded, and prefinished.

Prefinishing can be a big help when it comes to making flat door or drawer panels. As was the case with presanding, the best assembly practice for prefinishing a door panel is to follow a rabbeted approach. We cut plastics-clad material for the body of the door and then fit this panel into a rabbeted frame. Once the panel is fit perfectly, we can remove it from the frame and do our final sanding and finishing work on the wood.

Eliminate Flush Joints. As just mentioned, we can make things easier on ourselves if we are willing to design nonflush joints into our cabinetry. Nonflush joining makes sanding easier and allows easier releasable fastening. It should be fairly evident that it makes postassembly finishing easier, too.

Alter the Finishing Tools. Regardless of which techniques you employ for joining components together, you may wind up having to do some postassembly finishing anyway. Then you will very likely have to alter your usual finishing application techniques.

The first and most obvious procedure is to mask off portions of the cabinet where you do not want stains and clear coats to be applied. In the ensuing discussion, we will see that it is not terribly difficult to remove finishing materials from plastics cladding, but it's still far better to avoid overspraying or overapplying stains and clear coats in the first place. Thus, wherever you have wood and plastic meeting on the assembled cabinet, the best practice is to mask off the plastic up to 4 in. or even more.

Stains can still be applied in several ways when we have to stain wooden components that are immediately adjacent to plastics-clad parts. In fact, this is much easier to accomplish than postassembly sanding operations.

Smooth, especially glossy plastic surfaces may be unforgiving when it comes to marks or scratches left by a carelessly worked scraper or piece of sandpaper. But most oil-based stains will have very little permanent effect on the commonly used plastic-sheet coverings. The stain will wipe off with relative ease because most plastics such as melamine are designed to resist staining in general; the plastics neither react with the stain nor allow it to penetrate. Unless you have covered nearly all the nearby plastic with masked paper or tape, you should probably apply the stain with a brush or cloth rather than a spray gun. Otherwise, any time you save by spraying will be lost in wiping the oversprayed stain off the plastic. (See Illus. 195.)

Illus. 195. Most stains can be fairly easily removed from plastics cladding. Masking off is still a good idea, however.

After the necessary stain-penetration time, you should wipe off any excess liquid-coloring material. If you are confident that the mask has effectively sealed out stain seepage, you can leave it in place to keep oversprayed clear coatings from getting on the plastic.

If you think some stain has seeped beneath the masking, remove the paper or tape immediately and clean off the excess color. Considering the impenetrability of most plastic-cladding materials, this is probably not essential, but cleaning is certainly easier before the stain has dried.

Another method for tinting a project is to add color to the clear-coating material, resulting in the elimination of two steps of the usual finishing process, because you not only get the first coat of lacquer on along with the stain but you also don't have to wipe off any excess stain. Of course, to make the system work, the following procedural changes are necessary.

- Mask off larger areas of the plastic, since the stain-lacquer mixture will probably be sprayed.
- Mix finish components properly; the color and the clear material must be miscible, and a correct balance must be used.
- Avoid all but the lightest sanding upon the first coat so as not to remove color.

The mixed-component finishing method can make a lot of sense for cabinetmakers who are very concerned with speed and efficiency, but others tend to reject the practice.

After proper curing time, finishing can continue with sealing and lacquering. Except for masking off the plastics-clad components, clear coating is a very conventional operation. The finest finishes are sprayed finishes, particularly those applied by suction-feed guns. These will yield the most waste, however, and will require the most thorough job of masking off. With a brush, the finisher has better control over where the coating is applied. This factor, along with the reduced amount of waste, can lead the finisher of European cabinetry to prefer brushing, especially when only limited areas of a particular job are in need of clear coating.

All in all, the process of finishing European cabinetry is not as difficult as it might first appear. Good planning helps to reduce the amount of after-assembly sanding and finishing. Some common sense in adapting our conventional cabinetmaking and finishing will help us in our choice of tools and techniques for the procedures that remain.

INSTALLATION

We have already observed the main technological contributions of the European installation system: base-cabinet levelling legs and wall-cabinet hangers. We saw several advantages to these two hardware items, but we also noted that both systems were necessary because of the basic nonrigidity of European designed furniture and cabinetry. The first important matter to consider is not how to employ European installation but rather when to employ it.

Questions of Rigidity and Adjustment

If there was ever any sort of problem with the traditional installing system, it tended to be with door and drawer adjustment.

In very general terms, traditional installation progresses with the following steps.

1. Determine correlated units; that is, decide which cabinet units must be located in relation to others.
2. Place all correlated units in their positions and measure critical spacings; for example, in a U-shaped kitchen, we might set all base cabinets approximately where they go and measure out spaces, such as 30-in. openings between cabinet units for placement of a range/oven.
3. Level all the correlated units at once in conjunction with each other; use shims to raise sections of cabinetry off the floor or to lower them from the soffit or ceiling.
4. Drive fasteners to fix cabinet units to walls; wherever there are spaces between the rear of the cabinet and the wall, insert shims to fill them.

This completes the installation of a section of cabinetry. The installer proceeds in the same way for other groups of correlated units. The wall units might all be levelled and attached now, for instance. With all cabinetry fastened in place, the installer trims the job with mouldings. The purposes of moulding are to enhance doors and to cover small gaps between the cabinets and the walls, floors, and ceilings. Finally, the installer goes through the job, door by door and drawer by drawer, to make any adjustments that might be necessary.

This last step—adjustment—has been, if not eliminated, at least extremely simplified by the European system. This results partly from the very different installation system used in the European approach.

Perhaps one rationale for choosing the European installation system is the desire to avoid the extra step of adjusting.

European cabinets are often constructed without nailers. It ought to be fairly obvious that we usually can't install by conventional means without nailers in our cabinets. There are exceptions, such as island cabinets that must be attached to the floor or ceiling, but a nailerless cabinet is one circumstance that seems to call for European installing methods.

Much European cabinetry is also frameless. If we put nailers into frameless units and attempt to install them with shims and screws, we may not meet with perfect success. European system installers believe that cabinetry with no frames and no nailers is subject to more distortion and twisting than traditional cabinetry when wall-mounted by conventional shimming and screwing. They are undoubtedly correct. The distortion problem is the result of combined influences, not merely the nonrigidity of European cabinets.

Of the several types of walls we might find in buildings, wallboard over two-by-four studs is one of the most common. This kind of wall may not only have some irregularities, but it also may conceal these irregularities, since the wallboard may not fully contact a warped, twisted, or crooked stud. Shims can be used to solve the problem of unflat walls, but because of the hidden wall problems we cannot always tell where to place them. The other problem with shims is that they, too, are subject to some shrinkage and expansion, both from pressures exerted in the initial installation and from moisture gains and losses over time. When we mount conventional cabinetry upon such a wall, we sometimes tighten screws or fasteners so much that the cabinet's back and nailer, the wallboard, and the stud are all cinched taut. The tension upon our cabinet piece can be unnatural, twisting the entire unit out of its rectangular shape. Perfectly aligned doors suddenly do not sit flat in their openings, and drawers do not glide in and out properly.

Generally, the problem of installation-caused distortions is worse on wall cabinets, where more fasteners are usually driven and where the fasteners are often driven very tight in efforts to ensure secure mounting. On the other hand, the problem is normally not a major one. One big help is the use of hardware that makes adjustments easy. Nearly all the European hardware is very easy to adjust, and some of the drawer-gliding-hardware systems include side cam action to permit easy postinstallation adjustments. Of course, frame-type cabinet construction emphasizes rigidity, and cabinetry of this type is less affected by conventional installation than are frameless boxes.

To generalize from all this, we might benefit from European installation methods when:

- cabinetry is frameless,
- cabinetry has no nailers,
- drawers and doors are not easily adjustable,
- walls to be used for mounting/fastening either have very irregular surfaces or lack rigidity, or
- climatic conditions vary so much in terms of humidity that wooden shims will be adversely affected.

European installation methodology was developed particularly for hanging frameless cabinet boxes. If your "European styling" on a particular job is primarily a matter of appearance, including such features as flat doors mounted with narrow reveals with fully concealed hinges, then you may want to stay with your regular face-frame and nailer techniques. In that case, you would be more likely to rely on traditional installing methods, too. Most small shop woodworkers will want to be able to perform equally well with both systems.

European Installation Principles

Regardless of whether you are installing base, wall, or tall cabinetry, there are a few specialized European hardware systems and methods that apply.

Cabinet Connectors. Since so much of the European cabinetry we have been discussing is modular, several pieces must usually be joined to make an entire length of cabinet. For instance, in the north elevation of our sample modular kitchen, the length of the wall cabinet consists of three separate units joined together. (Refer back to Illus. 36.) This is very different from traditional custom cabinetmaking in which the entire length of the cabinets would be built as a single piece.

To facilitate the interconnection of cabinet units, the European system employs special cabinet-connecting screws. These are naturally designed to work well as part of the hole-line system. Many consist of two pieces: the screw itself, threaded much like a machine screw, and a matching threaded sleeve. (See Illus. 196.)

Illus. 196. A cabinet connecting screw. (Courtesy of Julius Blum, Inc.)

Alignment of the separate cabinet units is extremely easy for the installer via use of the special cabinet connectors, providing that holes were accurately drilled in the line-boring operation. Both screw and sleeve are self-centering because their size is perfectly matched to the line-bored holes. These connectors are available in various lengths, depending on whether they must extend through two 5⁄8-in. or two 3⁄4-in. end panels.

Generally, it's best to align and join individual base units into a length of cabinetry before you attempt to situate and mount them. This will speed up the levelling and alignment because, just as in conventional installing methodology, correlated units are levelled and aligned all at once, not separately. With wall cabinetry, we do not attach individual boxes to one another until all the pieces have been suspended from their hangers.

To join individual cabinet units, we must usually drill all the way through the end panels for placement of connecting screws. We locate matching holes that can be utilized for this purpose and simply extend the holes all the way through both panels with a portable drill. Bit diameter should be large enough to function as a clearance hole, but it should probably be slightly less than the original line-bored hole. We might extend an 8-mm hole with a 6-mm bit, and thus preserve the accuracy of the original line-boring. It should be pointed out that some connectors are available that can be driven without the additional drilling by the installer. This type of connector employs a self-threading tip to create its own passage through both panels and into its matching threaded sleeve. When units are set next to one another and joined with the screw-sleeve connectors, they will align perfectly along the front and top. (Here again, the importance of straight-cut components is fairly obvious.) Four or five connectors are usually enough to connect the units.

Fillers and Filler Panels. With any modular-installed cabinets, there is a good likelihood that the installer will need to place and attach several fillers and filler panels. This is true because modular cabinets are not designed for specific rooms or locations. Instead, they are designed in predetermined sizes. When several of these units are linked together for attachment to one wall, they may or may not fill the space properly.

Suppose we are intending to install cabinets, wall to wall, in a space that is 110½ in. in length—½ in. longer than the west elevation in our sample kitchen from Chapter 2. (Refer back to Illus. 30.) If we are making a custom kitchen, we have no problem here whatsoever. We simply plan the total wall of cabinets to be 110 in. long (perhaps 111 in. if we are intending to scribe ends). With modular cabinets, though, we will need fillers. If our predetermined cabinet lengths are all in multiples of 3 in., then we can design our total wall of cabinetry no longer than 108 in., meaning that we need to fill up a leftover space of about 2½ in. A quality-minded woodworker would undoubtedly mount the cabinets so that this leftover space is split in half—that is, with 1¼-in. spaces on both ends to be enclosed with fillers.

With large gaps to cover, an installer operating in the conventional system would be likely to use wide mouldings, at least to cover spaces up to 1½ in. or so. Wider gaps are dealt with by virtue of nailed-on or screwed-on filler pieces, which must be fitted and attached before the cabinetry is placed and mounted.

Once again, the European system employs special fasteners to cope with this situation. Most of these fasteners work by virtue of simple friction and allow the fillers to be pressed into place even after the cabinet is installed. Naturally, these fittings can be mounted by making use of the vertical hole line, or they can be attached with wood screws. (See Illus. 197.)

When gaps are fairly narrow, most traditionalist woodworkers cover by means of mouldings, perhaps ¼ in. × ¾ in. solid stock made from the same species as the cabinet's facing. In the European system, it is often considered acceptable to leave the gap "as is." The dark space between the cabinet and wall is supposed to render a finished appearance, referred to as a "shadow line." There are many cabinetmakers who have trouble with this notion, though, insisting that simply renaming an untrimmed section of cabinetry is not sufficient to call the work finished.

Illus. 197. Push-in fittings can be used for attachment of fillers and other site-installed panels. (Courtesy of Häfele America Co.)

In general, moulding upon European cabinets is kept to a minimum, especially vertical strips, where a conventional installer is primarily concerned with covering irregular gaps between the wall and cabinet. Flexible rubberized plastic seals can also be used to give a clean cabinet-to-wall appearance. Such seals have a right angle that wraps around the cabinet edges, and they have a protruding flexible flap that extends to the wall. (See Illus. 198.)

Crown mouldings are more common on installed European cabinets, and there are even connectors available to join mitred strips of

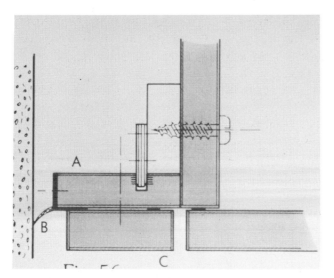
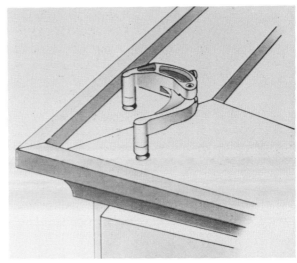

Illus. 198 (left). Use of a wall seal. A is a joining strip or filler. B is the seal. C is a false door panel. (Courtesy of Mepla Inc.) Illus. 199 (right). Crown moulding connector. (Courtesy of Mepla Inc.)

the crown moulding at corners. These fittings help to ensure a good mitre joint without glue and nails. (See Illus. 199.)

Larger filler panels are sometimes necessary on the European cabinet, particularly where there is a corner-return situation. (There are three return corners in the sample kitchen drawn out in Chapter 2; refer again to Illus. 30, 36, and 38.) Since modular cabinets meeting in a corner will generally be placed a couple of inches apart to allow doors, slide-out shelves, and appliances to operate properly, returns will need two varieties of filler. One is the narrow type we have already looked at. We can attach a narrow filler strip to extend the facing of one unit so that it fills the space between return cabinets the same way that it would fill a space between the cabinet and wall.

The other type of filler panel might be called a cover panel. It closes off the front of a cabinet box behind the return. If it were not for this panel, stored items could fall through the space between the cabinets. The panel can be attached with any of the convenient connectors we have described, connecting angles and press-in fittings being two of the better choices. Such a panel would protrude beyond the face of the return cabinet, establishing the required space for accessories and appliances to function. Proper planning will yield the same amount of space, from door edge to corner, on each cabinet. (See Illus. 200.)

Constants. Regardless of the installation methodology you choose, there are certain constants—that is, certain concerns and techniques that pertain to both systems.

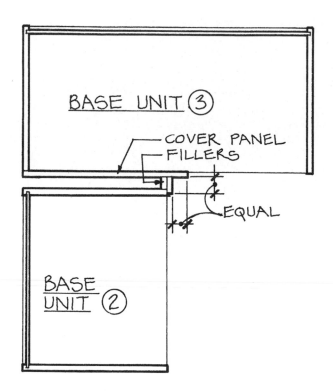

Illus. 200. The top view of base-units two and three from our sample kitchen. Note the two types of fillers and the equalized spacings.

One constant is the importance of determining cabinet location. We have to plan out the exact locations of all cabinets so that we have reference points established in the kitchen. The first need we will have for this information is for determining locations of holes that must be cut. In many cabinets, and particularly sink base cabinets, it is necessary to cut holes through the back panels for pipe access. (See Illus. 201.) We do not want these holes to be any larger than necessary, nor do we want them in the wrong place. This is one reason for determining exact locations of certain reference points.

Wherever a base cabinet's end must line up exactly with the end of a wall cabinet, above it is another cabinet situation that demands the exact determination of a reference point. In our sample kitchen, such a place is the plumb line at the immediate left of base unit 1 and the wall cabinet directly above it. (Refer back to Illus. 36.) These must line up perfectly because they both attach to the oven cabinet at their left. In fact, we usually need a reliable reference point, in the form of a plumb line, wherever there is a tall cabinet adjoined by other cabinet pieces.

Appliances may also require exact placement. Some, such as eye-level, oven-range combinations, require exact placement for the same reason as tall cabinets. Ends of bases and wall cabinets need to align perfectly.

The cabinet installer should also take care to make sure that return

Illus. 201. Sink cabinets must have their back panels cut for the entry of pipes.

cabinetry sits at right angles, especially base cabinets that will be overlaid with mitred countertops. What seems like a slight imperfection in squareness, when extended over several feet of installed base cabinet, can actually cause the countertop not to fit.

There are a variety of other matters (listed below) with which the installer must be concerned.

- Appliance size and location—some appliances, such as 24-in.-wide dishwashers, will fit fairly tight; others, like refrigerators, may require several inches of clearance.
- Reveals should be equalized next to doors and windows, if possible, for pleasing symmetry.
- Base cabinets must be attached to walls, and island cabinetry may have to be attached to the ceiling or floor.
- Built-in cabinetry must be installed level, regardless of the quality of the floor and walls; we accomplish this with a conventional level.

In reality, the traditional and the European installing methods have much in common, despite the very clear differences in wall-cabinet attachment and base-cabinet levelling systems.

Hanging Wall Cabinets

Although the European method for hanging wall cabinets is radically different from the traditional approach, it is quite simple to master.

The first matter is to determine the height of the cabinets. If they are to be mounted right at the ceiling or soffit, the height is determined for us. Another reference here might be the height of an adjacent oven unit or other tall cabinet. The tops of wall units and tall units must be even. If there is open space above the wall cabinets and no adjacent tall cabinet, we can use the traditional standard—84 in. from the finished floor to the top of the wall cabinetry.

With the finished height determined, next figure out the height at which to mount the hanging rail. It is important to take some care here if we are installing to a soffit, since we will usually have only about ½ in. of vertical adjustment built into our suspension fittings.

When the wall cabinets have a free end, an end with plenty of adjacent open space, we can actually slide single cabinet units onto the rail and into position from this free end. In the sample kitchen (Illus. 30), the wall cabinets on both the north and east walls can be slid into place this way.

In a wall-to-wall situation, we will not be able to slide the units into position as described. Instead, we have to slip the fittings' suspension hooks over the rail from the front. The rail must be low enough to allow this but also high enough to allow the installer to raise cabinets all the way to the soffit by means of the height-adjustment screws. Blum's system specifies a minimum space of 1¾ in. between the ceiling and the hanging-rail screw holes.

With rail height determined, we simply get it level and attach it to the wall with our usual fasteners. Naturally, it is important to hit the studs of hollow walls whenever possible.

A notch must be cut into the end panel of each wall cabinet suspended from the hanging rail. Because of this, the length of the hanging rail can be a critical determination. If it is too short, the last suspension fitting may not catch it; if too long, it will not allow proper positioning of a cabinet with a finished end. (See Illus. 202.) With all cabinets hanging from the rail, the installer has only to raise and align them by use of the suspension fittings' adjustment screws. Then the individual units are fastened together with connecting screws, as described earlier.

Illus. 202. The suspension-fitting-and-hanging-rail system. Notice the notch in the end panel. (Courtesy of Julius Blum, Inc.)

Levelling Floor Cabinets

By floor cabinets, we mean any units that rest upon the floor (both bases and tall cabinets) because they are levelled in the same way.

We deal with floor cabinetry somewhat differently than we do with wall cabinets in that we generally join them together as much as possible before attempting to level and attach them. In this way, several cabinet units are transformed into a single, somewhat rigid length of cabinetry. The two-part connecting screws are installed, and fillers and cover panels are attached where appropriate.

If it has not already been accomplished, the installer inserts the actual legs into fixing blocks that have been installed on the cabinet's bottom. As pointed out in Chapter 6, only two legs are needed at the junction of two cabinets. Most models of the levelling legs have fixing blocks with a flange that can be turned to support two end panels instead of one. (Refer again to Illus. 159.) Superfluous legs and fixing blocks can be removed and saved for another job.

With the legs in place, and with all cabinets raised to approximately the same height, we position all correlated cabinetry where it goes in the room. In a U-shaped kitchen, all components of the U should be placed before we make an attempt to level the cabinets. The installer then rests a level along the cabinetry and begins adjustment. Instead of driving shims beneath a section of cabinetry to raise it, we can raise or lower the leveller legs to get the top perfectly aligned. Anyone who has done a good deal of cabinet installation will appreciate the up-and-down capability. With shims, we can only adjust upwards, and we have to begin at the highest spot on the floor. This is usually not necessary with levellers. With all the correlated cabinets sitting level, a few fasteners should be driven to hold the cabinet in its correct position. Most times, these must be driven through the back panel and into the wall, just as if we were using nailers. Of course, these should be placed as close as possible to the rear top rails and bottom panels where the box is most rigid. Most importantly, the fasteners must not be overtightened. It should be fairly obvious that we will need some shims, anyway, not to raise the cabinets off the floor, but rather to fill the gaps between the rear of the cabinet boxes and the wall. Though our woodworking project is undoubtedly sitting flawlessly plumb and level, the wall may not be.

The best type of shim is probably the plastic variety marketed by some of the European style manufacturers. They cost more than the kind you can cut for yourself, but they will not be affected by climatic changes in temperature and humidity.

Snap-on toeboards are snapped in place after the cabinets have been mounted. These can present one difficulty for the installer of island base cabinets. In conventional cabinet installation, we almost always mount island base cabinets by attaching them to cleats fastened to the floor. The cabinet-to-cleat attachment is made by driving fasteners through the rigid toe kick. This will obviously not work for European cabinets with clip-attached toe kicks. If you are planning this sort of kick on your island, you will have to devise an attachment technique. One method is to attach an extra-thick cleat to the floor and to drive fasteners into it from above, through the bottom panel.

ALTERNATIVES

Earlier, we pointed out that frameless, nailerless cabinetry seems to call for European installation methods, whereas more rigid boxes seem to call for the traditional methodology. Thus, our most obvious set of options to wall-cabinet hangers and levelling legs is, when appropriate, the use of shims, nailers, and conventional fasteners. There are some occasions that suggest we use a blended approach, though.

In the description of attachment techniques for European base cabinetry, you may have noted an inconsistency. I stated that it was necessary to drive a few fasteners for the sake of stability and that the installer should drive these fasteners close to the most rigid portions of the back: the bottom panel or top rail, and especially where these components meet the end panels. The first difficulty that may have occurred to you is that this arrangement will not allow us to drive fasteners into studs as often as we would like. Further, this fastening system is perhaps not generally as firm and reliable as we might want to make it.

Nailers can be a good solution to this problem. The nailers do not have to be a major departure from European cabinetmaking; they do not even have to be visible on the installed cabinetry if your back panels are installed into slots rather than overlaid. We can put a nailer behind the back panel and between the ends as we would when constructing a premium-grade traditional cabinet. In fact, this nailer can often be wood glued firmly to the rear side of the back because that surface is frequently unclad particleboard. In Chapter 2, we suggested a European design that created a 13-mm space behind the back panel. That is, we called for installation of the back panel into slots located 13 mm from the back edge. This is obviously perfect for placing a ½-in. nailer. It is extremely easy for the assembler to cut a length of ½-in. stock to the exact length between the end panels, and to attach it with some glue and a few fasteners. A staple gun is probably the fastest method of attaching the nailer to the back. Of course, with some ½-in. stock, the installer can actually cut and place nailers at the job site, but site attachment is not nearly as efficient.

Nailers allow us to drive more fasteners and to drive them more snugly, leading to firmer, more reliable installation, but we do have to be careful to preserve the squareness of the cabinet.

Visible (mounted in front of the back panel) nailers are also an option when we are installing cabinets with back panels that are flush with the rear edges of other cabinet members. Such back panels can overlay the rear edges of the ends, top, and bottom, or they can be rabbeted into these other cabinet components. This type of nailer functions quite well for attaching base units and tall cabinets, even frameless units, because we join base cabinetry into lengths prior to attachment. Easily adjustable door and drawer hardware also reduces the significance of slight distortions. Visible nailers can also be built into wall cabinets and used for attaching them, particularly longer units—units without doors, or framed units. (See Illus. 203.)

It's important to note that the use of plastic shims will solve one of the problems we can encounter with conventional installation. These plastic wedges can be trusted to retain their size regardless of changes in humidity and temperature. Of course, the settling of a building can be another factor that influences the levelled condition of cabinetry, and the European hardware systems allow the user to make some adjustments virtually forever.

Illus. 203. Nailer mounting works well for long, doorless wall cabinets.

SUMMARY

It is possible to make cabinets that require absolutely no sanding or finishing by excluding wood and veneer entirely from the cabinet project. However, the popularity of wood—of its appearance and texture—will undoubtedly keep it in the custom cabinetmaker's designs for the foreseeable future. Thus, we need techniques that will allow us to sand and finish cabinetry made from both wood and plastic.

Even though we will want to include some wood components on our European styled cabinets, we can take certain measures to eliminate a lot of sanding. Much can be done to reduce sanding by making sure that the components to be joined have perfectly straight, smooth edges. This eliminates the need for filler and the problem of excess glue. We can also presand the wooden components if we can achieve flat joints without sanding and if we can avoid damaging the sanded wood surfaces while working with them during installation. As an aid in this, the woodworker can use releasable fasteners, thus eliminating glue and allowing parts to be trial-fitted. Certain types of milling are a help, too, especially rabbeting of wood parts for placement of a thin panel. Milled joining methods, such as dowelling, are only helpful if you have very precise tools and skills.

Avoiding flush joints can be another aid in sanding. If postassembly sanding is necessary, it is easier when wood and plastic parts don't need to be flush.

We should make every effort to ensure that postassembly sanding is kept to a minimum—if possible, that it be only touch-up sanding. When we need to sand after components are joined, we can make the job easier by masking off plastics that might be damaged by abrasives, by using a properly sharpened flat scraper, and by using shaped, "lock-on" sanding blocks.

The finishing of wood components is not similar in every way to the sanding of these parts. Some prefinishing is possible through the use of releasable joints, but the emphasis here is on postassembly methods. This is because finishes such as stain and lacquer are easily damaged during assembly, and because it's fairly easy to protect plastic surfaces from overspray. Stains and clear finishes usually do not adhere to plastic very well, either.

The main differences between the European and the traditional installing methodologies are the use of levelling legs on base cabinetry and the use of suspension hangers and hanger rails for wall cabinets in the European methodology. The purpose for using these two hardware systems is to eliminate the twists and distortions created by traditional installing. The hanger and levellers help to eliminate the need for adjusting the doors and drawers. European modular-cabinet units are connected to one another with special connectors that are installed by means of the vertical hole line.

The design of European cabinetry also suggests the use of several fillers and cover panels, as well as removable toe kicks, on a given job.

RECOMMENDATIONS

When we reach the installation stage of the cabinetmaking process, decisions concerning installing methods have probably already been made. Levelling legs and suspension fittings are either in place or they are not. Both can also be fairly easily installed with conventional drilling equipment as well as with a good-quality jig.

For frameless wall cabinets, especially modular units with doors, the suspension-and-hanger system is really a good one. It allows the wall cabinetry to be installed without introducing twists and distortions. The main reason to use the levelling legs, though, is not to avoid distortion but rather to make the process easier for the installer. Both systems are good, but neither is a huge improvement over the traditional approach. Your choice might be based on overall cabinet design. There is no great tooling investment that will lock you into the European approach if you decide to use it. Therefore, you might continue using a traditional approach for framed cabinets and take up the European system for cabinets where you want no face frame.

When it comes to sanding and finishing, manufacturers will often take care of these subprocesses by eliminating the need for them. When woods are included in their cabinetry, they will generally require the kind of sanding that a unisystem edge bander will be able to accomplish. Those of us operating in smaller shops will continue to use woods that need sanding and finishing. Incorporating woods will remain a labor-intensive task in small and medium-sized shops.

8
ADAPTING TO EUROPEANIZATION

THE ULTIMATE DEFINITION

We have now looked at a number of possible definitions for the European system. In fact, each of the seven preceding chapters began with some kind of definition for the system. But there are probably only four general definitions that can provide traditionalist cabinetmakers with entry points into the system. That is, these four definitions can give them a basis for beginning to incorporate the European style into their own methodology and to make appropriate tooling and design decisions without an immediate or complete changeover. The four possibilities for identifying European cabinetry are as follows.

1. Cabinetry incorporating components made from preclad particleboard, with cladding that is usually plastic; this will lead the cabinetmaker towards tooling capable of producing smooth, accurate, chip-free cuts.
2. Cabinetry put together in a new way—with components simply butted together and joined by means of dowels or connectors; acceptance of this definition will direct you towards hole lines and the necessary boring tools.
3. Cabinetry that is faced only with a thin edging rather than a face frame; this will lead you towards an initial involvement with an edge-banding system.
4. Cabinetry that conveys the unbroken European look, involving closely spaced flat doors, European hardware, and continuous horizontal alignment; this will bring you to initial involvement with some type of drilling equipment and other tooling specifically designed for mounting European hinges and drawer guides.

Before you choose your ultimate definition—your own point of entry into the European system—consider a couple of matters. First, ask a few acquaintances what comes to mind when they think of European furniture design. Chances are that they will mention matters that have to do with appearance: door design and gap, concealed hinges, and the like. Second, remember that cut quality will dictate the quality of all other subsystems within the European approach. Therefore, it is not wise to choose edge banding or line boring as your entry point into the European system unless you are also prepared to ensure excellent cut quality.

Naturally, some people will say that we should not call a product European unless it involves the entire 32-mm technology: modularized dimensioning, hole lines, banded edges, and so on. All-or-nothing thinking like that is not too realistic for the small shop, though. Many traditionalist cabinetmakers are being persuaded to incorporate European elements into their products, but usually only one step at a time.

In this chapter, it will become evident that the two best definitions for European cabinetry are the one based on incorporating plastics-clad particleboard and the one based on bringing the European look into your cabinetmaking projects. These two definitions are probably not considered to be as essential to 32-mm technology as edge banding and line boring, but they are the easiest for the traditional cabinetmaker to begin using.

A FEW PREDICTIONS

I am a cabinetmaker and not a prophet, so it may be a bit presumptuous of me to try reading the future. Yet, there are a few matters that seem like excellent predictors of the continued expansion of the European influence.

First of all, as world forests continue to shrink, there will be a greater emphasis on plastics, and frameless design will dominate the trade. Face frames are in fact a superfluous use of wood if we employ some means to make the cabinet box rigid. It is not that face-frame cabinetry will totally disappear; instead, framed cabinets will be the rarer variety, perhaps prized because of their luxurious use of wood and the extra labor that they reflect. Plastics-clad sheet goods will grow even more popular because they are so functional and because they will also remain relatively inexpensive.

The European styling is also here to stay because consumers are demonstrating that they like it. The style's look is clean, simple, and lovely. European cabinetry is spacious and easy to care for. Some of it can be taken apart, shipped flat, and then reassembled—important features in certain kinds of furniture, such as entertainment cabinetry and "wall systems."

Another reason that it makes sense to predict the continued expansion of the European influence is that the 32-mm-based technology is such a great benefit to modularizers. Most large producers of modular cabinetry will undoubtedly embrace the system because it will save them money in production. There may be some large initial investments for these producers, but such capital outlays can be recovered very quickly in high-volume situations. And since so much cabinetry will be built according to the 32-mm methodology, woodworkers in smaller shops will be providing their own renditions of the style. Middle-sized shops will be trying to compete with the biggest producers, while the craftsmen in small shops will simply want to be able to choose—to move back and forth between styles and systems.

However, we can probably assume that the traditional approach to cabinetmaking will not be entirely replaced in the near future. European cabinetry is functional and strong, but it is not everyone's preference. Many people still prefer the traditional styling and construction details, claiming that the European style "lacks something." This is a matter of taste, thus beyond disputation. The point is that some people will continue to prefer the traditional look, and though it is possible to render this look on 32-mm constructed boxes, some cabinetmakers will still employ face frames, overlaid backs, and fixed toe kicks.

The demand for perfected and highly customized products will also continue to grow. This means that hobbyists and other small shop operators will probably still find plenty of projects to do, in both the European and the more traditional styles. Small shops will still be free to switch from one methodology to the other, and even to blend the two techniques. If any woodworking business operations are threatened by the growth of the European influence, they are the middle-sized plants. This is because mid-sized shops are generally not able to afford all the machinery necessary for a modularized, assembly-line approach, yet they depend on maintaining certain production levels to survive. Such operations may be caught in the middle—they may be too small for a real modular approach and too large for doing a lot of customizing.

BASIS FOR DECISION MAKING

We have said a good deal about the advantages and disadvantages of several cabinetmaking systems with both methodologies. However, in terms of deciding which systems are best suited to you, it is just as important to know your own goals as it is to know all the choices open to you. In fact, it's a good idea for cabinetmakers to ask themselves why they go into the shop in the first place.

I once attended a woodworking seminar at which one of the main speakers said: "We don't build cabinets because we like the smell of sawdust." He was basically saying that the goal of a cabinetmaker is and ought to be to make money. Of course, the speaker was addressing craftspeople whose livelihood depended on woodworking, and so the comment was largely appropriate. Some of us do like the smell of sawdust, though, even some of us who are dependent on the trade for our living. To help you clearly identify your own cabinetmaking objectives, you should give careful answers to the following five questions.

Are You Essentially a Tradesman or an Artisan?

The difference here is based on the types of motives we have been discussing. A tradesman can be thought of as someone who practices woodcraft mainly to make money, whereas you can think of an artisan as someone who is primarily interested in the cabinet product itself. Artisans are generally more willing to invest extra time in the cabinetmaking process, while tradesmen often prefer to invest more money in tooling, so long as the investment will save time and labor.

As an illustration, suppose we know an artisan and a tradesman who both own small shops that operate at about the same production level. To mount the European style hinges, the tradesman would probably prefer to buy a boring/insertion machine, while the artisan might decide to buy only the 35-mm bit needed for drilling a hinge-cup hole.

What Is the Status of Your Current Tooling?

This may be the most significant question for you to consider right now. Woodworking tradesmen and artisans alike are already aware that their craft requires more space and more monetary investment than virtually any other craft. The new generation of tools has not made much of a difference in this regard.

In one sense, the 32-mm system has simplified the entire notion of tool selection. In fact, the European approach requires fewer tools than the traditional approach. Think about it: If you are building only European type cabinetry, and if you possess good panel-processing equipment, then you no longer need many of the tools you currently use—sanders, jointer, radial arm saw, and so on. In spite of this, converting to 32-mm-based tooling won't change the fact that we need a fair amount of money as well as space to engage in woodworking. The good panel-processing equipment just mentioned is expensive, and it certainly requires no less space to use than our conventional equipment.

Throughout this book, we have pointed out ways that the woodworker can use some types of conventional tooling to achieve "European" results. But in addition to considering ways that you can employ your current tools to build European cabinetry, you must also do some honest appraising of these tools. There is, after all, an extremely wide range in terms of quality in the equipment currently available.

To put any portion of the European system in place, you will have to make sure that your cutting operations are capable of producing panels that are accurately sized and free of chipped edges. Some conventional saws will provide reasonably good results, although you may have to upgrade a bit with hollow-ground blades, stabilizers, and a high-quality rip fence that allows accurate dimensioning—and you may have to invest more time in cutting than the bigger shops that possess panel saws. However, there are some saws that simply are not up to the type of work that is called for in constructing European cabinet boxes. Be honest with yourself when you evaluate your saw and your other pieces of equipment. Inferior tools will not yield the level of precision that is required for European style cabinets; they will lead instead to frustration, annoyance, and substandard articles of furniture.

As you think about tools, do not overlook the importance of your available space. More than craftspeople in any other trade, the cabinetmaker needs room: room to store sheet goods properly, room for tools to function, room to construct cabinets, and perhaps room to store and finish projects. For example, you may see a lot of value in having a reliable line borer but opt for a set of boring jigs because you don't have the necessary space for the stationary tool right now.

What Is Your Level of Production?

Naturally, the more you produce and the more consistent your flow of work, the more likely you will be to buy automatic and specialized European equipment. For example, if every job that you have done recently has required that you do hundreds of feet of edge banding, then it may be time for you to start shopping for a hot-melt edge-band applicator. If you have had to hire someone to do edge banding for you—especially if you've had to hire a skilled worker to perform the job—this is particularly good advice. As any machine salesperson will tell you (and quite accurately), when there is a choice, it is almost always better to pay for tools than to pay for additional skilled labor.

How Flexible Do You Want to Remain?

Whether you have read this book from page one or simply picked it up to thumb through, you have obviously acquired some interest in the European system. At this point, it may be pertinent for you to consider whether you want to convert to the 32-mm approach, even on a small scale, or rather merely add some European tools and techniques to your repertoire. I assume that most of you will be taking the latter approach, at least for the time being, but some woodworkers may feel that European cabinet design is so superior that they will want to embrace it more completely. It certainly has advantages, as we have seen.

If you believe that you will someday be building only European furniture, then you will undoubtedly recognize the need for beginning your conversion by upgrading the cut quality in your shop. In this situation, you want to keep trying to make your 10-inch table saw overachieve. Instead, you will want to begin using a saw that is equipped to achieve perfect cuts without time-consuming extra steps, such as reverse feeds or secondary milling.

What Are Your Plans?
To answer this question, it is clearly not sufficient to look at just your current status in the trade. Many tradesmen were once hobbyists; many shop owners were once tradesmen earning a wage.

You need to identify the direction in which you are headed. Suffice it to say that the more business-oriented you are, the more you will want to simplify your production system, and nowadays, this will mean utilizing 32-mm production techniques.

Your answers to these five questions should help you shape your definition of European cabinetmaking, at least in your own shop.

BEGINNING THE TRANSITION

Although the woodworking world may one day be dominated by modular 32-mm cabinets, there is probably no need for the hobbyist or other customizer to make a complete conversion to the system. Still, there are a few transitions that we will be making, either because these modifications make the most sense or because they will be thrust upon us.

Hinging

Your induction into European cabinet design may come as you start mounting doors with European style hinges. I am sure that many of you have already been introduced to the system by virtue of using these hinges. This is quite logical since the hinges are so good. They are so good, in fact, that it's hard not to like them. Consumers and designers like them mainly because they are "invisible," while cabinetmakers like them because they're strong, reliable, and easy to adjust. These hinges are undoubtedly the dominant system in today's hardware.

Since you are probably already using European door hardware, and since you will surely be mounting more and more of these hinges, it makes sense for your first investment in European tooling to be equipment to facilitate hinging. If you already have a good-quality drill press, the most sensible thing to do is to buy a boring gearbox and insertion mechanism that will work on the machinery that you already have. If you enter the system in this way, make sure that you keep the principle of versatility near the top of your priorities. That is, keep in mind that you may eventually want your gearbox to do some other jobs besides drill for and insert hinges. Locate a boring gearbox that will allow you to drill for knock-down or eccentric fittings. (Refer back to Illus. 145.)

If you do not already have a great deal of money tied up in a drill press, or you are about to purchase drilling equipment, then the best thing to do is to locate the type of machine that will allow you to do line boring as well as hinge boring. Purchase equipment that allows easy switching of gearboxes. Many of the European hinge producers market drilling machines with this capability built in, but be sure to check this feature out before making a purchase. Again, tool versatility is important, especially in small shops. Naturally, tool specialization is more important to modularizers and other high-volume shops.

Once you have made a commitment to a European hinging system and the relevant hardware, you will probably begin using other elements of the 32-mm approach. One reason for this is the tool versatility that we have already discussed. Another reason is that the concealed hinges themselves will encourage further development of the European look. You will soon want to experiment with vinyl-coated drawer guides, a continuous bar pull, and narrow reveals between doors and drawers.

European drawer guides have some desirable features—features that consumers and cabinetmakers alike will find beneficial: quiet operation, easy adjustment with some models, and locking capability with the drawer pulled out, to name a few.

All the factors that contribute to the European door and drawer look may lead us towards some other tools, such as the profile mounting tool. They may lead us towards some hole-line assembly, as well, so that rendering the Euro-look (concealed hardware, flat doors, and narrow reveals) is certainly a good way to enter the European system.

Using Preclad Particleboard

Whether or not you decide to stay with the traditional look in your cabinet work, you may be drawn towards using melamine-covered sheets or other preclad materials in your shop. They are tough, stain-resistant, and easy to clean, and certainly worth including in many cabinet projects.

It's probably fairly apparent that plastics-clad particleboard is appropriate in the kitchen and bathroom, especially for cabinet interiors. Traditionalist cabinetmakers can certainly use this material in these locations very easily, as we have observed. A few modifications are necessary, mainly because of the nonglueability of the plastics claddings. But, if the woodworker is willing to sacrifice some time, he or she can use essentially conventional methods to construct cabinetry. In fact, when only cabinet interiors are clad in plastic, nearly the entire traditional cabinetmaking system can be used: face frames, nailers, hold-downs, overlaid backs, and glue-and-nails construction. When there will be plastics claddings on the cabinet's exterior, such as on finished ends or door faces, a few more modifications in technique will allow us to stay with our traditional tools and approaches. For instance, we can perform jointing or other secondary milling to get perfect panel edges on door panels, and we can perhaps use deep rabbets along the top and bottom edges of finished ends in order to avoid having to nail through their faces. (Refer back to Illus. 104.)

The serious woodworker should think of plastics claddings on the outside of the cabinet as a real demarcation point. That is, when you start having to make finished ends and doors out of plastics-clad particleboard, it may be time to start thinking about upgrading your saw. I do not mean that the first time you get a request for doors with a plastic face and a wide solid-oak edging, that you need to go out and buy a CNC panel saw. What I do mean is that a consistent need to make such doors will suggest your getting either a vertical panel saw or a table saw with a scoring blade. This is the sense in which preclad particleboard panels will bring about a means of entry into the European cabinetmaking system.

The price of either a good vertical panel saw or a good dimension saw with a scoring blade is what leads the cabinetmaker deeper into the European system. The size of such an investment may well push the cabinetmaker towards higher volume.

Entering the world of European cabinetmaking either by virtue of incorporating preclad panels or by attempting to render the European look will bring about some fine results for almost any cabinetmaker. The central benefit, in addition to the lovely articles that can be created, is that we can make a single-step entry. That is, there are no prerequisites—we can invest in a saw with a scoring blade or in a boring-and-insertion machine, and derive immediate benefits without having to buy other equipment.

Furthermore, as we have observed, these machines will give us extended benefits. With the scoring-blade saw, we can cut not only plastics-clad materials, but also the finest plywood. By lowering the scoring blade, we can also still use the saw for cutting solid stocks. (Refer back to Illus. 14.) In addition, establishing fine-cut quality will free us to adopt other precise equipment, such as an edge bander or line borer, when we choose to do so. As we have noted, the boring machine can be used for several purposes.

Building Frameless/Using the Hole Line

Frameless design and hole-line technology may be the very heart of the European system, but neither is probably the point at which to begin building European. Both edge banding and line boring have an important prerequisite: accurate, chip-free cutting. Therefore, to make use of edge bands rather than face frames, or to employ hole lines for assembly or accessory attachment, we need to purchase not only tooling that will drill holes or equipment that will band edges—but, in addition to these, we need to invest in good cutting tools. If you want to get involved with edge banding or line boring right away and you have limited resources, it would be best to sink those resources into a good saw and then use some less expensive varieties of banding or boring tools. For instance, you might want to buy a good, vertical panel saw for dimensioning materials and then invest in a modest hot-air table-mounted edge bander or a drilling jig that can be used in conjunction with a portable power drill.

Ultimately, only you can be the judge of which 32-mm systems are suitable for you and your own shop. Hobbyists and many other low-volume producers may want to remain with their current tool systems to a very large extent. That is why this book contains so many alternatives involving traditional tooling.

Still, it should be fairly clear that you can build cabinets and furniture within the European system without investing unreasonable amounts of money. Begin with your saw: let's say, a vertical panel saw in the small shop, or the best upgrading you can manage of the table saw that you currently own. If you intend to incorporate any European design elements at all, other than perhaps basic hinging, you must naturally begin by doing all you can to ensure precisely dimensioned panels that have chip-free edges. With cut quality established, you can attain other facets of the 32-mm system with fairly inexpensive tool systems: edge banding that involves preglued edgings that can be applied with an iron or a hot-air tool, line boring via jigs and hand-held drills, and assembly with glueless fasteners.

The European cabinetmaking system has brought new techniques and new technologies to our trade. It is the craftsman's job to make the best use of these contributions.

METRIC EQUIVALENCY CHART

MM—MILLIMETRES   CM—CENTIMETRES

INCHES TO MILLIMETRES AND CENTIMETRES

INCHES	MM	CM	INCHES	CM	INCHES	CM
⅛	3	0.3	9	22.9	30	76.2
¼	6	0.6	10	25.4	31	78.7
⅜	10	1.0	11	27.9	32	81.3
½	13	1.3	12	30.5	33	83.8
⅝	16	1.6	13	33.0	34	86.4
¾	19	1.9	14	35.6	35	88.9
⅞	22	2.2	15	38.1	36	91.4
1	25	2.5	16	40.6	37	94.0
1¼	32	3.2	17	43.2	38	96.5
1½	38	3.8	18	45.7	39	99.1
1¾	44	4.4	19	48.3	40	101.6
2	51	5.1	20	50.8	41	104.1
2½	64	6.4	21	53.3	42	106.7
3	76	7.6	22	55.9	43	109.2
3½	89	8.9	23	58.4	44	111.8
4	102	10.2	24	61.0	45	114.3
4½	114	11.4	25	63.5	46	116.8
5	127	12.7	26	66.0	47	119.4
6	152	15.2	27	68.6	48	121.9
7	178	17.8	28	71.1	49	124.5
8	203	20.3	29	73.7	50	127.0

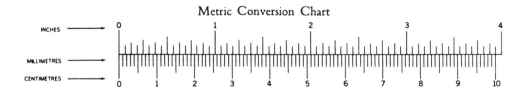

Metric Conversion Chart

INDEX